I0012696

Mastering Generative AI

Design Patterns
Frameworks
Real-World Applications

Singh, Rajni

DEDICATION

To my father, who believed in me always. You are always with me *Papa!*

Table of Contents

This book isn't just about learning GenAI System Design; it's about preparing yourself for the present and future in tech. No matter where you stand in your career, the insights and knowledge present in this course can empower you to contribute to the AI landscape.

Generative AI System Design is for you if you are a:

Software engineer: This course will equip software engineers (SEs) of various levels (associate SEs to principal SEs) with a strong foundation to build cutting-edge GenAI systems and solve real-world challenges. Whether just starting or leading a team, you can equip yourself with the knowledge of designing large-scale GenAI systems.

Machine learning (ML) engineer: As an ML engineer, you'll gain valuable insights into how your models fit into the broader system architecture. This course will bridge the gap between model development and deployment, familiarising you with designing scalable and reliable systems that effectively utilise GenAI models. You'll learn about infrastructure considerations, optimisation techniques, and best practices for integrating ML models into real-world applications.

Engineering and product managers: These managers or leaders can gain a deeper technical understanding of how Genai systems work to make informed decisions, plan effectively, and lead cross-functional teams.

Interviewee: Mastering these concepts puts you ahead in the competitive tech job market, particularly for AI-focused roles where System Design is critical. System Design interviews now emphasise futureproofing, with GenAI becoming one of the key topics to be discussed.

Learning enthusiast: Are you a techie who's curious about generative AI? This course allows you to immerse yourself in the design principles powering GenAI advancements. In today's tech landscape, staying ahead is key; this course will be a great asset in staying ahead of the curve. Also, if you are interested in the inner workings of modern GenAI systems like Chatgpt, Stable Diffusion, etc., this course is for you.

Introduction to Generative AI System Design

This course is designed to introduce the core concepts of GenAI and then dive into specific real-world examples. The structure of the course is given below:

Fundamental concepts: This section lays the groundwork for understanding the intricacies of generative AI System Design. It provides a comprehensive overview of the essential concepts, equipping learners with foundational knowledge. By exploring core machine learning principles, evaluation techniques tailored for generative AI, the power of parallelism in training large models, and optimization strategies for efficient inference, learners will understand the building blocks of generative AI systems.

GenAI System Design framework: Designing GenAI systems is not straightforward, but having a framework that defines a common strategy for designing different systems can set the tone for a good solution. This section discusses a 6-step framework to help you design GenAI systems.

GenAI System Design case studies: This section takes you behind the scenes of fascinating real-world GenAI systems. You'll understand the architectural decisions, design-level trade-offs, estimations, and deployment details through in-depth case studies. You'll gain valuable insights and practical knowledge by exploring how we can tackle the challenges of building and deploying large-scale GenAI systems."

Prerequisites for the GenAI System Design

We assume that you have a fundamental knowledge of key concepts of distributed systems. An understanding and knowledge of the following courses will enable you to learn the core concepts and systems discussed in this course:

To successfully navigate the world of GenAI System Design, a solid grasp of generative AI itself is crucial. You should be familiar with the core concepts of generative models, their applications, and the underlying technologies that drive them. This includes understanding transformer networks and their variants, such as vision transformers for image generation and multimodal transformers for tasks involving multiple data types. You'll also have practical experience with hands-on exercises, like experimenting with large language models (LLMs) for text generation, which will further solidify your understanding and prepare you for the System Design challenges ahead.

Generative AI systems are rapidly changing the world around us. From creating stunningly realistic images to composing captivating music, these systems are pushing the boundaries of what's possible with artificial intelligence. Behind these systems, however, lies a combination of two technologies: **distributed machine learning (DML**) for training generative models and System Design for deploying these models.

DML has revolutionized how we train the massive machine learning models that power generative AI. By distributing the computational workload across numerous machines, DML allows us to handle the enormous datasets and complex models required for generative AI. This approach, inspired by the principles of distributed systems, enables us to train models faster and more efficiently.

However, training these models is only half the complexity. To realize their power, we need robust and sophisticated systems to deploy and manage them. This is where System Design comes in. By applying core System Design principles like modularity, scalability, and reliability, we can build the infrastructure needed to support real-world generative AI applications.

Generative AI System Design: Blending traditional System Design principles with emerging GenAI concepts like DML
What is generative AI System Design?
The combination of generative AI and System Design gives rise to a new discipline: Generative AI System Design. This emerging field focuses on training and deploying complex systems that power generative AI applications, ensuring these systems are robust, efficient, scalable, and reliable.

Generative AI System Design is already impacting various industries. For instance, Elon Musk's xAI rapidly developed "Grok," a sophisticated AI system, by leveraging the principles of generative AI System Design. This demonstrates the power of the principles inherent to GenAI and System Design to accelerate innovation and deliver cutting-edge AI solutions.

As generative AI continues to evolve, so will the generative AI System Design field. This field will be essential in tackling the challenges and harnessing the opportunities of rapidly advancing technology, shaping the future of AI and its applications across various domains.

"Generative AI is the key to solving some of the world's biggest problems, such as climate change, poverty, and disease. It has the potential to make the world a better place for everyone." – Mark Zuckerberg.

The rise of large-scale GenAI applications, such as chatbots, image-generation models, and code-generation tools, has highlighted the need for a systematic approach to their development. The principles guiding the development of these large-scale systems need to be defined. Additionally, addressing the industry's skill gap is essential to achieving the goal of delivering applications in a short period. This course aims to fill that knowledge gap by exploring the System Design of a real-world generative AI system.

System Design

A strong foundation in **System Design** is crucial for building efficient, scalable, and reliable software. Let's break down the key principles in simple terms:

1. Scalability - How do we handle more users and data smoothly?
2. Availability - Can users access the system anytime they need it?
3. Low Latency - How fast does the system respond?
4. Reliability - Can the system keep working even if something fails?
5. Maintainability - Can developers easily update or fix the system?

Scalability

Scalability means designing a system that can **grow** without breaking. If more users start using the system or data increases, it should still work well.

Example:

Imagine an online store during a big sale. If thousands of people suddenly visit at the same time, the website shouldn't crash. To handle this, companies use:

- **Horizontal Scaling**: Adding more servers (like hiring more cashiers in a busy store).

- **Vertical Scaling**: Upgrading servers to be more powerful (like training a cashier to work faster)

Availability

Availability means the system should be up and running **most of the time** (ideally 99.99% uptime).

Example:

Think about an online banking app. If you need to transfer money but the app is down, it's frustrating. To ensure availability, systems use:

- **Redundant Servers**: Extra backup servers that take over if one fails.

- **Load Balancers**: Devices that distribute user traffic across multiple servers to prevent overload.

Latency

Latency is the time it takes for a request to get a response. A lower latency means **faster performance**.

Example:
When you search on Google, results appear almost instantly. That's because:

- **Data is stored in multiple locations (CDN)** to serve users from the nearest server.

- **Efficient indexing** allows quick search retrieval.

Principle	What It Means	Real-World Example
Scalability	Handles more users & data	E-commerce sites during sales
Availability	Stays online as much as possible	Online banking apps
Low Latency	Responds quickly	Google search, video streaming
Reliability	Works even if something fails	Cloud storage with backups
Maintainability	Easy to update & fix	Adding features to apps smoothly

Reliability

Reliability means **preventing failures** or recovering quickly when they happen.

Example:
If one database crashes in an online payment system, transactions **shouldn't be lost**. Companies ensure reliability by:

- **Replication**: Keeping copies of data in multiple places.

- **Failover Mechanisms**: Automatically switching to a backup system when the main one fails.

Maintainability

A system should be easy to **understand, modify, and scale** over time.

Example:
If a social media app wants to add a new feature (like disappearing messages), developers should be able to do it **without breaking existing features**. This is achieved by:

- **Modular Design**: Breaking the system into small, independent services (microservices).

- **Clear Documentation**: Keeping track of how the system works for future engineers.

Generative AI System Design core component

A **Generative AI system** is a complex architecture designed to create new content, such as text, code, images, or even music, based on input prompts. To understand how such a system works, it's essential to break it down into its **core components**. These components work together to enable the system to generate high-quality, contextually relevant outputs.

Core components of a Generative AI system:

1. Input Layer (Prompt Interface)

This is where the user interacts with the system. The input layer captures the user's prompt, which is a natural language description of what they want the AI to generate.

- **Examples of Prompts:**
  - "Write a Python function to calculate the Fibonacci sequence."
  - "Generate a blog post about the benefits of renewable energy."
  - "Create a logo for a tech startup."
- **Key Features:**

o   User-friendly interface (e.g., text box, voice input).
o   Ability to handle multi-modal inputs (text, images, audio).

2. Natural Language Understanding (NLU) Module

The NLU module processes the user's prompt to extract intent, entities, and context. This step ensures the AI understands what the user wants.

- Functions:
  - o   **Intent Detection:** Identifies the goal of the prompt (e.g., generate code, write content, create art).
  - o   **Entity Extraction:** Identifies key details (e.g., programming language, topic, style).
  - o   **Contextual Understanding:** Captures additional context or constraints (e.g., tone, length, format).
- Technologies Used:
  - o   Pre-trained language models (e.g., BERT, GPT).
  - o   Named Entity Recognition (NER) systems.

3. Generative Model (Core AI Engine)

The generative model is the heart of the system. It uses the processed prompt to create new content.

- Types of Generative Models:
  - o   **Text Generation:** Models like GPT (Generative Pre-trained Transformer) for generating text, code, or dialogue.
  - o   **Image Generation:** Models like DALL·E, Stable Diffusion, or MidJourney for creating images.
  - o   **Audio Generation:** Models like WaveNet or Jukebox for generating music or speech.
- How It Works:
  - o   The model is trained on vast datasets (e.g., books, code repositories, images).
  - o   It uses patterns learned during training to predict and generate outputs that match the input prompt.
- Key Features:
  - o   **Fine-Tuning:** The model can be fine-tuned for specific tasks (e.g., medical text generation, legal document drafting).
  - o   **Multi-Modal Capabilities:** Some models can handle multiple types of inputs and outputs (e.g., text-to-image, text-to-audio).

4. Knowledge Base (Training Data)

The knowledge base is the dataset used to train the generative model. It provides the foundational knowledge and patterns the AI uses to generate outputs.

- Types of Data:
    - **Text Data:** Books, articles, code repositories, and conversational datasets.
    - **Image Data:** Labelled images, art collections, and design templates.
    - **Audio Data:** Music tracks, speech recordings, and sound effects.
- Key Considerations:
    - **Quality:** High-quality, diverse datasets lead to better outputs.
    - **Ethics:** Ensuring the data is free from biases and respects copyright laws.

5. Post-Processing Layer

After the generative model produces an output, the post-processing layer refines it to ensure it meets quality standards and user requirements.

- Functions:
    - **Syntax Checking:** Ensures code or text is error-free.
    - **Style Adjustment:** Aligns the output with the desired tone or style.
    - **Formatting:** Structures the output for readability or usability (e.g., adding headings, bullet points).
- Technologies Used:
    - Grammar and spell-checking tools.
    - Code linters and formatters.
    - Image editing tools (e.g., cropping, colour correction).

6. Validation and Feedback Mechanism

This component ensures the generated output is accurate, relevant, and meets user expectations.

- Functions:
    - **User Feedback:** Allows users to rate or refine the output.
    - **Automated Validation:** Uses rules or AI to check for errors, biases, or inconsistencies.
    - **Iterative Improvement:** Incorporates feedback to improve future outputs.
- Key Features:

- Explainability: Provides insights into how the output was generated.
- Bias Detection: Identifies and mitigates biases in the output.

7. Output Layer (Delivery Interface)

The output layer delivers the generated content to the user in a usable format.

- Examples of Outputs:
  - Text: Code snippets, articles, or reports.
  - Images: Logos, illustrations, or designs.
  - Audio: Music tracks, voiceovers, or sound effects.
- Key Features:
  - Multi-modal delivery (e.g., text, image, audio).
  - Integration with other tools (e.g., IDEs, design software).

8. Orchestration and Workflow Management

This component manages the flow of data and tasks between the other components, ensuring the system operates smoothly.

- Functions:
  - Task Scheduling: Coordinates the sequence of operations (e.g., prompt processing → generation → validation).
  - Resource Management: Allocates computational resources (e.g., GPU, memory) efficiently.
  - Error Handling: Detects and resolves issues during the generation process.
- Technologies Used:
  - Workflow automation tools (e.g., Apache Airflow).
  - Containerization (e.g., Docker, Kubernetes).

9. Security and Compliance Layer

This component ensures the system operates securely and complies with legal and ethical standards.

- Functions:
  - Data Privacy: Protects user data and prompts.
  - Content Moderation: Filters inappropriate or harmful outputs.
  - Compliance: Ensures adherence to regulations (e.g., GDPR, copyright laws).

- **Key Features:**
  - Encryption for data security.
  - Audit trails for accountability.

10. Continuous Learning and Adaptation

Generative AI systems improve over time by learning from new data and user feedback.

- **Functions:**
  - **Reinforcement Learning:** Uses feedback to fine-tune the model.
  - **Data Augmentation:** Expands the knowledge base with new datasets.
  - **Model Updates:** Regularly updates the generative model to improve performance.
- **Key Features:**
  - Self-improving systems that adapt to user needs.
  - Ability to handle new tasks or domains over time.

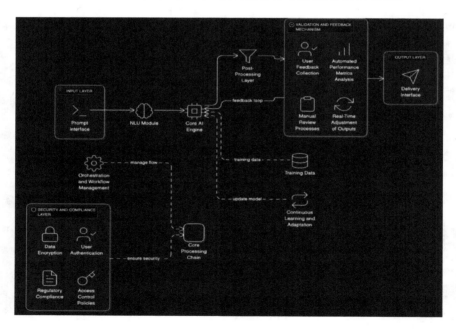

The core components of a Generative AI system work together to transform user prompts into high-quality outputs. By understanding these components, teams can design, build, and optimize systems that leverage the power of Generative AI to solve real-world problems. Whether it's generating code, creating art, or drafting content, these systems are revolutionizing how we interact with technology.

Fundamental Concepts in Generative AI

Understanding the fundamental principles of neural networks and their various forms is essential for building large-scale Generative AI (GenAI) systems that can perform tasks such as text, image, speech, and video generation. In this lesson, we will delve into the following key concepts:

- Neural networks
- Convolutional neural networks (CNNs)
- Recurrent neural networks (RNNs)
- Transformer networks
- Attention mechanisms

These machine learning concepts form the foundation of modern GenAI systems, enabling machines to recognize patterns, produce creative outputs, and operate at scale. By grasping these principles, we can more effectively design and optimize the intricate system architectures needed for real-world GenAI applications.

Let's begin by exploring each of these concepts, starting with neural networks.

Neural network

Neural networks are computational models inspired by the human brain, designed to recognize patterns and make predictions by processing data through interconnected layers of nodes (neurons). The architecture of a neural network refers to its structure and organization, including the arrangement of layers, neurons, and connections. This architecture determines how data flows through the network, enabling it to learn and make predictions or decisions.

Key Components of a Neural Network

Below are the fundamental components of a neural network, though we will focus on only a few in this discussion:

- **Neurons:** The basic processing units of a neural network, also known as nodes. Each neuron receives an input feature vector $(x1,x2,...,xm)(x\_1, x\_2, ..., x\_m)(x1,x2,...,xm)$, multiplies it with corresponding weights $(w1,w2,...,wm)(w\_1, w\_2, ..., w\_m)(w1,w2,...,wm)$, adds a bias, and sums them up. The result is then passed through an activation function σ\sigma$\sigma$ to introduce nonlinearity. The mathematical formulation is:

  output=σ(Bias+∑i=1mxiwi)=σ(Bias+x1w1+x2w2+...+xmwm)\text{outp ut} = \sigma(\text{Bias} + \sum_{i=1}^{m} x_i w_i) = \sigma(\text{Bias} + x_1w_1 + x_2w_2 + ... + x_mw_m)output=σ(Bias+i=1∑mxiwi)=σ(Bias+x1w1+x2w2+...+xmwm)

- **Activation Functions (σ\sigmaσ):** These functions introduce nonlinearity, enabling the network to learn complex patterns. Common activation functions include sigmoid, ReLU (Rectified Linear Unit), and softmax.

- **Weights and Bias**: Weights determine the strength of connections between neurons, while bias allows shifting of the activation function, improving the model's ability to fit the data.

Neural Network Architecture

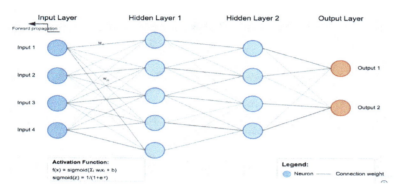

Neurons in a neural network are organized into layers, each responsible for processing information at a different stage:

- **Input Layer:** Receives raw data or features (x1,x2,...,xm)(x_1, x_2, ..., x_m)(x1,x2,...,xm). The number of neurons in this layer corresponds to the number of features in the dataset.

- **Hidden Layers:** Perform computations using weights and activation functions to extract meaningful features. The number of hidden layers varies based on the complexity of the network.

- **Output Layer:** Produces the final output, such as predictions or classifications.

The Foundation of Modern AI

Neural networks serve as the backbone of advanced AI systems. From deep learning to transformer-based models, all modern AI architectures build upon these fundamental principles. Their ability to learn patterns and adapt is what powers today's most sophisticated generative AI technologies.

Next, let's explore **Convolutional Neural Networks (CNNs)**—an advanced neural network architecture designed for processing structured and image data.

Convolutional Neural Networks (CNNs)

Definition:
CNNs are specialized neural networks designed for processing structured data like images. They automatically extract features from raw data using convolutional layers.

Key Components:
1. **Convolutional Layer:** Applies filters to the input to extract local features.

   - Applies learnable filters (kernels) to extract local patterns

   - Creates feature maps highlighting detected features (edges, textures, shapes)

   - Early layers detect simple features (edges, corners)

   - Deeper layers combine these to detect more complex patterns

   - Each filter specializes in detecting specific patterns
     - **Example:** Detecting edges in an image.

2. **Pooling Layer:** Reduces spatial dimensions, making the model invariant to small changes.

   - Reduces spatial dimensions through down sampling

   - Max pooling: retains the maximum value from each region

   - Average pooling: computes the average of values in each region

   - Provides robustness to small translations and transformations

   - Reduces computation and helps prevent overfitting
     - **Example:** Max pooling retains the maximum value in a region.

3. **Fully Connected Layer:** Combines features to make predictions.

- Connects every neuron to all neurons in the next layer

- Combines all extracted features for final decision making

- Typically located near the end of the network

- Final layer uses Softmax activation for classification problems
  - **Example:** Classifying an image as a cat or dog.

Example: A CNN for facial recognition might use convolutional layers to detect eyes, nose, and mouth, pooling layers to reduce dimensionality, and fully connected layers to identify the person.

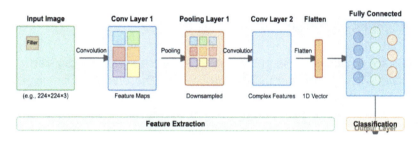

Recurrent Neural Networks (RNNs)

A **Recurrent Neural Network (RNN)** is a type of artificial neural network that incorporates loops within its hidden layers, allowing information to persist over time. Designed for processing sequential data, RNNs maintain a memory of previous inputs, making them particularly effective for tasks involving temporal or contextual dependencies.

How RNNs Work

Unlike traditional feedforward neural networks, which process inputs independently, RNNs utilize a looping mechanism that updates an internal state at each time step. This enables the network to retain and use information from earlier elements in a sequence, making it ideal for handling sequential patterns.

Applications of RNNs

RNNs are widely used in:

- **Natural Language Processing (NLP):** Text sequencing in conversational AI and machine translation.

- **Generative Models:** Creating descriptive text in text-to-image models.

- **Time Series Analysis:** Predicting trends in stock markets, weather forecasting, and other temporal data applications.

Challenges and Advancements

While RNNs are powerful for sequential tasks, they struggle with long-term dependencies and lack efficient parallel processing. These limitations have led to the rise of more advanced architectures, such as **transformer networks**, which leverage attention mechanisms to revolutionize sequence modelling.

Next, let's explore **transformer networks** and how they have transformed the field of deep learning.

Transformer Network

Definition:
Transformers are deep learning models that handle sequential data using self-attention mechanisms. They are the backbone of many NLP models.

Key Components:

1. **Tokenization and Input Encoding:**
   What it does: The transformer breaks down the input text into smaller pieces called **tokens** (which can be words or parts of words). Each token is then converted into a numerical representation called a **vector** (a list of numbers). For example, each word might be turned into a vector of 512 numbers.
   Why it's important: This step helps the model process text as numbers, which is necessary for computers to understand language.

Example: For the sentence "MYSTERIOUS FOOTSTEPS ECHOED IN THE SILENT FOREST," each word (like "Mysterious" or "footsteps") is turned into a vector of 512 numbers.

2. **Positional Encoding:**

What it does: Since transformers don't process words in order (like humans do), they need a way to understand the **position** of each word in a sentence. Positional encoding adds information about the order of words to the vectors created in the previous step.

Why it's important: Without this, the model might treat sentences with the same words but different orders as identical. For example, "THE SUN SETS BEHIND THE MOUNTAIN" and "THE MOUNTAIN SETS BEHIND THE SUN" would look the same to the model without positional encoding.

How it works: Each word's vector (from step 1) is combined with another vector that represents its position in the sentence. This ensures the model knows where each word belongs.

3. **Attention Mechanism:** Captures relationships between words.

What it does: The attention mechanism helps the model focus on the most important words in a sentence when processing a specific word. It captures relationships between words, even if they are far apart in the sentence.

Why it's important: This allows the model to understand context. For example, in the sentences:

> "SHE POURED MILK FROM THE JUG INTO THE GLASS UNTIL IT WAS FULL."
> "SHE POURED MILK FROM THE JUG INTO THE GLASS UNTIL IT WAS EMPTY."
> The word "IT" refers to the glass in the first sentence and the jug in the second. The attention mechanism helps the model figure this out by looking at the relationships between words.

- o **Self-Attention:** Computes the importance of words within a single sequence.
  What it does: Self-attention is a specific type of attention mechanism where the model looks at all the words in a sentence and decides how much importance to give to each word when processing another word. For example, when

processing the word "IT," the model might pay more attention to "GLASS" or "JUG" depending on the context. **Why it's important**: It helps the model understand the meaning of a word based on its relationship with other words in the sentence.

1.
- o **Multi-Head Attention:** Runs self-attention in parallel multiple times to capture different aspects.

What it does: Instead of using just one attention mechanism, transformers use multiple attention mechanisms (called "heads") in parallel. Each head focuses on different parts of the sentence, allowing the model to capture a richer understanding of the text. **Why it's important**: This makes the model more powerful and capable of understanding complex language patterns.

Cross-attention is a mechanism that helps one set of data (called the **query**) focus on and connect to another set of data (called the **key-value pair**). Think of it like highlighting the most relevant parts of one conversation to make sense of another. It ensures that the two sides work together smoothly.

Here's how it works:
1. **Query (Q)**: This is what you're currently focusing on or what you're looking for in the other dataset. For example, if you're translating a sentence, the query might be the word you're trying to translate next.
2. **Key (K)**: This is like a tag or label that represents information in the other dataset. It helps determine how relevant a piece of information is to the query.
3. **Value (V)**: Once the relevance is determined, this is the actual information you want to extract or use.

Self-Attention vs. Cross-Attention

- **Self-attention** works within a single sequence (like one sentence). It helps each word in the sentence understand its relationship with the other words. For example, in the sentence "SHE POURED MILK INTO THE GLASS," self-attention helps the word "SHE" understands its connection to "POURED" and "GLASS."
- **Cross-attention**, on the other hand, connects two different sequences. For example, when translating the sentence "SHE

POURED MILK INTO THE GLASS" into French ("ELLE A VERSÉ DU LAIT DANS LE VERRE"), cross-attention helps the French words focus on the relevant parts of the English sentence.

Transformers are a deep learning model that handles sequential data, such as text. They use a self-attention mechanism to capture the relationship between words in a sequence. They are the backbone of many NLP models. The transformer network (model), introduced in the paper "Attention Is All You Need," was presented in 2017. The following figure demonstrates its architecture.

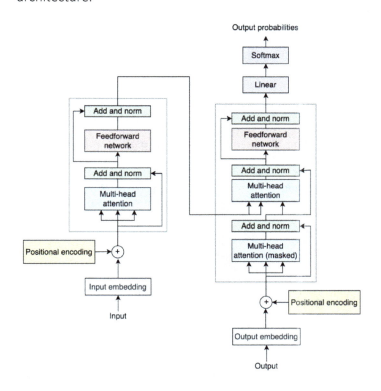

The **Transformer model** was introduced in 2017 in the paper **"Attention Is All You Need"** by Vaswani et al. It revolutionized natural language processing (NLP) by replacing traditional sequence models like RNNs (Recurrent Neural Networks) and LSTMs with a more efficient mechanism: **self-attention**.

Why Was the Transformer Model Created?

Before transformers, models like RNNs and LSTMs struggled with:

Slow training – RNNs processed words one by one, making them inefficient.

Difficulty handling long sentences – Information from earlier words was often lost.

Parallelization issues – RNNs couldn't process words simultaneously.

The **Transformer** solved these problems using **self-attention** and **parallel processing,** making it faster and more effective.

Architecture of the Transformer

The transformer consists of **two main parts**:

1️ **Encoder (Left Side in the Image)** – Processes the input sentence.
2️ **Decoder (Right Side in the Image)** – Generates the output (like a translated sentence).

Each **encoder and decoder** are made up of multiple **layers** containing key components:

Step 1: Input Processing

- The input sentence (e.g., *"She poured milk into the glass."*) is converted into numerical representations (**word embeddings**).

- **Positional encoding** is added so that the model understands word order (since transformers don't process sequentially).

Step 2: Encoder (Left Side of the Diagram)

Each encoder layer has:

Multi-Head Self-Attention – Helps the model understand relationships between words in the sentence.
Add & Normalize – Keeps values stable for better learning.
Feedforward Network – Further processes the attention output.

Each word attends to all other words, not just nearby ones, making the model understand **long-range dependencies**.

Step 3: Decoder (Right Side of the Diagram)

The decoder generates output step by step. It has:

Masked Multi-Head Attention – Ensures the model doesn't "peek" at future words during training.
Multi-Head Attention (Cross-Attention) – Connects the encoder's understanding with the decoder's generation.
Feedforward Network – Further processes data before generating words.
Softmax & Linear Layer – Converts numbers into actual words.

How Does the Transformer Work? (Step-by-Step)

1️⃣ **The encoder reads the entire input sentence at once** and understands relationships between words using **self-attention**.
2️⃣ **The decoder starts generating words** one at a time, using previously generated words and attention from the encoder.
3️⃣ **The process repeats until the full output sentence is generated** (e.g., translating to another language).

Key Benefits of Transformers

- Processes entire input at once (faster than RNNs).
- Understands long-range relationships between words.
- Parallelized training, making it efficient on GPUs.
- Achieved state-of-the-art performance in NLP tasks like GPT and BERT.

Transformer Architecture

"Attention Is All You Need"

"Mysterious footsteps echoed in the silent forest"

Word Embeddings (512 dimensions per word)

+

Positional Encoding (512 dimensions per position)

Combined Embeddings (Embeddings + Positional Encoding)

Multi-Head Attention
8 Attention Heads Working in Parallel

Feed-Forward Neural Network

Tokenization and input encoding

When working with text in AI models like transformers, the first step is to convert words into a format that the computer can understand. This process is called **tokenization and embedding**. Here's how it works:

1. **Tokenization**: The input sentence is broken down into smaller units called **tokens**. In most cases, each word becomes a token. For example, the sentence "MYSTERIOUS FOOTSTEPS ECHOED IN THE

SILENT FOREST" is split into 7 tokens: "MYSTERIOUS," "FOOTSTEPS," "ECHOED," "IN," "THE," "SILENT," and "FOREST."

2. **Embedding**: Each token (word) is then converted into a numerical representation called a **vector**. A vector is just a list of numbers. In this case, each word is turned into a vector of 512 numbers. This is important because computers can only work with numbers, not words.

3. **Why It Matters**: By converting words into vectors, the model can process and analyse the text. The numbers in the vector capture information about the word's meaning and its relationship to other words. This step is crucial for the model to understand the complexities of language.

Why Is This Important?

1️⃣ Transforms words into a machine-readable format.
2️⃣ Captures relationships between words (e.g., "silent" and "forest" might be closely related).
3️⃣ Allows the model to process long and complex sentences efficiently.

Word Tokenization and Embedding

| "Mysterious footsteps echoed in the silent forest" |

| Mysterious | footsteps | echoed | in | the | silent | forest |

| 512-dimension vector | 512-dimension vector | 512-dimension vector | 512-dimension vector | 512-dimension vector | 512-dimension vector | 512-dimension vector |

Each word is converted into a numerical vector of 512 dimensions
These vectors represent the meaning of each word

Example with the Sentence

Let's take the sentence: "MYSTERIOUS FOOTSTEPS ECHOED IN THE SILENT FOREST."

- Each word in the sentence is a token.
- Each token is converted into a vector of 512 numbers.

Here's a simplified representation of what happens:

Word (Token) Vector Representation (512 numbers)

Word (Token)	Vector Representation (512 numbers)
Mysterious	[8539.12, 1643.78, ..., 4201.56]
footsteps	[18976.32, 532.87, ..., 1894.23]
echoed	[456.78, 1502.34, ..., 3456.78]
in	[8765.43, 9876.54, ..., 5101.56]
the	[539.24, 173.79, ..., 601.67]
silent	[1459.10, 6413.09, ..., 1034.67]
forest	[189.12, 143.78, ..., 4201.56]

Imagine each word is turned into a long list of 512 numbers. These numbers represent the word in a way that the AI model can understand and work with. Here's a simple diagram to illustrate this:

Sentence: "Mysterious footsteps echoed in the silent forest"

Tokens: ["Mysterious", "footsteps", "echoed", "in", "the", "silent", "forest"]

Embeddings:
- "Mysterious" → [8539.12, 1643.78, ..., 4201.56]
- "footsteps" → [18976.32, 532.87, ..., 1894.23]
- "echoed" → [456.78, 1502.34, ..., 3456.78]
- "in" → [8765.43, 9876.54, ..., 5101.56]
- "the" → [539.24, 173.79, ..., 601.67]
- "silent" → [1459.10, 6413.09, ..., 1034.67]
- "forest" → [189.12, 143.78, ..., 4201.56]

Positional encoding

Positional encoding is a technique used in AI models, like transformers, to help the model understand the **order** of words in a sentence. Without it, the model might treat sentences with the same words but different orders as the same, which can lead to confusion.

Positional Encoding

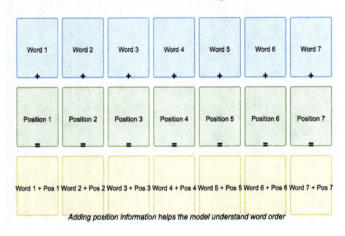

| Word 1 | Word 2 | Word 3 | Word 4 | Word 5 | Word 6 | Word 7 |

+ + + + + + +

| Position 1 | Position 2 | Position 3 | Position 4 | Position 5 | Position 6 | Position 7 |

= = = = = = =

Word 1 + Pos 1 Word 2 + Pos 2 Word 3 + Pos 3 Word 4 + Pos 4 Word 5 + Pos 5 Word 6 + Pos 6 Word 7 + Pos 7

Adding position information helps the model understand word order

Why Positional Encoding Matters

- **Word Order is Important**: In language, the order of words changes the meaning of a sentence. For example:
  - "THE SUN SETS BEHIND THE MOUNTAIN" means something very different from "THE MOUNTAIN SETS BEHIND THE SUN."
  - Without positional encoding, the model might think these two sentences are the same because they contain the same words.
- **How It Works**: Positional encoding adds information about the position of each word in the sentence to its numerical representation (embedding). This way, the model knows not just what the words are, but also where they appear in the sentence.

How Positional Encoding is Applied

1. **Embeddings**: First, each word in the sentence is converted into a numerical vector (a list of numbers) called an **embedding**. For example, the word "SUN" might be represented as [8539.12, 1643.78, ..., 4201.56].
2. **Positional Encoding**: A second vector, representing the word's position in the sentence, is added to the embedding. For example,

if "SUN" is the second word in the sentence, its positional encoding might look like [53.40, 3186.10, ..., 1929.14].

3. **Combining Embeddings and Positional Encoding**: The embedding and positional encoding vectors are added together. This combined vector now contains information about both the word's meaning and its position in the sentence.

Example with the Sentence

Let's take the sentence: "MYSTERIOUS FOOTSTEPS ECHOED IN THE SILENT FOREST."

- Each word is first converted into an embedding (a vector of 512 numbers).
- Then, positional encoding (another vector of 512 numbers) is added to each word's embedding.

Here's a simplified representation:

Word (Token)	Embedding (512 numbers)	Positional Encoding (512 numbers)	Combined Vector
Mysterious	[8539.12, 1643.78, ...]	[53.40, 3186.10, ...]	[8592.52, 4829.88, ...]
footsteps	[18976.32, 532.87, ...]	[3186.10, 452.76, ...]	[22162.42, 985.63, ...]
echoed	[456.78, 1502.34, ...]	[4596.90, 1872.35, ...]	[5053.68, 3374.69, ...]
in	[8765.43, 9876.54, ...]	[85.93, 761.43, ...]	[8851.36, 10637.97, ...]
the	[539.24, 173.79, ...]	[1506.01, 1073.9, ...]	[2045.25, 1247.69, ...]
silent	[1459.10, 6413.09, ...]	[1049.87, 1540.10, ...]	[2508.97, 7953.19, ...]
forest	[189.12, 143.78, ...]	[1929.14, 1113.90, ...]	[2118.26, 1257.68, ...]

Imagine each word's embedding and positional encoding as two lists of 512 numbers. These lists are added together to create a new combined vector that includes both the word's meaning and its position in the sentence.

Word: "Mysterious"
Embedding: [8539.12, 1643.78, ...]
Positional Encoding: [53.40, 3186.10, ...]
Combined Vector: [8592.52, 4829.88, ...]

Key Takeaways

- Helps Transformer models **understand word order** without sequential processing.

- Ensures words like **"sun" and "mountain"** don't swap meanings due to position loss.

- Uses **mathematical patterns** (like sine & cosine functions) to encode position efficiently.

The attention mechanism

The **attention mechanism** is a key part of transformer models that helps the model understand how words in a sentence relate to each other. It allows the model to focus on the most important words when processing a specific word, even if those words are far apart in the sentence.

Why Attention is Important

- **Context Matters**: In language, the meaning of a word often depends on the words around it. For example:
  - In the sentence "SHE POURED MILK FROM THE JUG INTO THE GLASS UNTIL IT WAS FULL," the word "IT" refers to the "GLASS."
  - In the sentence "SHE POURED MILK FROM THE JUG INTO THE GLASS UNTIL IT WAS EMPTY," the word "IT" refers to the "JUG."
  - The attention mechanism helps the model figure out these relationships.
- **Long-Range Dependencies**: Sometimes, words that are far apart in a sentence are closely related. The attention mechanism helps the model capture these relationships, even if the words are not next to each other.

How Attention Works

1. **Self-Attention**: This is the core of the attention mechanism. It calculates how much attention each word in a sentence should pay to every other word. For example:

    o   When processing the word "IT," the model might pay more attention to "GLASS" or "JUG" depending on the context.

    o   This is done by creating a **score** that represents how important one word is to another.

2. **Attention Scores**: The model creates a matrix (like a table) that shows how much attention each word gives to every other word. For example, in the sentence "MYSTERIOUS FOOTSTEPS ECHOED IN THE SILENT FOREST," the attention scores might look like this:

Word	Mysterious	footsteps	echoed	in	the	silent	forest
Mysterious	0.25	0.2	0.15	0.1	0.05	0.1	0.15
footsteps	0.13	0.21	0.12	0.18	0.1	0.08	0.18
echoed	0.15	0.20	0.25	0.12	0.10	0.08	0.10
in	0.12	0.18	0.14	0.26	0.10	0.08	0.12
the	0.15	0.08	0.14	0.20	0.30	0.07	0.06
silent	0.10	0.15	0.12	0.18	0.14	0.22	0.09
forest	0.08	0.10	0.15	0.12	0.10	0.13	0.20

    o   Each number in the table represents how much attention one word pays to another. For example, the word "MYSTERIOUS" pays 0.25 attention to itself, 0.2 attention to "FOOTSTEPS," and so on.

3. **Multi-Head Attention**: Instead of using just one attention mechanism, transformers use multiple attention mechanisms (called "heads") in parallel. Each head focuses on different parts of the sentence, allowing the model to capture a richer understanding of the text.

Why This Matters

The attention mechanism helps the model:

-   Understand the context of each word in a sentence.
-   Focus on the most relevant words when processing a specific word.

- Handle long-range dependencies, where words far apart in a sentence are closely related.

This is why transformers are so powerful for tasks like translation, summarization, and answering questions. They can understand and generate human-like text by paying attention to the right words at the right time.

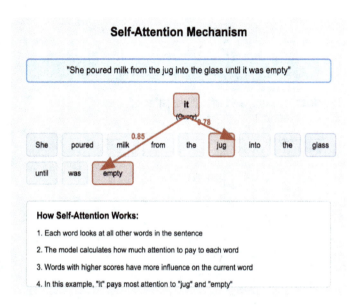

Self-Attention Mechanism

"She poured milk from the jug into the glass until it was empty"

How Self-Attention Works:

1. Each word looks at all other words in the sentence

2. The model calculates how much attention to pay to each word

3. Words with higher scores have more influence on the current word

4. In this example, "it" pays most attention to "jug" and "empty"

Multi-headed model

Multi-head attention is a technique used in transformers (like GPT models) to help them better understand the relationships between words in a sentence. Instead of looking at just one type of relationship, it looks at multiple perspectives at the same time.

Imagine you are reading a sentence:
"SHE POURED MILK FROM THE JUG INTO THE GLASS UNTIL IT WAS EMPTY."

If you were trying to understand what "IT" refers to, you might think about different possibilities:

- One perspective might focus on "THE JUG."

- Another perspective might focus on "WAS EMPTY."

Instead of using just one way to determine meaning, **multi-head attention** runs several attention mechanisms (called "heads") in parallel. Each head focuses on different aspects of the relationships between words.

What a Multi-Head Attention Works (Step-by-Step)

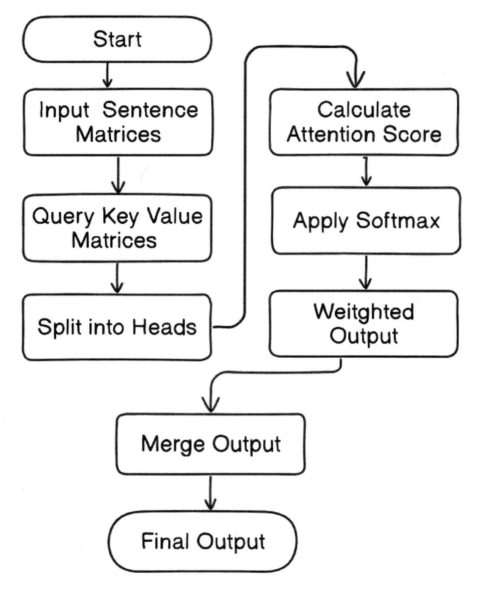

Step 1: Convert Words into Queries (Q), Keys (K), and Values (V)

Each word in the input is represented as a numerical vector. These vectors are used to create three matrices:

- **Q (Query):** Represents the current word we are focusing on.

- **K (Key):** Represents all words in the sentence and their importance.

- **V (Value):** Stores the actual word meaning to pass forward.

Step 2: Create Multiple Heads (Splitting the Input)
Instead of using just one attention mechanism, the model **splits the input into multiple smaller parts (heads)**.
For example, if we have **512** total input features and **8 heads**, each head gets **64 features** (512 ÷ 8 = 64).

Step 3: Perform Self-Attention in Each Head
Each head calculates self-attention independently. The steps for each head are:

1. Multiply **Q** with **K** (to get attention scores).

2. Apply **SoftMax** to normalize the scores (so they add up to 1).

3. Multiply the scores with **V** (to get the final weighted values).

Step 4: Combine the Results from All Heads
Each head captures different types of relationships between words. After processing, the outputs from all heads are **combined into a single matrix (C)**.

Step 5: Apply Final Weight Matrix (WC) and Output the Context
The final matrix (C) is multiplied by another set of weights (**WC**) to create the final representation of the input, now enriched with context from all attention heads.

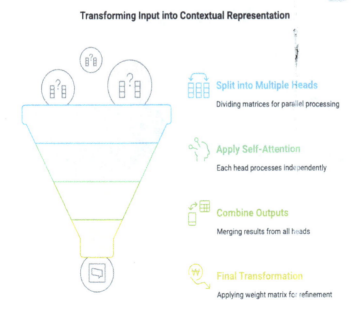

Transforming Input into Contextual Representation

Split into Multiple Heads
Dividing matrices for parallel processing

Apply Self-Attention
Each head processes independently

Combine Outputs
Merging results from all heads

Final Transformation
Applying weight matrix for refinement

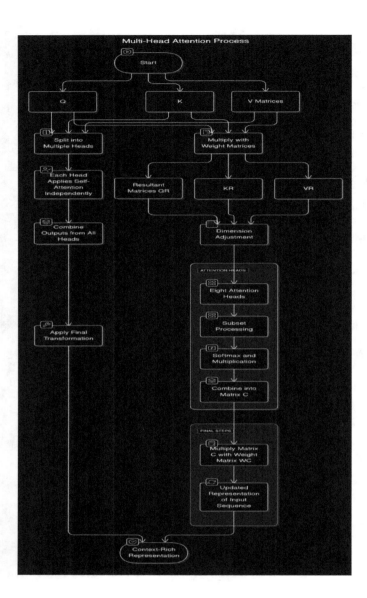

Why is Multi-Head Attention Important?

1️⃣ **Captures Different Meanings** – Each head learns different relationships, improving the model's understanding.
2️⃣ **Handles Complex Dependencies** – Helps track long-range relationships in a sentence.
3️⃣ **Improves Model Accuracy** – More precise word associations lead to better text generation and translation.

Takeaway

Mastering neural network architectures, including CNNs, RNNs, and transformers, is crucial for designing advanced GenAI systems. These concepts enable machines to learn patterns, generate creative outputs, and scale efficiently, forming the backbone of modern AI applications.

Evaluating Generative AI Systems

Evaluating Generative AI systems is crucial to ensure they produce high-quality, reliable, and safe outputs. As these systems become more integrated into various applications, understanding how to assess their performance becomes essential.

Why Evaluate Generative AI?

- **Quality assurance**: Ensure your AI meets basic quality standards

- **Comparison**: Compare different models to select the best one for your needs

- **Improvement**: Identify areas where your AI needs to be improved

- **Safety**: Detect harmful or biased outputs before deployment

- **Benchmarking**: Compare your AI against industry standards

Types of Evaluation

Evaluation Type	Description	When to Use
Automatic	Uses algorithms and metrics to evaluate outputs	When you need quick, consistent, large-scale evaluation
Human	Uses human reviewers to judge outputs	When subjective quality assessment is needed
Hybrid	Combines automatic and human evaluation	For balanced evaluation incorporating both perspectives

Key Evaluation Dimensions

1. **Accuracy**: How factually correct is the output?

2. **Relevance**: How well does the output address the prompt?

3. **Coherence**: How logical and well-structured is the output?

4. **Fluency**: How natural and grammatically correct is the language?

5. **Diversity**: How varied are the outputs for similar inputs?

6. **Safety**: Is the output free from harmful content?

7. **Fairness**: Is the output free from bias against specific groups?

8. **Helpfulness**: How useful is the output for solving the user's problem?

Key Evaluation Metrics

1. **Perplexity**: Measures how well the AI predicts a sample. A lower perplexity indicates better performance.

2. **BLEU (Bilingual Evaluation Understudy) Score**: Evaluates the similarity between the AI-generated text and reference texts, commonly used in translation tasks.

3. **ROUGE (Recall-Oriented Understudy for Gisting Evaluation) Score**: Assesses the overlap between the generated text and reference summaries, often used in summarization tasks.

4. **Human Evaluation**: Involves human reviewers assessing the AI's output based on criteria like fluency, coherence, and relevance.

5. **Task Success Rate**: Determines how effectively the AI completes a given task, such as answering questions correctly.

GenAI Evaluation Methods

1. Automatic Metrics

- **What it is**: Using mathematical formulas to evaluate outputs without human intervention.
- **Common Metrics**:
    - o **BLEU Score**: Measures how close the generated text is to a reference text (used in text generation).
    - o **Perplexity**: Measures how well the model predicts a sequence of words (lower is better).
    - o **FID (Fréchet Inception Distance)**: Evaluates the quality of generated images.
- **Example**: Use BLEU score to evaluate how similar an AI-generated summary is to a human-written summary.

Inception Score (IS)

- Evaluates image diversity and realism using a pretrained classifier.

- Higher scores indicate better diversity and recognizability.

- Formula involves:

    - o Computing label distribution.

    - o Finding the marginal distribution.

    - o Calculating Kullback-Leibler (KL) divergence.

    - o Taking the exponential of KL divergence.

2. Fréchet Inception Distance (FID)

- Measures similarity between generated and real images based on feature embeddings.

- Uses a pretrained model to compare the mean and covariance of image features.

- Lower FID scores indicate greater similarity.

- Can be adapted for text by encoding sentences into vectors and computing distances.

Fréchet Inception Distance (FID)

The diagram illustrates how Fréchet Inception Distance (FID) is calculated to compare generated images with real images. Here's the workflow:

1. Both a generated image (top) and a real image (bottom) of a tree with autumn foliage are passed through an Inception v3 neural network.

2. The Inception v3 model extracts feature vectors from both images.

3. For both feature sets, the system calculates:

   o The mean (μx for generated, μy for real)

   o The standard deviation (σx for generated, σy for real)

4. The FID is then calculated using the formula: $d(X,Y) = (\mu x - \mu y)^2 + (\sigma x - \sigma y)^2$

This metric measures the similarity between the distributions of real and generated images. A lower FID score indicates that the generated images are more similar to real images.

Fréchet Inception Distance (FID) is a widely used metric for evaluating the quality of images created by generative models. It measures how similar the distribution of generated images is to the distribution of real images.

How FID Works:

1. **Feature Extraction**:
   - Both real and generated image sets are passed through a pre-trained neural network (typically Inception v3)
   - This network acts as a feature extractor, converting images into feature vectors

2. **Statistical Analysis**:
   - For both real and generated feature sets, two statistical properties are calculated:
     - Mean (μ): The average of all feature vectors
     - Covariance (σ): How the features vary and correlate with each other

3. **Distance Calculation**:
   - The FID formula computes the distance between these statistical distributions:
   - $FID = ||\mu x - \mu y||^2 + Tr(\sigma x + \sigma y - 2\sqrt{(\sigma x \cdot \sigma y)})$
   - Where:
     - μx, σx: Mean and covariance of generated images
     - μy, σy: Mean and covariance of real images

- Tr: Trace of a matrix (sum of diagonal elements)

4. Interpretation:

   o   Lower FID scores indicate better quality and diversity

   o   A score of 0 would mean the distributions are identical

Advantages of FID:

- More comprehensive than older metrics like Inception Score

- Sensitive to image quality issues like blurriness and artifacts

- Can detect mode collapse (when a generator produces limited varieties)

- Correlates well with human perception of image quality

Limitations:

- Depends on the choice of feature extractor

- Requires a large batch of images for accurate estimation

- Cannot detect certain types of issues like memorization of training data

FID has become the standard evaluation metric for generative models like GANs, VAEs, and diffusion models because it provides a single number that effectively captures both the quality and diversity of generated images.

3. BLEU Score (Bilingual Evaluation Understudy)

- Measures similarity between generated and reference texts using n-gram comparisons.

- Precision-based; best for translation tasks.

- Penalizes short outputs to prevent artificially high scores.

BLEU (Bilingual Evaluation Understudy) is a way to measure how similar a generated text is to a reference text by comparing chunks of text called n-grams.

What is BLEU?

BLEU measures how similar a computer-generated text is to a reference text (like a human translation). It's especially useful for evaluating machine translations.

How N-grams Work in BLEU

N-grams are simply sequences of n words:

- 1-gram: Looking at single words ("edulive", "is", "an", etc.)

- 2-gram: Looking at pairs of words ("edulive is", "is an", etc.)

- 3-gram: Looking at triplets of words ("edulive is an", etc.)

Simple Example Calculation

Let's compare:

- Reference: "edulive is an e-learning platform with hundreds of courses"

- Generated: "edulive is an online platform with hundreds of courses"

Step 1: Count the Matching N-grams

1-gram (single words):

- 8 words match out of 9 total words in the generated text

- Precision = 8/9 = 0.89

2-gram (word pairs):

- 6 pairs match out of 8 total pairs in the generated text

- Precision = 6/8 = 0.75

3-gram (word triplets):

- 4 triplets match out of 7 total triplets in the generated text

- Precision = 4/7 = 0.57

Step 2: Calculate Geometric Average Precision

We take the cube root of the product of all three precision values (giving equal weight to each):

$$\sqrt[3]{0.89 \times 0.75 \times 0.57} = \sqrt[3]{(0.89)^{1/3} \times (0.75)^{1/3} \times (0.57)^{1/3}} \approx 0.723$$

Step 3: Apply Brevity Penalty (if needed)

Since our generated text (9 words) is the same length as the reference (9 words), there's no penalty:

- Brevity penalty = 1

Step 4: Calculate Final BLEU Score

BLEU = Brevity penalty × Geometric average precision BLEU = 1 × 0.723 = 0.723

In Simple Terms

The BLEU score of 0.723 (on a scale of 0 to 1) tells us the sentences are quite similar but not identical. This makes sense because they differ primarily by one word ("e-learning" vs "online").

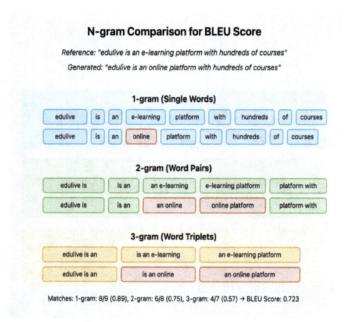

4. ROUGE Score (Recall-Oriented Understudy for Gisting Evaluation)

- Measures how much content from the reference text appears in the generated text.

- Variants include:

  - ROUGE-N: Matches based on n-grams.

  - ROUGE-L: Uses longest common subsequence.

  - ROUGE-S: Uses skip-bigram comparison.

- Best suited for summarization tasks.

5. Perplexity Score

Perplexity measures how "surprised" a language model is by a piece of text. In simple terms:

- **Low perplexity (close to 1):** The model confidently predicts the text

- **High perplexity (above 20):** The model finds the text unexpected or difficult to predict

How to Calculate Perplexity

1. **Get word probabilities:** For each word, calculate how likely the model thinks that word would appear next

2. **Multiply all probabilities:** Get the overall probability of the entire sequence

3. **Normalize by length:** Take the nth root where n is the number of words

4. **Calculate perplexity:** Perplexity = 1 ÷ normalized probability

Example: "My name is Edward"

In our example with vocabulary ["Hello", "Cat", "my", "Dog", "name", "is", "Edward"]:

1. P("My") = 0.3

2. P("name" | "My") = 0.5

3. P("is" | "My name") = 0.9

4. P("Edward" | "My name is") = 0.7

Total probability = 0.3 × 0.5 × 0.9 × 0.7 = 0.0945 Normalized probability = 0.0945^(1/4) = 0.5549 Perplexity = 1/0.5549 = 1.80

The perplexity of 1.80 indicates the model is quite confident in predicting this phrase.

When Perplexity Calculation is Critical

Perplexity is especially important when:

- Evaluating language model quality

- Comparing different models

- Detecting "off-distribution" text (content unlike what the model was trained on)

- Fine-tuning models to improve performance on specific domains

- Identifying when a model might be generating nonsensical or incoherent text

Remember that perplexity should be used alongside qualitative evaluation to get a complete picture of language model performance.

- Evaluates the fluency and confidence of text generation models.

- Lower perplexity indicates better predictions and coherence.

- Calculated using the probability distribution of words in a sequence.

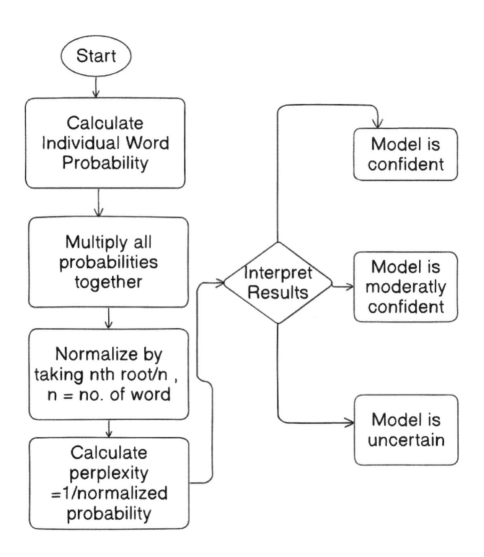

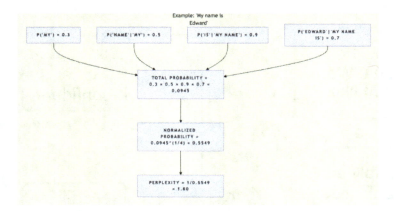

Example: 'My name is Edward'

| P('MY') = 0.3 | P('NAME'|'MY') = 0.5 | P('IS'|'MY NAME') = 0.9 | P('EDWARD'|'MY NAME IS') = 0.7 |

TOTAL PROBABILITY =
0.3 × 0.5 × 0.9 × 0.7 =
0.0945

NORMALIZED
PROBABILITY =
0.0945^(1/4) = 0.5549

PERPLEXITY = 1/0.5549
= 1.80

5. CLIP Score (Contrastive Language-Image Pretraining)

CLIP works like a translator that converts both images and text into the same "language" (numerical vectors) and then measures how close they are in meaning. It's similar to how we might judge if a caption accurately describes a photo but using mathematical precision.

How CLIP Score Works

The diagram shows the CLIP scoring process with these key components:

1. **Input:**

   o An image (a tree with orange/red autumn leaves in a field)

   o A text description ("A single tree in a field with orange leaves")

2. **Processing through CLIP**:

- o The image and text are passed through the CLIP neural network (shown as a brain with circuitry)

- o CLIP creates standardized vector representations (embeddings) for both the image and text

- o These embeddings capture the semantic meaning in a mathematical format (shown as matrices of 0s and 1s)

3. **Similarity Calculation**:

- o The cosine similarity formula calculates how aligned these embeddings are

- o Formula: Cosine similarity = $(A \cdot B)/(||A|| \cdot ||B||)$

- o Higher similarity means better text-image alignment

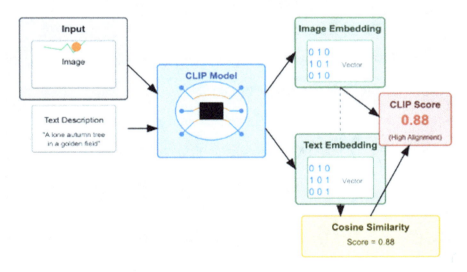

CLIP Score: Measuring Text-Image Alignment

- Assesses text-to-image alignment using cosine similarity between embeddings.

- Scores range from -1 (opposite) to 1 (perfect alignment).

- Higher scores indicate better semantic coherence.

CLIP Service Design

CLIP can be integrated into various services and applications:

1. **Content Validation Service**

   o Input: Image and caption pairs

   o Process: Calculate CLIP score

   o Output: Validation if the caption properly describes the image

   o Use case: Verifying accessibility descriptions for images

2. **Image Search Engine**

   o Input: Text query

   o Process: Compare query embedding against database of image embeddings

   o Output: Images ranked by CLIP score

   o Use case: Finding images based on detailed descriptions

3. **AI Image Generation Quality Control**

   o Input: Text prompt and generated image

   o Process: Measure alignment via CLIP score

   o Output: Accept/reject decision based on threshold

   o Use case: Ensuring text-to-image models produce relevant results

Technical Details of CLIP

CLIP (Contrastive Language-Image Pre-training) was developed by OpenAI and has several important characteristics:

- **Pre-training**: Trained on 400 million image-text pairs from the internet

- **Zero-shot learning**: Can perform tasks without specific training examples

- **Multi-modal understanding**: Bridges the gap between visual and textual information

- **Embedding space**: Projects both text and images into a shared 512-dimensional vector space

- **Contrastive learning**: Trained to maximize similarity for matching pairs while minimizing it for non-matching pairs

Practical Applications

CLIP score is particularly useful for:

1. **Text-to-image generation**: Evaluating if models like DALL-E, Midjourney, or Stable Diffusion are producing images that match text prompts

2. **Multimodal content analysis**: Assessing if image captions are accurate

3. **AI alignment research**: Measuring if AI systems interpret human instructions correctly

4. **Content moderation**: Detecting mismatches between images and descriptions that might indicate misleading content

The beauty of CLIP is that it understands both the semantic meaning of text and the visual content of images, allowing it to judge their alignment in a way that's similar to human judgment but can be automated at scale.

Metric	What It Measures	Calculation	Best For
BLEU	Precision of n-grams	Count matching n-grams between output and reference	Translation, text generation
ROUGE	Recall of n-grams	Overlap between output and reference texts	Summarization
METEOR	Word matching with synonyms	Alignment between output and reference with synonymy	Translation
BERTScore	Semantic similarity	Cosine similarity between BERT embeddings	General text quality
Perplexity	Prediction probability	$2^{\wedge}(\text{-average log probability})$	Language modeling

2. Human Evaluation

Human assessment captures aspects like creativity, coherence, and user satisfaction that automated metrics often miss.

1. Mean Opinion Score (MOS)

- Evaluators rate outputs on a fixed scale (e.g., 1-5).

- Common in speech synthesis, text generation, and image evaluation.

2. Task-Specific Quality Evaluation (TSQE)

- Focuses on key dimensions such as:

    o **Fluency** (grammatical correctness and natural flow).

    o **Relevance** (alignment with input prompt/context).

    o **Creativity** (originality and novelty).

3. Pairwise Comparison

- Evaluators compare two model outputs and select the superior one based on specific criteria.

- Useful for ranking models and identifying best-performing variations.

Pairwise Comparison: Compare outputs from two different systems:

- **What it is**: Comparing two outputs (e.g., from different models or versions) to determine which one is better.
- **How to conduct**:
    - Present two outputs to evaluators and ask them to choose the better one.
    - Use criteria like quality, relevance, and creativity.
- **Example**: Compare two AI-generated book outlines and ask which one has a better flow and structure.

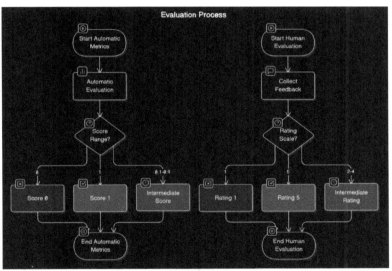

A snapshot of automatic vs. human evaluation

3. Benchmark Datasets

- **MMLU** (Massive Multitask Language Understanding)

- **HELM** (Holistic Evaluation of Language Models)

- **BIG-bench** (Beyond the Imitation Game benchmark)

- **GLUE/SuperGLUE** (General Language Understanding Evaluation)

Task-Specific Evaluation

- **What it is**: Evaluating the system based on how well it performs a specific task (e.g., generating a book outline, creating an image).
- **How to conduct**:
  - Define clear criteria for success (e.g., coherence, relevance, creativity).
  - Use human evaluators or automated metrics to assess the outputs.
- **Example**: For a book outline generator, evaluate if the chapters are logically ordered and relevant to the theme.

Task	Key Metrics	Evaluation Method
Text Summarization	ROUGE, BERTScore	Compare to reference summaries, check for factuality
Text Generation	BLEU, Perplexity, Human ratings	Check coherence, fluency, creativity
Translation	BLEU, chrF, COMET	Compare to reference translations
Question Answering	F1 score, Exact Match	Check answer correctness against gold standard
Chatbots	Response relevance, Human satisfaction	Conversation-level metrics, user feedback
Code Generation	Functional correctness, Pass@k	Test if generated code executes correctly

Conducting an Evaluation

Step-by-Step Process

1. **Define objectives**: What aspects of the AI system are you evaluating?

2. **Select metrics**: Choose appropriate automatic and human metrics

3. **Prepare test data**: Create diverse examples covering use cases

4. **Run evaluations**: Apply metrics and gather human evaluations

5. **Analyze results**: Identify strengths, weaknesses, and patterns

6. **Compare to baselines**: How does your system compare to others?

7. **Document findings**: Record methods and results for future reference

Practical Tips for Evaluation

1. Use **diverse test sets** that represent real-world use cases

2. Include **adversarial examples** to test robustness

3. **Balance automatic and human** evaluation for comprehensive assessment

4. Ensure **consistent instructions** for human evaluators

5. **Track progress over time** to measure improvement

6. Define **clear acceptance criteria** for quality thresholds

When to Use Different Evaluation Approaches

- **Development stage**: Use automatic metrics for rapid iteration

- **Pre-release**: Use comprehensive human evaluation

- **Production**: Monitor with automatic metrics and periodic human review

- **Comparison**: Use pairwise evaluations to select between systems

- **Specialized tasks**: Use task-specific metrics and expert evaluators

Safety and Ethical Evaluation

1. **Test for harmful outputs** across categories (violence, hate speech, etc.)

2. **Evaluate bias** across demographic dimensions

3. **Check for hallucinations** and factual correctness

4. **Test with adversarial inputs** designed to elicit problematic responses

5. **Evaluate data privacy** compliance

Evaluation Framework Diagram

Generative AI Evaluation Framework

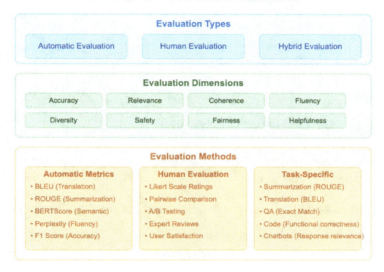

Sample Quiz Questions

1. What is the difference between BLEU and ROUGE metrics?

2. Why might human evaluation be preferred over automatic metrics?

3. What does perplexity measure in language models?

4. How would you evaluate the safety of a generative AI system?

5. What is the advantage of using pairwise comparisons over Likert scales?

Evaluating Generative AI systems is essential to ensure they produce high-quality outputs. By using task-specific evaluation, pairwise comparison, and automated metrics, you can measure the performance of your GenAI system and make improvements. Regular evaluation helps maintain the system's effectiveness and user satisfaction.

Metrics for Text Generation

Text generation metrics assess how well AI-generated text aligns with human expectations across dimensions like relevance, fluency, and coherence.

BLEU (Bilingual Evaluation Understudy)

BLEU measures the precision of n-grams (sequences of n words) in generated text compared to reference texts.

When to use: Translation tasks, summarization, and other tasks where exact word matching is important.

Calculation:

1. Count matching n-grams between generated and reference texts

2. Apply brevity penalty for short outputs

3. BLEU = Brevity Penalty × (Precision of n-grams)

Example:

- Reference: "The cat sat on the mat"

- Generated: "The cat is sitting on the mat"

- Unigram matches: "The", "cat", "on", "the", "mat" (5/7)

- BLEU-1 score: ~0.71 (simplified)

ROUGE (Recall-Oriented Understudy for Gisting Evaluation)

ROUGE focuses on recall of overlapping units like n-grams between generated and reference texts.

When to use: Summarization tasks where coverage of key information is critical.

Types:

- ROUGE-N: N-gram overlap

- ROUGE-L: Longest common subsequence

- ROUGE-S: Skip-bigram overlap

Calculation (ROUGE-N):

ROUGE-N = (Number of matching n-grams) / (Total n-grams in reference)

Perplexity

Perplexity measures how well a model predicts a sample, representing the model's uncertainty.

When to use: Language modeling evaluation, comparing models' predictive power.

Calculation:

Perplexity = 2^(-average log likelihood)

Lower perplexity indicates better predictions.

Human Evaluation Metrics

- **Fluency**: How natural the text reads

- **Coherence**: Logical flow and consistency

- **Relevance**: Appropriateness to the prompt

- **Informativeness**: Amount of useful content

Metrics for different generative AI modalities—text, image, audio, and video

Metrics for Image Generation

FID (Fréchet Inception Distance)

FID measures the similarity between distributions of generated and real images.

When to use: Evaluating the quality and diversity of generated images.

Calculation:

1. Extract features using a pre-trained network (typically Inception-v3)

2. Calculate mean and covariance for real and generated image features

3. $FID = ||\mu r - \mu g||^2 + Tr(\Sigma r + \Sigma g - 2\sqrt{(\Sigma r \Sigma g)})$

Lower FID scores indicate better image quality.

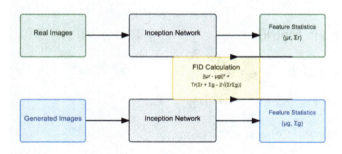

IS (Inception Score)

IS measures the quality and diversity of generated images using class probabilities from an Inception model.

When to use: When you need a quick assessment of image quality and diversity.

Calculation: Higher IS indicates better quality and diversity.

$IS = exp(E[KL(p(y|x) \mid\mid p(y))])$

SSIM (Structural Similarity Index)

SSIM assesses the perceptual similarity between images based on luminance, contrast, and structure.

When to use: When comparing generated images to specific target images.

Calculation:

$SSIM(x,y) = [l(x,y)]^\alpha \cdot [c(x,y)]^\beta \cdot [s(x,y)]^\gamma$

where l, c, and s are luminance, contrast, and structural components.

LPIPS (Learned Perceptual Image Patch Similarity)

LPIPS uses deep networks to measure perceptual similarity between images.

When to use: When human perceptual judgment is the primary concern.

Calculation: Distance between deep features of images, weighted by learned parameters.

Metrics for Audio and Video Generation

Audio Metrics

PESQ (Perceptual Evaluation of Speech Quality)

PESQ compares a reference audio signal with a generated one.

When to use: Speech generation, speech enhancement, and audio restoration.

Scale: -0.5 to 4.5, with higher scores indicating better quality.

MOS (Mean Opinion Score)

MOS involves human raters evaluating audio quality on a 1-5 scale.

When to use: When human perception of audio quality is critical.

Scale:

- 1: Bad

- 2: Poor

- 3: Fair

- 4: Good

- 5: Excellent

STOI (Short-Time Objective Intelligibility)

STOI measures the intelligibility of distorted speech signals.

When to use: Speech enhancement, speech synthesis evaluation.

Scale: 0 to 1, with higher values indicating better intelligibility.

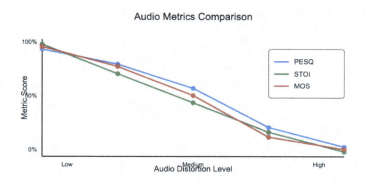

Audio Metrics Comparison

Video Metrics

PSNR (Peak Signal-to-Noise Ratio)

PSNR measures the pixel-by-pixel difference between frames.

When to use: Video compression, restoration, and generation tasks.

Calculation:

PSNR = 10 * log10(MAX²/MSE)

where MAX is the maximum pixel value and MSE is the mean squared error.

VMAF (Video Multimethod Assessment Fusion)

VMAF combines multiple quality metrics using machine learning to align with human perception.

When to use: Video streaming quality assessment, video compression.

Scale: 0 to 100, with higher scores indicating better perceptual quality.

FVD (Fréchet Video Distance)

FVD extends FID to video by capturing spatiotemporal characteristics.

When to use: Evaluating video generation models.

Calculation: Similar to FID but applies to video features extracted from 3D CNN models.

Bias & Fairness Considerations

Demographic Parity

Ensures that the probability of a positive outcome is the same across different demographic groups.

When to use: When equal representation is the primary fairness goal.

Calculation:

$$P(\hat{Y}=1|A=a) = P(\hat{Y}=1|A=b)$$

where A represents demographic attributes.

Equality of Opportunity

Ensures that the true positive rates are equal across demographic groups.

When to use: When equal opportunity for qualified individuals is the fairness goal.

Calculation:

$$P(\hat{Y}=1|Y=1,A=a) = P(\hat{Y}=1|Y=1,A=b)$$

Equalized Odds

Requires equal true positive rates AND equal false positive rates across demographic groups.

When to use: When both opportunities and error rates should be balanced.

Calculation:

$P(\hat{Y}=1|Y=y,A=a) = P(\hat{Y}=1|Y=y,A=b)$ for $y \in \{0,1\}$

Counterfactual Fairness

Ensures that predictions would be the same in a counterfactual world where the individual belonged to a different demographic group.

When to use: When causal relationships between attributes are important.

Fairness Evaluation in Generative AI

For generative AI specifically, consider:

1. **Representation Bias**: Evaluate how often different demographic groups appear in generated content

2. **Attribute Association**: Measure stereotypical associations in generated content

3. **Quality Disparity**: Compare quality metrics across demographic groups

4. **Harmful Content Rate**: Track differential rates of harmful content generation across groups

When to Use Which Metrics

Text Generation Use Cases

1. **Translation**: BLEU, human evaluation

2. **Summarization**: ROUGE, human evaluation

3. **Creative writing**: Human evaluation, perplexity

4. **Chatbots**: Human evaluation, task completion metrics

Image Generation Use Cases

1. **Photorealistic images**: FID, IS, human evaluation

2. **Style transfer**: LPIPS, SSIM, human evaluation

3. **Image-to-image translation**: SSIM, LPIPS, FID

Audio Generation Use Cases

1. **Speech synthesis**: PESQ, MOS, STOI

2. **Music generation**: Human evaluation, custom domain metrics

3. **Audio enhancement**: PESQ, STOI

Video Generation Use Cases

1. **Video prediction**: FVD, PSNR, VMAF

2. **Video synthesis**: FVD, human evaluation

3. **Video enhancement**: PSNR, VMAF

Use Case	Recommended Metric(s)
Machine Translation	BLEU, ROUGE, METEOR
Text Summarization	ROUGE, BERTScore
Open-ended Text	Perplexity, Human Evaluation
Image Generation	FID, IS, CLIP Score
Audio Quality	PESQ, MOS
Bias Detection	WEAT, Demographic Parity

Example Metric Calculations

BLEU Calculation Example

Reference: "The quick brown fox jumps over the lazy dog" **Generated**: "A quick brown fox jumps over a lazy dog"

1. Count 1-gram matches: 7/9 (missing "The" and using "A" twice)

2. Apply brevity penalty: 9/9 = 1 (same length)

3. BLEU-1 = 1 × (7/9) = 0.778

FID Calculation Example

1. Extract features from 1000 real images using Inception-v3

2. Extract features from 1000 generated images

3. Calculate mean and covariance for each set

4. Calculate FID using the formula

5. Example result: FID = 18.65 (lower is better, under 20 is generally good)

PESQ Calculation Example

1. Process reference and degraded audio through PESQ algorithm

2. Map raw scores to MOS-like scale

3. Example result: PESQ = 3.8 (on scale of -0.5 to 4.5)

Best Practices for Evaluation

1. **Use multiple metrics**: No single metric captures all aspects of quality

2. **Include human evaluation**: Automated metrics don't always align with human perception

3. **Consider task-specific metrics**: Different applications need different evaluation approaches

4. **Evaluate for fairness**: Check performance across demographic groups

5. **Analyze failure cases**: Understanding where models fail provides insights for improvement

Parallelism in Generative AI Models

Data Parallelism: Key Concepts and Challenges

Data parallelism distributes the dataset across multiple processing units while maintaining a complete copy of the model on each unit. This approach is widely used for handling large datasets efficiently.

Data Parallelism Architecture

In data parallelism, the process works as follows:

1. The dataset is divided among multiple GPUs/nodes

2. Each GPU independently processes its data portion and computes gradients

3. Gradients are synchronized across all nodes

4. Model parameters are updated using aggregated gradients

Synchronization Techniques in Data Parallelism

Parameter Server (Centralized) Architecture

- A dedicated server manages all parameter updates

- GPUs send gradients to the server and receive updated parameters

- **Challenge**: Creates a single point of failure and potential bottleneck

- **Resolution**: Implement redundant parameter servers and optimize communication patterns

Peer-to-Peer (Decentralized) Architecture

- GPUs communicate directly with each other without a central server

- Common implementations include AllReduce and Ring-AllReduce

AllReduce

- Each GPU shares gradients with all other GPUs

- **Challenge**: Communication overhead grows quadratically with number of GPUs

- **Resolution**: Use optimized communication libraries and algorithms

Ring-AllReduce

- GPUs arranged in a virtual ring topology, communicating only with neighbors

- **Challenge**: Sequential updates mean system speed limited by slowest GPU

- **Resolution**: Implement dynamic scheduling and hardware monitoring

Hierarchical AllReduce

- GPUs organized into clusters with coordinators

- Gradients aggregated within clusters first, then between coordinators

- **Challenge**: Adds complexity to system design

- **Resolution**: Careful system design with automated coordination mechanisms

How Data Parallelism Works

1. The dataset is divided among multiple GPUs or nodes.

2. Each GPU trains on its respective portion of the data, computing gradients independently.

3. The gradients from all GPUs are synchronized using various communication strategies.

4. The model is updated using the aggregated gradients, ensuring that all GPUs remain in sync.

Data Parallelism Architectures

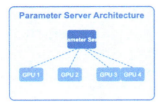

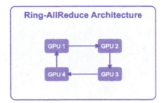

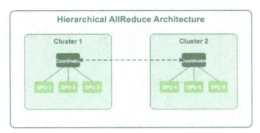

Model Parallelism: Types and Approaches

Unlike data parallelism, model parallelism splits the model itself across multiple devices, which is crucial when models are too large to fit in a single GPU's memory.

Types of Model Parallelism

While data parallelism distributes the dataset across multiple GPUs, model parallelism **splits the model itself** across devices. This technique is useful when the model is too large to fit into a single GPU's memory.

1. Layer-wise Partitioning

- Different layers of the neural network are assigned to different GPUs

- Each GPU processes its assigned layer and passes activations to the next GPU

- **Challenge**: Sequential processing creates synchronization bottlenecks

- **Resolution**: Pipeline parallelism with micro-batches to keep all GPUs busy

2. Operator-wise Partitioning

- Individual operations (e.g., matrix multiplications) are distributed across GPUs

- Suitable for complex computations that benefit from fine-grained parallelism

- **Challenge**: Requires careful data flow management to prevent bottlenecks

- **Resolution**: Automatic partitioning algorithms that optimize operation placement

3. Tensor Parallelism

- Computation for individual tensors is split across multiple devices

- Used for large matrix operations in transformer models

- **Challenge**: Increased communication overhead for tensor synchronization

- **Resolution**: Optimized communication patterns and hardware-aware partitioning

4. Pipeline Parallelism

- Combines layer-wise partitioning with micro-batches

- Different GPUs process different stages of the model simultaneously

- **Challenge**: Pipeline bubble inefficiencies at start and end of processing

- **Resolution**: Optimal micro-batch sizing and scheduling algorithms

Hybrid Parallelism: Combining Approaches

For extremely large models and datasets, combining multiple parallelism techniques is necessary. Hybrid parallelism combines data parallelism with various forms of model parallelism to optimize performance.

Hybrid Parallelism Implementation

- Dataset split across multiple groups of GPUs (data parallelism)
- Within each group, the model is split using model parallelism techniques
- Enables efficient handling of both enormous datasets and massive models
- This allows for efficient handling of **both large datasets and large models**.

Example: GPT-4, which contains trillions of parameters, uses hybrid parallelism during training.

Benefits of Hybrid Parallelism

- Overcomes memory limitations of single devices
- Improves computational efficiency
- Enables training of trillion-parameter models
- Provides flexible scaling options for different architectures

When to Use Hybrid Parallelism

- When the dataset is **too large** for a single GPU but can be split across multiple GPUs.

- When the model is **too large** for a single GPU's memory but can be split across multiple GPUs.

- When aiming for **maximum scalability** across large clusters.

Implementations in Modern GenAI Systems

- GPT-4 uses a combination of pipeline, tensor, and data parallelism

- Stable Diffusion models leverage hybrid approaches for faster training

- Advanced LLMs like Claude implement custom hybrid parallelism strategies

Model Parallelism Approaches

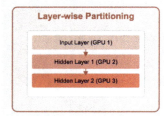

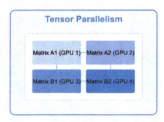

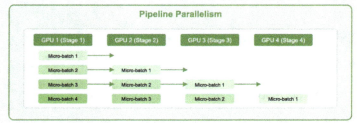

Common Challenges in Parallelism and Their Resolutions

1. Communication Overhead

- **Challenge**: High bandwidth requirements for gradient synchronization
- **Resolution**:
    - o   Optimize communication patterns (Ring-AllReduce)
    - o   Gradient compression techniques
    - o   Asynchronous communication where applicable

2. Synchronization Bottlenecks

- **Challenge**: Waiting for all nodes to complete computation
- **Resolution**:
    - o   Implement asynchronous updates where possible
    - o   Dynamic load balancing
    - o   Adaptive batch sizing

3. Memory Management

- **Challenge**: Efficient use of limited GPU memory
- **Resolution**:
    - o   Gradient checkpointing to trade computation for memory
    - o   Mixed-precision training

o   Offloading optimizer states to CPU

4. Fault Tolerance

- **Challenge**: Handling node failures in large clusters
- **Resolution**:

    o   Regular checkpointing of model state

    o   Redundant computation for critical components

    o   Graceful degradation strategies

5. Load Imbalance

- **Challenge**: Some GPUs process more data or complex operations than others
- **Resolution**:

    o   Dynamic workload allocation

    o   Hardware-aware partitioning

    o   Adaptive scheduling algorithms

Here's a summary of the different architectural concepts we discussed in data parallelism:

Aspect	Centralized Parameter Servers	Peer-to-Peer (P2P)(Decentralized)
Architecture	Uses a central parameter server to aggregate model updates and distribute parameters.	Peer-to-peer communication (no central coordinator).
Communication Pattern	One-to-many (workers to server and vice versa).	Many-to-many (workers communicate with neighbors).
Scalability	Limited by the central server's capacity (network, CPU, memory).	Highly scalable; no central bottleneck.
Fault Tolerance	The centralized server is a single point of failure.	More resilient to individual node failures; no single point of failure.
Synchronization	Easier to implement synchronous or asynchronous updates through the server.	Challenging to synchronize without global coordination.
Implementation Complexity	Low	High

Parallelism is a **fundamental concept** in training large-scale GenAI models. By distributing computation across multiple GPUs or entire clusters, we can **significantly accelerate training times** while overcoming hardware limitations.

- **Data parallelism** is widely used for **scaling dataset processing**.

- **Model parallelism** is crucial for handling **large models** that exceed a single GPU's memory.

- **Hybrid parallelism** combines the two for **maximum efficiency** in large-scale training.

However, challenges such as **communication overhead, fault tolerance, and load balancing** must be carefully managed to maximize efficiency. With optimized parallelism techniques, modern AI systems can train on massive datasets in a fraction of the time, enabling rapid advancements in generative AI

Inference System Design for GenAI Systems

Imagine you've trained a really smart robot to solve puzzles. Now you want to show it off to your friends! But there's a problem - the robot is slow, uses too much battery power, and sometimes gets the answers wrong. This is where "inference optimization" comes in.

Understanding Inference and Its Optimization in AI Systems

Machine learning models are like trained experts that learn from examples to solve specific problems. Once a model completes its training, we need to put it to work on real data - this process is called **inference**.

Inference simply means feeding new information to your trained AI model and watching it do its job - whether that's identifying objects in photos, translating text, or generating creative content. It's like giving a test to your AI to see how well it performs on information it hasn't seen before. During inference, we can measure things like how quickly the model responds and how accurate its answers are.

Let's say your AI model passes all your tests with flying colors - it gives great answers! The next challenge becomes making this impressive technology available to many users. This is where things get tricky.

Your users don't just care about correct answers - they care about:

- How quickly they get those answers (latency)

- Whether the service is available when they need it

- If it can handle thousands of users at once

- And you, as the provider, need to worry about keeping costs reasonable and energy consumption manageable

This is why **inference optimization** is so important. It's all about fine-tuning how your AI model works in the real world to make it:

1. Faster

2. More scalable

3. More efficient

4. Cost-effective

All while maintaining the quality of results your users expect.

For any AI system that needs to operate in production environments - especially those handling lots of users during busy periods - these optimizations aren't optional extras. They're essential to delivering a service that people will actually want to use.

What is Inference?

Inference is simply when your trained AI model (your smart robot) looks at new information and tries to give you a helpful answer. For example:

- A language model like me seeing your question and writing this response

- An image model looking at a photo and telling you what's in it

- A translation model converting English to Spanish

Why Optimize Inference?

Think of optimization as making your AI model:

1. **Faster** - nobody likes waiting!

2. **Cheaper** - using less electricity and computer power

3. **More efficient** - handling more users at once

4. **Just as accurate** - maintaining quality while improving everything else

When your GenAI system goes from a cool experiment to a real product that thousands or millions of people use, these optimizations become crucial.

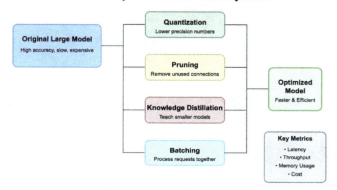

Inference Optimization in GenAI Systems

Key Inference Optimization Techniques

1. Quantization – Teaching the AI to Use Simpler Math

Quantization is a critical step in **model optimization** for real-world applications where resources (memory, power, latency) are constrained. By sacrificing minimal precision, models become more efficient without significantly compromising performance.

Imagine This:

You have a super-smart robot that does math with crazy precision – like measuring water to the **0.000001 liter** every time. Sure, it's accurate, but it takes ages and eats up tons of battery power. What if, instead, it just rounded to the nearest **whole number** or **tenths**? It would still do a pretty good job – but much faster and with less power.

That's **quantization** – making the AI use simpler, more compact numbers for its math.

What's Happening Under the Hood:

AI models use a lot of numbers – these are called **weights**. By default, these are stored as **32-bit floating-point numbers**. They are very precise, but also very bulky and slow to process. Quantization converts these into **8-bit integers** or **16-bit floats**, which are much faster and take less space.

Instead of:
Weight = 3.1415926535
It becomes:
Weight = 3

What it is: Converting the model's math from high precision (like using dollars and cents) to lower precision (just using whole dollars)

Why It Helps:

- Reduces model **size** (often by 4x or more)

- Speeds up computation by using simpler numbers

- Saves **memory** and **battery**

- Enables running AI on **edge devices** (phones, IoT devices)

Key Takeaway from Quantization

1. Reduced Precision:
   - High-precision numbers (e.g., 32-bit floats) are converted to lower-precision (e.g., 8-bit integers).
   - Some detail is lost (e.g., 7.91 → 7), but the overall structure of the data is preserved.
2. Benefits:
   - **Smaller Model Size**: Fewer bits per number reduce memory usage.
   - **Faster Inference**: Integer operations are computationally cheaper than floating-point ones.
   - **Hardware Efficiency**: Enables deployment on edge devices (e.g., smartphones, embedded systems).
3. Trade-offs:
   - Minor accuracy loss due to rounding, but often negligible for well-optimized models.

The Catch:

Quantization can slightly reduce **accuracy** if done poorly, especially in models that rely on very fine calculations (like complex vision or speech models). However, with smart techniques like **post-training quantization** or **quantization-aware training**, this accuracy drop can be minimized.

Real-World Example:

A company wants to deploy object detection in a drone that flies over farms. Initially, the model needs a GPU on a laptop. After quantization, the same model runs smoothly on a **Raspberry Pi**, using way less power and still spotting crops with 98% accuracy.

2. Pruning – Cutting the Useless Brain Wires

Imagine your robot's brain is like a giant spider web of wires. But not all wires are useful – some are like decorations, doing next to nothing. So why not snip them off?

That's **pruning** – cutting out the parts of the AI network that don't contribute much to the final decision.

How Pruning Works in Neural Networks

Pruning is like trimming away the unnecessary branches of a tree to make it healthier and more efficient. In neural networks, it works as follows:

1. **Start with a Fully-Trained Model**: First, train a complete neural network with all its connections and neurons until it performs well. This is your dense "overgrown" network.

2. **Identify Important Connections**: Analyse which connections are actually important by looking at their weight values. Strong weights (those with larger absolute values) contribute more to the model's decisions, while weak weights have minimal impact.

3. **Remove Weak Connections**: Cut away connections with small weights since they contribute little to the output. This is like removing the weakest branches from a tree. In some approaches, entire neurons may be removed if all their connections are weak.

4. **Fine-Tune the Pruned Model**: After removing connections, briefly retrain (fine-tune) the smaller network to allow it to adjust to the changes and regain any lost accuracy.

5. **Enjoy the Benefits**: The pruned model is now:

   o Much smaller in size (often 65-90% smaller)

   o Significantly faster at inference

   o Using less memory

   o Almost as accurate as the original model

The key advantage of pruning over other optimization techniques is its surgical precision. Rather than uniformly reducing the precision of all parameters (as in quantization), pruning selectively removes only what's truly unnecessary while preserving the critical parts of the network.

This results in models that are not just smaller and faster, but that maintain most of their original intelligence. It's like carefully editing a long essay to remove all unnecessary words while preserving its meaning, rather than just making all the words shorter.

How Neural Network Pruning Works

Step 1	Step 2	Step 3
Train the full model	Analyze connection importance	Remove weak connections

Step 4	Step 5: Compare Performance	
Fine-tune the pruned model	**Original Model**	**Pruned Model**

	Original Model	Pruned Model
Size:	100 MB	35 MB
Speed:	1.0x	2.7x faster
Accuracy:	95%	93%
Memory:	High	Low

What's Really Happening:

Deep learning models often have **millions or billions of parameters**. But research has shown that a lot of them are redundant or barely used. Pruning looks for:

- Weights that are **close to zero**

- Neurons that barely activate

- Layers that aren't pulling their weight

Then it removes them (like trimming a tree), making the model **lighter, faster**, and still smart.

Why It's Great:

- Reduces **model size**

- Speeds up **inference time**
- Uses **less memory and compute**

The Catch:

Prune too much and your model loses its "thinking power" – performance drops. That's why pruning is usually done gradually, followed by a quick **fine-tuning** to restore lost knowledge.

Real-World Example:

A language model trained for summarizing news articles is initially 65GB. After pruning out 70% of the least useful parameters, it's reduced to 20GB. It still produces great summaries, now runs 2x faster, and costs 60% less to host.

3. Batching – AI Becomes a Team Player

Imagine This:

Your robot is answering customer questions. But it handles one at a time, like a cashier who serves one person, takes a break, then serves the next. Now imagine that instead, it waits for 10 people, takes their questions together, and answers them all in one go.

That's **batching** – processing multiple inputs in one efficient go.

What's Happening Technically:

Instead of calling the model **for every single request**, we group several inputs into a **batch** and run them through the model in **parallel** on a GPU or TPU. This is way more efficient because modern hardware is designed for parallel operations.

Why It's Awesome:

- Improves **throughput** (more work done per second)
- Maximizes **GPU/TPU usage**

- Reduces **per-request cost**

The Catch:

- Some users may need to wait until a batch is full (adds latency).

- Complex to implement dynamically in real-time applications.

Real-World Example:

An AI that generates artwork from text gets 1,000 requests per minute. Instead of doing them one by one, it batches them in groups of 32, completing them in milliseconds per batch and lowering compute costs dramatically.

Knowledge Distillation – Passing the Torch

Knowledge distillation (KD) is an elegant technique that transfers the "wisdom" of a large, complex model (the teacher) to a smaller, more efficient model (the student). This process allows us to deploy powerful AI capabilities on devices with limited resources while preserving most of the original performance.

The Core Concept

Unlike the traditional approach of simply training smaller models from scratch, knowledge distillation leverages the insights already learned by larger, more powerful models. The teacher model, with its extensive neural architecture, captures complex patterns and nuances in the data that might be difficult for a smaller model to learn directly.

The genius of knowledge distillation lies in how it transfers this knowledge:

1. **Soft Targets**: Instead of just using hard labels (like "cat" or "dog"), the teacher provides probability distributions across all possible outputs. These "soft targets" contain rich information about similarities between categories.

2. **Temperature Scaling**: A temperature parameter controls how "soft" these probability distributions become. Higher temperatures create smoother distributions that better reveal the teacher's understanding of relationships between classes.

3. **Dual Loss Training**: The student model is typically trained with a combined loss function that balances mimicking the teacher's outputs with predicting the correct ground truth labels.

Why Knowledge Distillation Works

Large models often have substantial redundancy in their parameters. Knowledge distillation effectively compresses the essential patterns while discarding unnecessary complexity. The teacher model acts as a filter, highlighting which aspects of the data are most important for making accurate predictions.

Practical Applications

Knowledge distillation has revolutionized AI deployment in resource-constrained environments:

- Converting massive language models like GPT into versions that run on smartphones
- Deploying computer vision systems on edge devices and IoT sensors
- Creating efficient translation or voice recognition systems for offline use
- Reducing cloud computing costs while maintaining service quality

Evolution of the Technique

Since its formalization about two decades ago, knowledge distillation has expanded beyond simple classification tasks. Modern approaches include:

- **Feature-based distillation**: Transferring intermediate representations
- **Relation-based distillation**: Preserving relationships between different data points
- **Online distillation**: Teacher and student models learning simultaneously
- **Self-distillation**: Models teaching refined versions of themselves

The diagram illustrates how knowledge flows from training data through both teacher and student models, with the teacher guiding the student through soft targets while the student also learns from ground truth data, ultimately creating a compact model suitable for resource-constrained devices.

Knowledge Distillation Framework

Knowledge Distillation transfers insights from complex teacher models to compact student models, enabling deployment on resource-constrained devices while maintaining comparable performance through soft probability distributions.

Imagine This:

You've got a professor robot that knows everything – but it's slow, heavy, and can't fit in your pocket. What if the professor trained a smart student robot to mimic its answers – not perfectly, but good enough?

That's **knowledge distillation** – using a big model (teacher) to train a smaller model (student) to think in a similar way.

How It Works:

1. First, train a large and powerful model (the teacher).

2. Use the teacher to generate outputs (e.g., probabilities, classifications).

3. Train a smaller model (the student) to **mimic** those outputs.

4. The student ends up with much of the teacher's performance but is smaller and faster.

Why It Rocks:

- Great for **deployment on smaller devices**

- Keeps good **accuracy**

- Reduces **cost and energy usage**

The Catch:

- Student never becomes as smart as the teacher.

- Needs a good strategy to choose what knowledge is distilled.

Real-World Example:

OpenAI's GPT-3 (175B parameters) is distilled into a much smaller model (like GPT-2 size) that can run on a laptop and still perform many tasks well like answering emails, summarizing text, and chatting.

5. Model Caching – Robot's Short-Term Memory

Caching is a fundamental technique used across computational systems to enhance performance by storing and reusing previously computed results. In **Generative AI (GenAI) systems**, caching plays a crucial role in **reducing inference latency, minimizing computational overhead, and improving response times**—making AI-powered services faster and more efficient for end users.

Since GenAI models (e.g., LLMs, diffusion models) often process **repetitive or semantically similar queries**, caching avoids redundant computations by retrieving stored results instead of reprocessing inputs. Below, we explore key caching strategies optimized for GenAI inference.

1. Semantic Cache

How it Works:
Unlike traditional caches that require **exact input matches**, semantic caching retrieves results based on **meaning similarity**. It uses embeddings (vector representations) to compare queries and return cached responses if they meet a similarity threshold.

Example:
- Query 1: *"What is 1 + 1?"*
- Query 2: *"What's one plus one?"*
  Both trigger the same cached answer (*"2"*) because their semantic meanings align.

Use Case:
- Ideal for chatbots, search engines, and Q&A systems where users phrase questions differently.

[User Query: "Explain gravity"] → [Embedding Comparison] → [Cache Hit: Similar to "Define gravity"] → [Returns Cached Answer]

2. Prompt Cache

How it Works:
Stores responses for **identical or partially overlapping prompts**, avoiding reprocessing by the LLM. It breaks prompts into reusable modules (e.g., templates, common prefixes) for faster lookup.

Example:
- Cached Prompt: "TRANSLATE 'HELLO' TO FRENCH" → "BONJOUR"
- New Prompt: "TRANSLATE 'HELLO' TO FRENCH, AND ADD A SMILEY" → Reuses "BONJOUR" before appending ":)".

Use Case:
- Reduces latency in applications with repetitive prompt structures (e.g., code generation, templated responses).

Prompt: "Summarize this text: {A}"] → [Cached Summary]
[New Prompt: "Summarize this text: {A} in 10 words"] → Reuses summary, then trims

3. Key-Value (KV) Cache

How it Works:
Stores intermediate computations (keys and values from attention layers) during **autoregressive token generation**, allowing models to reuse past context instead of recomputing it for each new token.

Example:

- Generating "THE CAT SAT ON THE..." reuses cached KV pairs for earlier tokens to predict "MAT" faster.

Use Case:

- Critical for **real-time text generation** (e.g., ChatGPT, code autocompletion).

Trade-off:

- High memory usage, as KV cache grows with sequence length.

```
Tokens: ["The", "cat", "sat"] → [KV Cache Stores Attention Outputs]
Next Token: "on" → [Uses Cache to Compute "the mat"]
```

4. Exact Cache

How it Works:
Stores **fully identical inputs/outputs** (e.g., using Redis/Memcached) with eviction policies (LRU, FIFO) to manage storage.

Example:

- Caching a web search result for "CURRENT TIME IN PARIS" for 1 minute.

Use Case:

- Chain-of-thought reasoning, external API calls, or deterministic outputs.

```
• [Input: "2+2"] → [Exact Cache] → [Output: "4"]
• [Input: "2+2"] → [Cache Hit] → [Skips Computation]
```

Cache Layer Decision Process

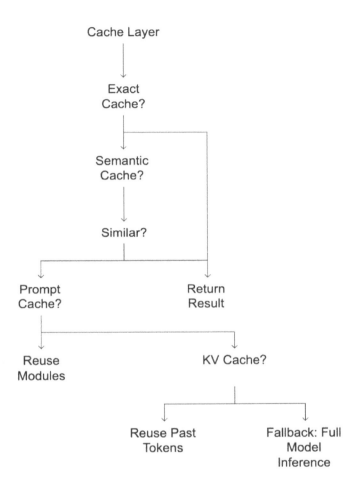

Imagine This:

You keep asking your robot, "What's 2+2?" Every time, it thinks hard and answers: "4." But isn't that a waste? Why not just **remember** the answer the first time?

That's **model caching** – storing frequently asked questions and their answers, so the model doesn't repeat work.

What's Actually Happening:

- Every time the model is asked something, the input and output are stored.

- Next time the same input is seen, the system returns the **stored result** instantly.

- No need to run the AI model at all for these queries.

Why It's Powerful:
1. **Latency Reduction**: Avoids reprocessing frequent/similar queries.
2. **Cost Efficiency**: Reduces cloud inference costs (e.g., GPT-4 API calls).
3. **Scalability**: Enables high-throughput applications (e.g., customer support bots).

The Catch:

- Not useful for new, creative, or unique inputs.

- Needs good cache management and storage space.

Comparison of Caching Strategies in GenAI

Criteria	Semantic Cache	Prompt Cache	KV Cache	Exact Cache
Scope	Similar queries (semantic meaning)	Repeated/overlapping prompts	Tokens within a single prompt	Identical queries (exact match)
Complexity	High (embedding comparisons)	Medium (heuristic matching)	Low (stores token-level data)	Low (direct key-value lookup)
Memory Demand	High (stores embeddings)	High (stores prompt modules)	Medium (scales with context)	Varies (depends on eviction policy)
Latency Benefit	Medium to High (similarity checks)	Very High (avoids re-computation)	High (reuses past computations)	High (instant retrieval)
Best Use Case	Fuzzy matching (e.g., chatbots, search)	Structured queries (e.g., code generation)	Autoregressive generation (e.g., ChatGPT)	Deterministic outputs (e.g., FAQs)
Scalability	Resource-intensive (clustering helps)	Limited by prompt diversity	Highly scalable (low overhead)	Effective with deduplication

Real-World Example:

A customer service chatbot answers thousands of "What's your refund policy?" queries daily. Instead of querying the model every time, the system just **reuses a saved response**, making it instant and free.

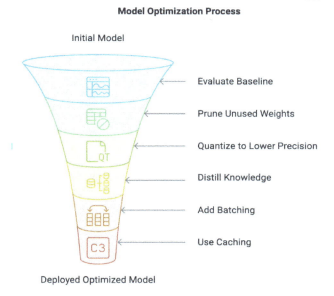

Model Optimization Process

Initial Model

- Evaluate Baseline
- Prune Unused Weights
- Quantize to Lower Precision
- Distill Knowledge
- Add Batching
- Use Caching

Deployed Optimized Model

Deep Comparison Table (Expanded)

Technique	Main Goal	Key Benefit	Accuracy Impact	Best For	Common Challenge	Real-World Example
Quantization	Reduce precision	Speed & size boost	Slight loss	Edge devices, mobile apps	May lower accuracy slightly	Phone runs vision AI locally
Pruning	Remove unused parts	Smaller, faster models	Low if done right	Large over-parameterized models	Risk of pruning too much	LLM shrinks from 65GB to 20GB
Batching	Process together	Higher throughput	None	High-traffic apps, APIs	Latency for single requests	AI image tool serves 32 requests at once
Distillation	Train smaller model	Faster inference, lower cost	Moderate loss	Running on cheaper hardware	Might miss deep logic	Student LLM mimics GPT-3 on small device
Model Caching	Avoid duplicate work	Zero-latency for repeats	None	Repeated queries, FAQs	Not good for unique prompts	Chatbot stores answers for common questions

Parameters for Measuring Optimization Success

When optimizing inference, engineers track these key metrics:

1. **Latency** - How fast does the model respond? (lower is better)

2. **Throughput** - How many requests can be handled per second? (higher is better)

3. **Memory Usage** - How much RAM is needed? (lower is better)

4. **Model Size** - How much storage space is required? (lower is better)

5. **Energy Consumption** - How much electricity is used? (lower is better)

6. **Accuracy Trade-off** - How much accuracy is lost during optimization? (less is better)

7. **Cost per Inference** - How much does each prediction cost? (lower is better)

Inference optimization isn't just for techies — it's what makes your smart assistants, recommendation engines, and creative AIs feel **magical and fast** instead of **slow and clunky**.

With these techniques:

- AI runs on **phones**, not just data centres

- More people get **access** to powerful tools

- Companies save **millions in compute**

- It's better for the **environment** too

Summary for Inference optimization

In this lesson, we explored essential **inference optimization techniques** that enable scalable, high-performance AI systems. While training and deploying models are critical steps, optimizing inference ensures these models run **efficiently at scale**— reducing costs, latency, and resource demands for end users.

Key techniques like **quantization, pruning, and caching** (semantic, prompt, KV, and exact) form the backbone of real-world AI deployments. Beyond these, methods such as:

- **Model compression** (reducing size without sacrificing accuracy),
- **Pipeline parallelism** (distributing workloads across devices),
- **Hardware-specific acceleration** (e.g., TPUs, GPUs, edge chips)

further push the boundaries of what's possible. Together, these strategies are the **building blocks of sustainable, future-proof AI systems**—balancing performance, cost, and user experience.

Key Improvements:

1. **Stronger Opening**: Clearly ties optimization to real-world impact.
2. **Conciseness**: Removes redundancy (e.g., "widespread applicability" →
    "scalable, high-performance").
3. **Structured List**: Breaks down "other techniques" for readability.
4. **Forward-Looking Tone**: Emphasizes sustainability and future-proofing.

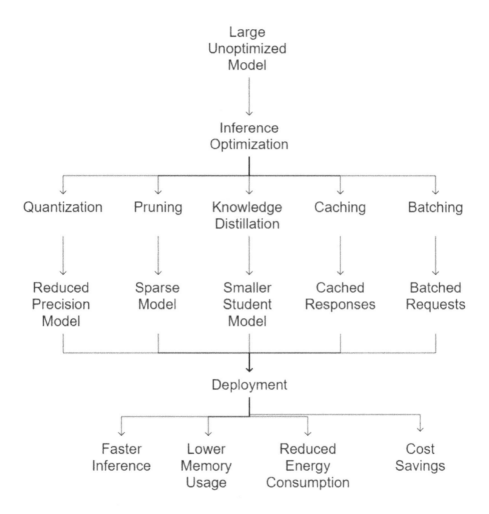

The diagram flows from top to bottom with the following structure:

1. At the top is "Large Unoptimized Model" - representing the starting point of
    a machine learning model before optimization.

2. This leads to a diamond-shaped node labelled "Inference Optimization" - the central process being explained.

3. From this central node, five optimization techniques branch out:

    o   "Quantization" → "Reduced Precision Model"

    o   "Pruning" → "Sparse Model"

    o   "Knowledge Distillation" → "Smaller Student Model"

    o   "Caching" → "Cached Responses"

    o   "Batching" → "Batched Requests"

4. All these optimized models/techniques converge to a node labelled "Deployment" - representing the implementation of the optimized model in a production environment.

5. The deployment then leads to four key benefits at the bottom of the diagram:

    o   "Faster Inference" - improved response time

    o   "Lower Memory Usage" - reduced RAM requirements

    o   "Reduced Energy Consumption" - better energy efficiency

    o   "Cost Savings" - economic benefits

This diagram effectively shows how various inference optimization techniques transform a large, inefficient model into a more streamlined solution with multiple performance and cost benefits. It visualizes the complete optimization pipeline from the original model to the final deployment advantages.

Key Concepts in Designing GenAI Systems

As Generative AI (GenAI) continues to advance, the ability to create high-quality, meaningful content—whether it's text, images, audio, or video—depends on a deep understanding of domain-specific concepts and techniques. These foundational ideas help us build systems that can interpret, process, and generate data in ways that closely resemble human creativity and perception.

This lesson introduces essential techniques used across different generative domains. From tokenization and embedding strategies in natural language processing, to phoneme conversion and acoustic modeling in speech synthesis, and fundamental ideas in video generation—each concept plays a vital role in transforming raw inputs into rich, context-aware outputs. These principles are at the heart of how modern GenAI systems work.

The table below outlines the key concepts we'll explore in each domain.

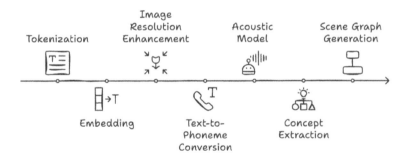

Tokenization

Tokenization is the fundamental process of breaking down text into smaller units called tokens that can be processed by machine learning algorithms. This critical first step in natural language processing (NLP) transforms raw text into a structured format that computers can analyse and understand. By converting continuous text streams into discrete elements, tokenization creates the building blocks that enable machines to process human language.

The Core Concept of Tokenization

At its heart, tokenization serves as a bridge between human language and computer processing. When we enter text into an AI system, that continuous stream of characters must be segmented into meaningful units. These units—or tokens—can vary in granularity depending on the specific requirements of the NLP task and the language being processed.

The tokenization process transforms unstructured text like "The five boxing wizards jumped quickly" into a structured sequence of discrete tokens. This transformation is essential because most machine learning models cannot directly process raw text; they require numerical representations derived from these tokens. Each token becomes a point of analysis that the model can examine individually and in relation to other tokens.

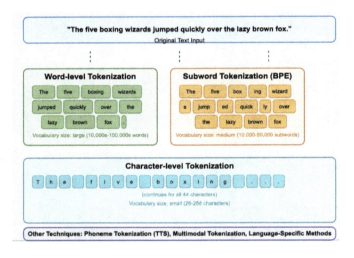

Diverse Tokenization Techniques

Word-Level Tokenization

Word-level tokenization splits text at word boundaries, typically using spaces and punctuation as delimiters. This is the most intuitive approach for languages like English that have clear word separators.

For example, the sentence "The cat sat on the mat." would be tokenized as: ["The", "cat", "sat", "on", "the", "mat", "."]

This method is straightforward but comes with significant limitations. It struggles with languages that don't use spaces between words (like Chinese or Japanese), and it creates extremely large vocabularies since each word form (including variations like "run," "runs," "running") becomes a separate token. Additionally, it has no elegant way to handle out-of-vocabulary words—terms that weren't seen during training.

Subworld Tokenization

Subworld tokenization addresses many limitations of word-level approaches by breaking words into meaningful components like prefixes, roots, and suffixes. This technique strikes a balance between the granularity of character-level tokenization and the semantic completeness of word-level tokenization.

Popular sub word tokenization methods include:

1. **Byte Pair Encoding (BPE)**: Starts with character-level tokens and iteratively merges the most frequent adjacent pairs to form new tokens.

2. **WordPiece**: Similar to BPE but uses likelihood rather than frequency to determine merges.

3. **SentencePiece**: Treats spaces as characters and works without pre-tokenization, making it suitable for languages without clear word boundaries.

For example, "unbelievable" might be tokenized as ["un", "believ", "able"], allowing the model to understand component meanings and handle rare words more effectively.

Character-Level Tokenization

Character-level tokenization represents the finest granularity, treating each character as a separate token. This approach creates a very small vocabulary (typically just 26 letters plus punctuation and special characters for English) and eliminates the out-of-vocabulary problem entirely.

The sentence "Hello!" would be tokenized as: ["H", "e", "l", "l", "o", "!"]

While this method is robust and language-agnostic, it produces much longer sequences of tokens, which can be computationally expensive and may require more sophisticated models to capture meaningful relationships between distant characters.

Specialized Tokenization Methods

Beyond these core approaches, specialized tokenization techniques exist for specific applications:

- **Phonetic Tokenization**: Used in text-to-speech systems to convert text into phonemes (sound units), ensuring proper pronunciation.

- **Multimodal Tokenization**: Handles mixed media inputs by tokenizing text alongside other data types like images or audio, creating unified representations for cross-modal understanding.

- **Language-Specific Tokenization**: Applies customized rules for languages with unique structures, such as morphologically rich languages (Finnish, Turkish) or languages without explicit word boundaries (Thai, Japanese).

The Impact of Tokenization Choices

The choice of tokenization strategy significantly impacts model performance and capabilities:

1. **Vocabulary Size**: Word-level tokenization typically results in vocabularies of tens or hundreds of thousands of tokens, while character-level approaches may need only dozens or hundreds. Subword methods usually fall in between with vocabularies of a few thousand to tens of thousands.

2. **Sequence Length**: Character-level tokenization produces longer sequences than word or subword approaches, affecting memory requirements and processing time.

3. **Out-of-Vocabulary Handling**: Subword and character-level approaches can represent previously unseen words by combining familiar components, while basic word-level tokenization cannot.

4. **Semantic Understanding**: Larger token units (words or common subwords) retain more immediate semantic meaning, while smaller units require the model to reconstruct meaning from multiple tokens.

Modern NLP systems like GPT, BERT, and others predominantly use subword tokenization methods, finding a balance between vocabulary size, sequence length, and semantic richness that enables powerful language understanding capabilities.

Tokenization remains a critical preprocessing step that shapes how machines interpret and generate human language, forming the foundation upon which sophisticated language models are built.

Embedding

Embeddings are a fundamental concept in machine learning and natural language processing that allow computers to work with words, sentences, or any discrete objects by converting them into numerical vectors. Let me explain this in simple terms with more detail.

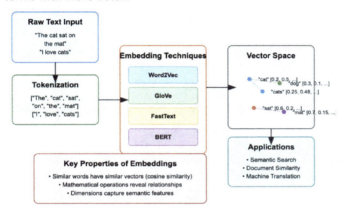

What Are Embeddings?

Embeddings are a way to represent words, sentences, images, or any discrete objects as continuous vectors of numbers. Imagine trying to explain what a "cat" is to a computer. The computer doesn't understand English words, only numbers. Embeddings bridge this gap by transforming words like "cat" into a list of numbers (like [0.2, 0.5, 0.1, -0.3, ...]) that computers can process.

These number sequences aren't random—they're carefully crafted to capture meaning. In a good embedding, words with similar meanings will have similar number patterns. For example, the vectors for "cat" and "kitten" would be closer to each other than the vectors for "cat" and "airplane."

Why Embeddings Matter

Embeddings solve a fundamental problem in machine learning: most algorithms can only process numerical data, but much of our information (text, images, etc.) isn't naturally numerical. By converting words into vectors, we enable computers to:

1. Measure how similar words are to each other
2. Discover relationships between concepts
3. Group related items together
4. Perform mathematical operations on words (like "king" - "man" + "woman" ≈ "queen")

Popular Embedding Techniques
Word2Vec

This technique learns word relationships by predicting either a word from its context (Continuous Bag of Words) or the context from a word (Skip-gram). Word2Vec trains a neural network that results in word embeddings that capture amazing semantic relationships.

GloVe (Global Vectors)

Unlike Word2Vec which focuses on local context, GloVe analyzes how often words appear together across an entire text corpus. It creates a co-occurrence matrix and generates embeddings that balance global statistics with local context information.

FastText

An extension of Word2Vec, FastText treats each word as a collection of character n-grams (subword units). This allows it to generate vectors even for words it hasn't seen before by combining the vectors of its subwords. For example, it could understand "untraceable" even if it never saw it during training.

BERT Embeddings

BERT revolutionized embeddings by making them contextual—the same word gets different embeddings depending on its context. For example, "bank" would have different embeddings in "river bank" versus "bank account." BERT uses transformer architecture to generate these rich, context-aware representations.

Universal Sentence Encoder (USE)

While the previous methods focus primarily on words, USE directly generates embeddings for entire sentences or paragraphs, capturing higher-level meaning and relationships.

How Embeddings Work in Practice

1. **Tokenization**: Text is broken down into words or subwords.
2. **Transformation**: Each token is mapped to a vector in a high-dimensional space (typically 100-300 dimensions).
3. **Learning**: Through various algorithms, these vectors are adjusted during training so that words used in similar contexts end up with similar vectors.
4. **Application**: The resulting vectors can be used for tasks like classification, clustering, or similarity measurement.

Real-World Applications

Embeddings power many technologies we use daily:

- **Search engines**: Finding semantically similar content beyond exact keyword matches
- **Recommendation systems**: Suggesting products or content based on embedding similarity
- **Translation services**: Understanding equivalent meanings across languages
- **Chatbots and virtual assistants**: Comprehending user queries and their intent
- **Image search**: Finding visually similar images (using image embeddings)

The Magic of Vector Math

One of the most fascinating aspects of embeddings is how they enable mathematical operations on language. In a well-trained embedding space:

- "France" - "Paris" + "Italy" ≈ "Rome"
- "King" - "Man" + "Woman" ≈ "Queen"

These mathematical relationships emerge naturally during training, demonstrating how embeddings capture meaningful semantic connections between concepts. Would you like me to elaborate on any particular aspect of embeddings or explain a specific technique in more detail?

Image Resolution Enhancement

Image resolution enhancement is about making pictures clearer and more detailed. Let me explain these techniques in simple terms with examples.

What is Image Resolution?

Image resolution refers to how much detail an image contains. Higher resolution means more detail and clarity. Think of it like this: a low-resolution image looks blurry when you zoom in, while a high-resolution image stays clear.

Why Enhancement Matters

When computers generate images from text descriptions, they need special techniques to make these images look good. These techniques help balance quality with processing power.

Key Enhancement Techniques

Super-resolution GANs (SR-GANs)

Super-resolution GANs work like a team of two computer programs:

- One program (the generator) tries to create high-resolution images from low-resolution ones

- Another program (the discriminator) checks if these created images look realistic

Instead of simply enlarging pixels, SR-GANs actually learn to add realistic details. For example, if you have a blurry photo of a cat, an SR-GAN doesn't just make the blur bigger—it creates whiskers, fur textures, and eye details that weren't visible in the original.

Perceptual Loss Functions

Regular image processing compares images pixel by pixel, but perceptual loss functions work differently:

- They use deep neural networks (like VGG) that "see" images more like humans do

- They focus on features and patterns rather than exact pixel matching

- This creates more natural-looking enhanced images

For example, when enhancing a landscape photo, these techniques prioritize making grass look like real grass rather than just making each pixel sharper.

Transformer-based Techniques

Transformers originally revolutionized language processing but now help with images too:

- They divide images into patches and analyze how these patches relate to each other

- They understand the "big picture" of what an image represents

- This global understanding helps them fill in details intelligently

For instance, when enhancing a face photo, transformer models understand that eyes have certain structures and textures, allowing them to generate realistic details even if the original was very low quality.

Image Resolution Enhancement Techniques

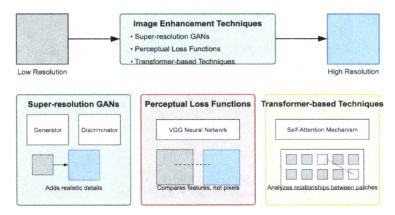

Practical Example

Imagine you have a photo of your grandparents that's small and blurry. Traditional enlargement would just make the blur bigger, but:

1. **SR-GAN** would study thousands of face photos to learn what details should be there, then add realistic wrinkles, eye details, and hair textures.

2. **Perceptual loss techniques** would ensure the enhanced photo looks natural to human eyes, focusing on making features look realistic rather than just mathematically precise.

3. **Transformer techniques** would analyse the whole image to understand the context (like recognizing it's an elderly couple) and use this understanding to add appropriate details.

The result is a larger, clearer photo that looks natural and preserves the identity and character of your grandparents, rather than just being a bigger version of a blurry image.

Modern image resolution enhancement goes far beyond simply enlarging pictures. These advanced techniques use artificial intelligence to actually create new details based on what the computer has learned about how images should look. This makes computer-generated images much more realistic and detailed than ever before.

Text-to-Phoneme Conversion: From Written Words to Speech Sounds

Text-to-phoneme conversion is the process of transforming written text into the actual speech sounds (phonemes) that would be used when pronouncing those words. Think of it as translating the spelling of words into a special code that represents exactly how they should sound when spoken aloud.

Why It Matters

Imagine you're learning English and come across these sentences:

- "I **read** a book yesterday."
- "I like to **read** every day."

The word "read" is spelled exactly the same in both sentences, but it's pronounced differently depending on whether it's past tense (/rɛd/ like "red") or present tense (/riːd/ like "reed"). Our brains automatically handle this distinction, but computers need special help to figure this out.

How Text-to-Phoneme Conversion Works

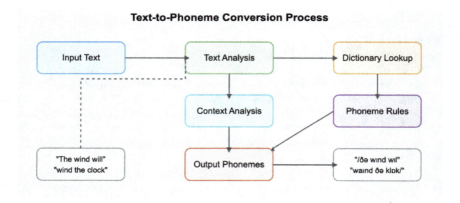

Text-to-Phoneme Conversion Process

The process typically follows these steps:

1. **Text Preprocessing**: First, the system normalizes the text by handling abbreviations, numbers, and special characters.

   o   "Dr." becomes "Doctor"

   o   "123" becomes "one hundred twenty-three"

2. **Dictionary Lookup**: Many common words are simply looked up in a pronunciation dictionary.

   o   English often uses CMU (Carnegie Mellon University) Pronouncing Dictionary

- Example: "hello" → /h ɛ l oʊ/

3. **Rule-Based Conversion**: For words not in the dictionary, rule-based systems apply language-specific patterns.

    - In English, "ph" usually makes the /f/ sound (phone → /foʊn/)

    - Double consonants often affect the vowel before them

4. **Context Analysis**: The system examines surrounding words to resolve ambiguities.

    - "The WIND blew hard" (noun: /wɪnd/)

    - "Please WIND up the toy" (verb: /waɪnd/)

5. **Machine Learning Approaches**: Modern systems use neural networks trained on large datasets to predict pronunciations with higher accuracy.

A Real-World Example

Let's break down the sentence: "The wind will wind the clock."

Text	Phoneme	Explanation
The	/ðə/	Simple dictionary lookup
wind	/wɪnd/	Context analysis identifies this as a noun (air movement)
will	/wɪl/	Simple dictionary lookup
wind	/waɪnd/	Context analysis identifies this as a verb (to turn)
the	/ðə/	Simple dictionary lookup
clock	/klɒk/	Simple dictionary lookup

The final phoneme sequence becomes: /ðə wɪnd wɪl waɪnd ðə klɒk/

Why This Matters In Everyday Life

Text-to-phoneme conversion powers many technologies we use daily:

- **Speech Synthesis (Text-to-Speech)**: Allows computers, phones, and virtual assistants to speak text aloud with natural pronunciation

- **Language Learning Apps**: Helps learners understand correct pronunciations

- **Assistive Technologies**: Enables screen readers for people with visual impairments

- **Voice-Based User Interfaces**: Powers voice assistants like Siri, Alexa, and Google Assistant

By correctly converting text to phonemes, these systems can correctly pronounce words like "read," "wind," "lead," and other confusing homographs based on their context in sentences.

Acoustic Model in Text-to-Speech Systems?

Imagine you're trying to teach a robot how to **speak naturally,** just like a human. You give it the sentence:
"Hello, how are you?"

Before it can actually **say** this sentence out loud, it needs to first understand **how** it should sound—what pitch to use, how long to stretch each word, how loudly to speak, and what kind of emotional tone or rhythm to follow.

This is exactly what an **acoustic model** does.

Role of the Acoustic Model

In a text-to-speech (TTS) system, once the text is processed (after tokenization, normalization, and linguistic analysis), the **acoustic model steps in** and **translates the processed text into acoustic features**—like a detailed instruction sheet for how the voice should sound.

These acoustic features include:

- **Mel-spectrograms** – A visual representation of sound over time (like a heatmap of voice).

- **Pitch (fundamental frequency)** – How high or low the voice sounds.

- **Duration** – How long each sound or syllable lasts.

- **Intensity (loudness)** – How soft or loud the voice is.

- **Formants / Harmonics** – Frequency components that shape the character of the sound.

These features don't produce audio **directly**—they are like a **blueprint**. A **vocoder** then takes these blueprints and **generates real audio** from them.

How Acoustic Models Work Internally

Acoustic models are typically **neural networks** trained on **large datasets** that contain:

- Text inputs (like transcripts or scripts)

- Paired audio recordings (real human speech)

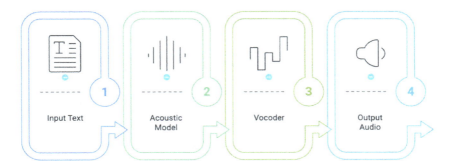

| Input Text | Acoustic Model | Vocoder | Output Audio |

The model learns the **subtle patterns** between **text** and the **way it sounds** when spoken. Over time, it gets really good at predicting how to pronounce any sentence—accurately capturing tone, pacing, and emphasis.

Popular Acoustic Models in GenAI

Here are some well-known models used in modern TTS pipelines:

Model Name	Description
Tacotron 2	A sequence-to-sequence model that generates mel-spectrograms from text, then passes them to a vocoder like WaveNet. Known for high naturalness.
FastSpeech 2	An improved model that speeds up training and inference by using duration prediction and parallel processing. Great for real-time use.
Fish-Speech	A more recent innovation that handles multiple TTS tasks, including emotion, speaker style, and multilingual capabilities, all at once.

These models form the **"brain"** behind the TTS system—deciding how the voice should sound based on the input sentence.

Example in Action

Let's walk through an example:

Input text: **"Good morning, everyone!"**

1. The **acoustic model** processes the input and generates a **mel-spectrogram** that includes:

    o   Rising pitch at the end (because it's cheerful)

    o   Slight pause after "morning"

    o   Emphasis on "everyone"

    o   Slightly higher volume to simulate enthusiasm

2. The **vocoder** (like HiFi-GAN or WaveGlow) converts this into actual audio.

Result: You hear a natural, expressive voice say: **"Good morning, everyone!"** — with the right tone and emotion.

Why Acoustic Models Matter in TTS

Importance	Why it Matters
Naturalness	Helps produce speech that feels real and expressive
Accuracy	Ensures correct pronunciation and stress patterns
Speed & Efficiency	Some models optimize for fast generation (important for live conversations)
Flexibility	Can learn multiple voices, accents, languages, and speaking styles
Generalization	Learns how to synthesize speech even for unseen words or names

Audio Samples

While I can't generate audio directly in this chat, here's how you can explore real samples:

🎧 Tacotron 2 Samples:

Google Tacotron 2 Demo:
https://google.github.io/tacotron/publications/tacotron2

Microsoft FastSpeech 2 Demo:
https://speechresearch.github.io/fastspeech2/

You can find samples on GitHub or Hugging Face under multi-speaker/multi-style TTS projects like ESPnet TTS Demos.

Scene Graph Generation

A **scene graph** is a powerful data structure that organizes visual information into a machine-readable format, enabling AI systems to understand complex scenes with multiple objects and their relationships. Think of it as a **visual knowledge graph** that breaks down an image or scene description into three core components:

1. **Nodes**: Represent objects or entities (e.g., "dog," "chair").
2. **Edges**: Define relationships between nodes (e.g., "sitting on," "next to").
3. **Attributes**: Describe properties of nodes (e.g., "red chair," "Siberian husky").

This structured representation helps AI models **interpret spatial layouts, contextual interactions, and semantic hierarchies**—critical for tasks like image generation, visual question answering, and robotics.

How Scene Graph Generation Works

The process converts raw input (text prompts or images) into a structured graph through these steps:

1. Concept Extraction

- **Input**: A textual prompt (e.g., "A SIBERIAN HUSKY SITTING ON A RED CHAIR IN A COOL LIVING ROOM").

- **Action**: NLP techniques (like dependency parsing) identify:

    o **Objects**: "husky," "chair," "living room."

    o **Attributes**: "Siberian," "red," "cool."

o   **Relationships**: "sitting on," "located in."

2. Graph Construction

- **Nodes** = Extracted objects + attributes.

- **Edges** = Relationships between nodes.

- **Example**:

Copy

```
[Dog (Siberian husky)] --(sitting on)--> [Chair (red)]
[Chair] --(located in)--> [Living room (cool)]
```

3. Semantic Enrichment

- **Knowledge Graphs**: Augment with external data (e.g., "Siberian husky" → breed of dog).

- **Hierarchy**: Nest sub-relationships (e.g., "chair" is part of "living room").

4. Output for AI Models

The final scene graph feeds into downstream tasks:

- **Image Generation**: Guides models like DALL-E to place objects correctly.

- **Video Synthesis**: Ensures consistency across frames.

Scene Graph Generation Process

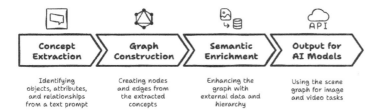

Concept Extraction	Graph Construction	Semantic Enrichment	Output for AI Models
Identifying objects, attributes, and relationships from a text prompt	Creating nodes and edges from the extracted concepts	Enhancing the graph with external data and hierarchy	Using the scene graph for image and video tasks

Technical Approaches

Scene graph generation typically employs:

1. **Deep Neural Networks**: Convolutional and transformer-based architectures extract visual features.

2. **Message Passing Networks**: Information flows between object nodes to refine relationship predictions based on context.

3. **Graph Neural Networks**: These learn to reason over the graph structure itself, improving relationship predictions.

4. **Knowledge Integration**: Pre-existing knowledge (like common object relationships) can be incorporated to improve accuracy.

Applications

Scene graphs serve as an intermediate representation that bridges visual understanding and downstream tasks such as:

- Image captioning

- Visual question answering

- Image generation from text

- Robot navigation and planning

- Augmented reality systems

By representing a scene as a structured graph rather than just a collection of objects, AI systems gain a deeper understanding of visual content that more closely resembles human comprehension.

Generative AI tech stack: Frameworks, infrastructure, models and applications

Developing generative AI applications at the enterprise level demands significantly higher standards. Organizations require frameworks that not only support large-scale AI deployments but also ensure robust security and seamless integration with existing IT ecosystems. These frameworks must be capable of managing the intricacies of enterprise environments while remaining adaptable to shifting business priorities.

Frameworks like TensorFlow and PyTorch have emerged as leading choices in this space, offering comprehensive libraries, strong community backing, and versatile integration options. Their scalability and flexibility make them well-suited for enterprise use, enabling the development of custom AI models tailored to specific business objectives. This empowers organizations to harness AI effectively and maintain a competitive advantage in their industry.

A 7-Step Framework for Designing GenAI Systems

7 Deployment &
Monitoring

Deploy the AI system and
establish monitoring processes
for ongoing performance.

6 Governance &
Compliance

Implement governance
frameworks to ensure safety
and compliance.

5 Evaluation &
Validation

Assess and validate the AI
system to ensure it meets
quality standards.

4 System Architecture

Design and integrate the
necessary system architecture for
AI implementation.

3 Model Selection &
Training

Choose and train the appropriate
AI models to meet objectives.

2 Data Strategy

Develop a comprehensive plan
for data collection,
management, and analysis.

1 Define Objectives

Establish clear goals and
desired outcomes for the AI
project.

Define Objective

At the foundation of any successful AI project lies a well-articulated objective. This step involves:

- Identifying the **business problem** or **opportunity**.
- Establishing **clear goals** and **measurable success criteria**.
- Involving stakeholders to ensure alignment with broader organizational strategy.

Example: A retail company may aim to improve customer retention by predicting churn using historical transaction data.

Every AI project begins by clearly defining what success looks like — not just technically, but in business and user terms.
For our legal assistant, the primary objective is to **improve the efficiency and consistency of legal contract workflows**. Legal teams often reuse boilerplate clauses, manually review long contracts, and must ensure compliance with jurisdiction-specific regulations. We aim to **automate clause generation, summarize legal texts**, and **identify non-compliant or high-risk clauses**.
Steps:

- Collaborate with in-house counsel and legal ops teams to identify bottlenecks.
- Define measurable KPIs:
  - Reduce contract drafting time by 30%

- o   Lower clause inconsistencies across documents
- o   Identify 90%+ of non-compliant clauses in a test set
- Determine project scope:
  - o   MVP: Clause generator using predefined clause types
  - o   Phase 2: Risk detection & legal term summarization

Data Strategy

Once objectives are defined, a comprehensive **data strategy** is key. Generative AI thrives on large, clean, and relevant datasets. For legal systems, the challenge is compounded by **data sensitivity, domain specificity,** and **annotation complexity**. We need diverse legal documents (e.g., NDAs, SLAs, SOWs) annotated by domain experts. These must include labels for clause types, summaries, and risk indicators. However, since contracts often contain sensitive data, **compliance and anonymization** are built into the data pipeline from day one.

Strategy Highlights:
- Collect data from internal repositories, legal tech vendors, and public sources like SEC filings.
- Anonymize PII using Named Entity Recognition (NER) tools.
- Use annotation platforms (e.g., Prodigy, Label Studio) with legal experts to:
  - o   Tag clauses by type (termination, indemnity, force majeure)
  - o   Identify risky language or non-compliance indicators
- Store structured data in a data lake or object store (AWS S3), and index for semantic search using vector DBs (e.g., Pinecone, Weaviate).
- Establish data versioning, lineage, and access controls from day one.

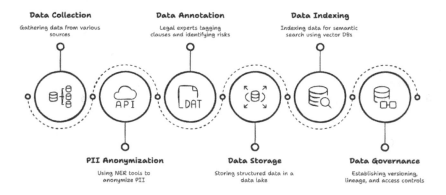

Data Collection
Gathering data from various sources

Data Annotation
Legal experts tagging clauses and identifying risks

Data Indexing
Indexing data for semantic search using vector DBs

PII Anonymization
Using NER tools to anonymize PII

Data Storage
Storing structured data in a data lake

Data Governance
Establishing versioning, lineage, and access controls

Model Selection & Training

With clean, labeled data in place, the next step is choosing the right models and training strategies. Generative AI requires more than just picking a foundation model — it requires choosing the **right tuning approach**, **evaluation framework**, and **inference strategy**.

We choose **Open-source LLMs** like GPT-NeoX or Falcon for full control, or API-based models (GPT-4, Claude) for rapid development. For legal clause generation, fine-tuning is essential to make the language precise and contextually aware.

Methodology:

- Use **Transfer Learning** by starting with a pretrained LLM.

- Apply **LoRA or QLoRA** for efficient fine-tuning on legal clauses.

- Use **Prompt Engineering** and **Chain-of-Thought prompting** for summarization.

- Train supporting models (BERT-based) for clause classification.

Key Evaluation Metrics:

- **ROUGE / BLEU** for summarization quality.

- **F1 Score / Accuracy** for clause classification.

- **Jaccard Similarity** to check clause reuse consistency.

- **Hallucination Rate** to ensure factual alignment.

Type	Examples	Use Cases
Text LLMs	GPT-4, Claude 3, Mistral, LLaMA, Mixtral, Falcon	Chatbots, writing, reasoning
Code Generation	Code LLaMA, Codex, StarCoder, Replit Code V1	Programming help, code synthesis
Image Generation	DALL·E 3, Midjourney, Stable Diffusion, SDXL	Artwork, design, avatars
Audio Generation	MusicGen, Bark, ElevenLabs, AudioCraft	Voice synthesis, music
Video Generation	Sora, Runway, Pika, Gen-2, Lumiere	Short video creation, animation
Multimodal	Gemini 1.5, GPT-4V, Kosmos, Florence	Vision + language tasks

Type	Examples	Use Cases
Domain-Specific	BloombergGPT, Med-PaLM, BioGPT	Finance, healthcare, biotech

Selecting the **right model for your use case in Generative AI** is a critical architectural and business decision. It affects performance, cost, compliance, accuracy, speed, and user experience. Here's a detailed guide explaining the **strategies and frameworks** you can use to decide **which Large Language Model (LLM)** or **generative model** to adopt, along with reference material and structured criteria.

Selecting the Right Generative AI Model: A Strategic Approach

Choosing the appropriate generative AI model is a critical decision that impacts everything from performance and cost to compliance and user experience. Let me walk you through a comprehensive strategy for model selection in straightforward terms.

Understanding Your Use Case

The foundation of model selection begins with clearly defining what you're trying to accomplish. Ask yourself:

- What specific task needs to be performed? (Customer support, code generation, creative writing)

- Who will be using the outputs?

- What kind of results do you expect?

- Is factual accuracy more important than creativity, or vice versa?

For example, if you're building a customer support chatbot, you'll prioritize accuracy and quick response times. For creative writing, you'll want models with stronger imagination and language fluency.

Matching Capabilities to Needs

Different model families have distinct strengths. For general reasoning tasks, models like GPT-4 and Claude 3 excel. If speed and cost efficiency are priorities, consider Mistral or GPT-3.5. For code generation, specialized models like Codex or Code LLaMA might be better choices.

124

When working with visual inputs, models with vision capabilities like Gemini or GPT-4V are necessary. For tasks requiring extensive context, Claude 3 Opus or Gemini 1.5 with their expanded context windows may be preferable.

Evaluating Practical Constraints

Non-functional requirements often narrow down your options significantly:

- **Budget**: The cost difference between models can be substantial. While GPT-4 offers powerful capabilities, it comes at a higher price point than alternatives like Mixtral.

- **Speed requirements**: Consider whether your application can tolerate some latency or needs near-instant responses.

- **Data privacy**: If handling sensitive information, you might need open-source models you can host privately.

- **Scalability**: Self-hosted models give you more control over scaling but require infrastructure management.

Generative AI Model Selection Framework

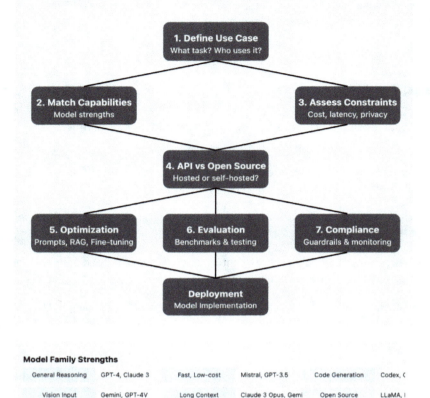

Model Family Strengths

General Reasoning	GPT-4, Claude 3	Fast, Low-cost	Mistral, GPT-3.5	Code Generation	Codex, (
Vision Input	Gemini, GPT-4V	Long Context	Claude 3 Opus, Gemi	Open Source	LLaMA, l

*Model capabilities and performance evolve rapidly. Always check latest benchmarks.

Model selection matrix, some example and parameters for reference

1. Define Your Use Case - Is it text generation, summarization, classification, Q&A, etc.? - What level of creativity vs. accuracy is needed? - Latency and throughput constraints? - Industry-specific requirements?
2. Selection Criteria (with Sample Weights) - Performance (30%) - Cost (15%) - Accuracy (25%) –

Criteria	Weight (1-5)	Model A (GPT-4)	Model B (Claude 3)	Model C (Mistral 7B)
Task performance	5	5	5	3
Domain alignment	4	5	5	3
Creativity vs factuality	3	4	5	3
Reasoning & coherence	5	5	4	3
Language fluency	4	5	4	4
Context window size	4	5	5	3
Knowledge freshness	3	4	5	3
Inference latency	4	4	5	5
Cost per 1K tokens	5	2	3	5
Token limits	3	5	4	3
API availability	5	5	5	4
Fine-tuning support	4	4	3	2
RAG compatibility	4	5	4	3
On-premise support	3	3	3	5
Moderation tools	4	5	4	3
Hallucination control	5	5	4	3
Compliance	5	4	4	2
Explainability	3	4	4	3
Community support	4	5	5	3
Active development	3	5	4	3
Tooling integrations	4	5	5	4
Total Score		377	360	280

3. Latency (10%) - Ecosystem & Tooling (10%) - Compliance & Safety (10%)
4. Common Model Choices - GPT-4: Best for general-purpose tasks, reasoning, content creation. - Claude 3: Known for safety, multi-turn conversation performance. - Mistral 7B: Open-source, fast, efficient for small-scale deployments.
5. Strategy - Define criteria & assign weights. - Score each model from 1-10. - Use SUMPRODUCT(weights, scores) to rank models. - Consider model size, token limit, and API vs. self-hosted options
6. Tools & References - Hugging Face Model Hub - Papers with Code (SOTA benchmarks) - OpenAI Cookbook & API Docs - LLMPerf for inference benchmarking

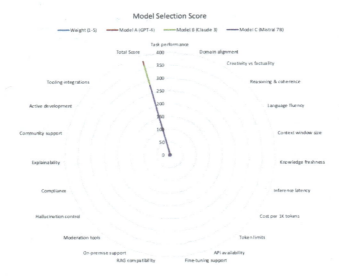

Model Selection Score

Tools to Help with Model Selection

- **Helicone** – for tracking cost/performance of models

- **LLM360** – for monitoring LLM usage, costs, and performance

- **PromptLayer** – manage and analyze prompt performance

- **MemGPT / LangChain Eval** – for memory-based evaluations

System Architecture

Designing the right **system architecture** is critical to support inference pipelines, scalability, user interaction, and model deployment.
For our use case, a **microservices-based architecture** with **agent orchestration** fits best. Each core task (generation, summarization, classification, risk detection) is broken into loosely coupled services. We use **LangChain or CrewAI** to route tasks intelligently between agents.
Architecture Overview:
- Each task (e.g., clause generation, summarization) is a containerized service (Docker).

- These are deployed on Kubernetes (EKS/GKE) for autoscaling and observability.
- LangChain router coordinates between services.
- Redis Queue or Kafka handles async task processing.
- Pinecone for clause similarity search.
- REST API Gateway with OAuth2, RBAC for secure access.

Comprehensive Generative AI System Architecture

Overview

Building a robust generative AI application requires a well-designed system architecture that handles everything from user interactions to model deployment and monitoring. A comprehensive architecture must balance performance, scalability, security, and cost while meeting specific business requirements. Let me break down the key components and considerations for designing such systems.

Core Components of Generative AI System Architecture

User Interface Layer

The front-end of a generative AI application serves as the critical interface between users and the underlying AI capabilities. This layer needs to:

- Provide intuitive ways for users to input prompts or queries (text, voice, or visual)
- Manage real-time feedback and progressive rendering of AI responses
- Handle various interaction patterns (chat interfaces, document editing, embedded components)
- Implement client-side optimizations like caching frequent responses

Modern generative AI applications often implement streaming responses rather than waiting for complete outputs, improving perceived performance and allowing for more interactive experiences.

API Gateway and Orchestration Layer

This middle layer manages the flow of requests, authentication, and access control:

- Routes requests to appropriate services
- Handles authentication and authorization
- Implements rate limiting and usage quotas
- Provides API versioning and documentation
- Orchestrates complex workflows that may involve multiple models or services

For enterprise applications, this layer often includes business logic and integration with existing systems like CRM, ERP, or knowledge management platforms.

Model Layer

The core of a generative AI system includes one or more models and their associated infrastructure:

- Model serving infrastructure (managed APIs or self-hosted environments)
- Model registry for tracking versions and configurations
- Prompt management systems to optimize and version prompts
- Caching mechanisms for frequent or similar queries
- Potential for model ensembles or routing between different models based on the task

This layer must balance performance needs (like low latency) with cost considerations, often implementing techniques like dynamic scaling based on demand.

Knowledge and Data Layer

Modern generative AI applications frequently augment models with external knowledge:

- Vector databases for retrieval-augmented generation (RAG)
- Document processors for ingesting and chunking content
- Knowledge graph integrations for structured information
- Database connectors for accessing enterprise data
- Data synchronization mechanisms to keep information current

This layer is essential for grounding model outputs in factual information and reducing hallucinations.

Monitoring and Feedback Layer

Operational visibility is critical for maintaining AI system quality:

- Performance monitoring (latency, throughput, error rates)
- Output quality assessment and feedback collection
- Usage analytics and cost tracking
- Drift detection to identify when model performance degrades
- Explainability tools to understand model decisions

This operational data feeds back into system improvement cycles, helping teams refine prompts, models, and integration points.

A detailed overview of the generative AI tech stack

Layer	Purpose	Examples/Components	Features/Types
Application Layer	Interfaces for end-users	Chatbots, Writing tools, Design tools	None
Orchestration & Agents	Coordinates tasks and model calls	Frameworks, Orchestrators, Agent Types	Tool calling, Task chaining
Model Layer	Core AI engines for content generation	Foundation models, Fine-tuned models	Text, Image, Audio, Video generation
Data Layer	Supplies memory and context	Vector databases, Document loaders	Semantic search, Long-term memory
Training Infrastructure	Train or fine-tune models	Training libs, Platforms, Dataset libraries	Distributed compute
Foundation Infrastructure	Base layer for hosting and scaling	Compute, Deployment, Storage	Auto-scaling, Model versioning

Key Architectural Patterns for Generative AI Systems
Retrieval-Augmented Generation (RAG)
RAG has become a foundational pattern for building more reliable generative AI applications:

1. **Content Processing Pipeline**: Documents are ingested, chunked, and embedded into vector representations.
2. **Vector Database**: These embeddings are stored in specialized databases optimized for similarity search.
3. **Retrieval Mechanism**: When a query arrives, relevant information is retrieved based on semantic similarity.
4. **Context Augmentation**: The retrieved information is added to the prompt before sending to the model.
5. **Response Generation**: The model generates responses grounded in the retrieved context.

This pattern significantly improves factual accuracy and reduces hallucinations by providing reliable context to the model.

Agent-Based Architecture
For more complex tasks, agent-based architectures allow models to:

1. **Decompose Problems**: Break complex tasks into manageable subtasks
2. **Plan and Execute**: Create a sequence of steps to accomplish goals
3. **Tool Usage**: Interact with external tools and APIs
4. **Self-Correction**: Review and revise outputs or approaches

This pattern is particularly valuable for applications requiring multi-step reasoning or integration with external services.

Parameter-Efficient Fine-Tuning (PEFT)
When customizing models for specific domains:

1. **Base Model Selection**: Choose an appropriate foundation model
2. **Adapter Definition**: Create specialized layers that can be trained efficiently

131

3. **Fine-Tuning Pipeline**: Optimize these adapters on domain-specific data
4. **Deployment Infrastructure**: Serve the fine-tuned model with adapters

This approach allows organizations to customize models without the expense of full retraining.

Infrastructure Considerations

Deployment Options

Generative AI applications can be deployed in several ways:

1. **Fully Managed**: Using services like OpenAI, Anthropic, or Google Vertex AI
   - Advantages: Quick to deploy, professionally maintained, continuously updated
   - Disadvantages: Less control, potential data privacy concerns, usage-based pricing
2. **Self-Hosted**: Running open-source models on your infrastructure
   - Advantages: Full control, fixed costs, data privacy
   - Disadvantages: Requires expertise, higher operational burden
3. **Hybrid**: Combining managed services with self-hosted components
   - Advantages: Flexibility, optimized cost-performance balance
   - Disadvantages: More complex architecture to maintain

Scaling Strategies

Generative AI applications face unique scaling challenges:

1. **Horizontal Scaling**: Adding more inference endpoints for handling increased load
2. **Caching**: Storing common responses to reduce computational load
3. **Quantization**: Using lower-precision models for faster inference
4. **Batching**: Processing multiple requests together for efficiency
5. **Load Balancing**: Distributing requests across multiple model instances

Security and Compliance Architecture

A robust security architecture includes:

1. **Input Validation**: Filtering harmful or malicious prompts
2. **Output Filtering**: Scanning model outputs for inappropriate content
3. **Access Controls**: Defining who can use which models and capabilities
4. **Audit Logging**: Recording all interactions for compliance and debugging
5. **Data Protection**: Securing sensitive information throughout the pipeline
6. **Prompt Injection Protection**: Preventing attacks that attempt to manipulate the model

Reference Architectures

Several patterns have emerged as industry standards:

1. **Simple API Integration**: Directly connecting applications to model providers via APIs
2. **RAG with Vector Database**: Adding knowledge retrieval capabilities
3. **Enterprise Integration**: Connecting AI capabilities with existing business systems
4. **Multi-Model Orchestration**: Using multiple specialized models for different aspects of a task
5. **Edge Deployment**: Running smaller models directly on devices for privacy and low latency

Evaluation and Validation

Model accuracy alone isn't enough in legal AI. We need robust **evaluation and validation** that blends automated scoring with human-in-the-loop reviews from legal experts.

Validation is done using curated test cases: input legal scenarios, expected outputs, and edge cases. Legal SMEs review model-generated outputs for correctness, risk, and tone. Red teaming is also done to test how the model responds to ambiguous or adversarial prompts.

Strategies:

- Human-in-the-loop scoring on a review dashboard.

- Simulate adversarial cases to uncover unsafe generations.

- A/B testing multiple model variants in sandbox environment.

- Implement fail-safe prompts and fallback logic.

Tools:

- **Evidently AI** for metric dashboards.

- **HumanEval or CheckList AI** for structured validation.

- **Jupyter dashboards or Gradio apps** for SMEs to interact and score.

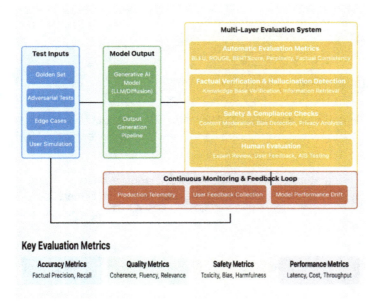

Key Evaluation Metrics

Accuracy Metrics	Quality Metrics	Safety Metrics	Performance Metrics
Factual Precision, Recall	Coherence, Fluency, Relevance	Toxicity, Bias, Harmfulness	Latency, Cost, Throughput

Proper evaluation and validation are critical components of building reliable generative AI applications. Unlike traditional software systems, generative AI outputs are probabilistic in nature, making thorough evaluation essential to ensure they meet quality, safety, and performance expectations. Let me walk you through comprehensive evaluation and validation approaches for generative AI systems.

The Challenge of Evaluating Generative AI

Evaluating generative AI presents unique challenges compared to traditional ML systems. While classification models can be assessed with clear metrics like precision and recall against ground truth, generative outputs are often subjective and context-dependent. A response may be grammatically perfect but factually incorrect, or vice versa. This necessitates multi-dimensional evaluation strategies that assess various aspects of model performance.

Multi-layered Evaluation Framework

Effective evaluation of generative AI requires examining performance across several key dimensions:

1. Task-Specific Performance Each application has unique requirements that dictate what "good" looks like. For a customer service bot, accuracy and helpfulness might be paramount. For creative writing, originality and coherence might matter most. Define metrics that directly align with your application's specific goals.

2. Factual Accuracy & Hallucination Detection Generative models can confidently present incorrect information. Implementing fact verification systems that cross-check outputs against trusted knowledge bases helps identify and quantify hallucination rates. This is especially critical for applications in domains like healthcare, legal, or finance where accuracy is non-negotiable.

3. Robustness & Reliability A robust system should perform consistently across diverse inputs and contexts. Testing should evaluate performance under various conditions including edge cases, adversarial inputs, and different phrasing of similar requests. Evaluate the model's ability to acknowledge uncertainty appropriately rather than making up answers.

4. Safety & Compliance Models should be evaluated for harmful content generation, bias, privacy risks, and regulatory compliance. This involves testing with potentially problematic inputs to ensure model guardrails are effective and implementing content classification systems to flag potentially unsafe outputs.

5. User Experience Metrics The ultimate measure of success is user satisfaction and engagement. Collect metrics on user interactions, including satisfaction scores, task completion rates, and engagement duration. A/B testing different model configurations helps optimize for real-world performance.

Automatic Evaluation Techniques

Several automated techniques help assess generative AI outputs at scale:

1. Reference-based Metrics These compare model outputs to human-generated "gold standard" references:

- **BLEU and ROUGE**: Measure word overlap with reference texts
- **BERTScore**: Uses contextual embeddings to measure semantic similarity
- **METEOR**: Evaluates matches including synonyms and stemmed words

2. Reference-free Metrics These evaluate outputs without requiring human-generated references:

- **Perplexity**: Measures how well a model predicts text
- **Coherence scores**: Assess logical flow and consistency
- **Grammatical error rates**: Identify linguistic mistakes

3. AI-assisted Evaluation Using other AI models to evaluate generative outputs:

- **Judge models**: Specialized models trained to rate quality aspects
- **GPT-4 Evaluation**: Using advanced models to critique outputs of other models
- **Classification models**: Detecting specific issues like factual errors or toxicity

Human-in-the-Loop Validation

Automated metrics alone are insufficient. Human evaluation remains essential for validating generative AI:

1. Expert Review Panels Subject matter experts can evaluate outputs for domain accuracy and appropriateness. This is especially important in specialized domains like medicine or law where factual correctness is critical.

2. Side-by-Side Comparisons Human evaluators compare outputs from different model configurations to identify strengths and weaknesses. These comparisons often use blind testing to prevent bias.

3. Real User Testing Gathering feedback from actual end-users provides insights into real-world performance and usefulness:

- **Task Completion Tests**: Measure if users can successfully accomplish goals
- **Satisfaction Surveys**: Collect qualitative feedback on model interactions
- **A/B Testing**: Compare different model versions in production environments

Continuous Monitoring Architecture

Evaluation shouldn't end after deployment. A robust monitoring architecture includes:

1. Telemetry Collection Gather operational metrics that indicate system health:

- Query patterns and response times
- Error rates and recovery patterns
- Usage patterns across different user segments

2. Feedback Collection Create mechanisms to collect ongoing user feedback:

- Explicit feedback (ratings, thumbs up/down)
- Implicit feedback (engagement time, follow-up questions)
- User corrections of model outputs

3. Performance Drift Detection Models may degrade over time due to:

- Changing user behavior or expectations
- Evolving language patterns
- New edge cases appearing in production
- World knowledge becoming outdated

Implementing systems to detect these changes allows for timely retraining or adjustments.

Validation Test Suites

Create comprehensive test suites that validate all critical aspects of your application:

1. Golden Dataset Tests Curate collections of representative inputs with known correct outputs. These tests ensure core functionality remains stable across model updates.

2. Adversarial Tests Design inputs specifically to challenge the model's weak points:

- Edge case handling (very long inputs, unusual formats)
- Robustness to slight input changes
- Resistance to prompt injection attacks

3. Red-Teaming Employ specialists to actively try to make the system fail or produce harmful outputs. This helps identify and patch vulnerabilities before they affect users.

Implementation Best Practices

For effective evaluation implementation:

1. Create a tiered evaluation strategy with different test depths for different development stages
2. Establish clear acceptance criteria for each metric before testing begins
3. Automate evaluation pipelines to run consistently across model versions
4. Document evaluation results with reproducible tests for future comparison
5. Balance quantitative metrics with qualitative human judgments

6. Focus on real-world performance rather than benchmark leaderboard.

Governance & Compliances

Since the assistant generates legal content, ensuring safety, fairness, and traceability is mandatory. We apply an **AI governance layer** to monitor risks, manage model versions, and log all inferences.

Access to the assistant is managed through **RBAC** and **audit trails** are maintained for every generation. Each model version, prompt, and input-output pair is stored and tagged for audit.

Governance Approaches:

- Maintain **model cards** with documentation on training data, risks, and intended use.

- Log every inference with metadata (user, prompt, output, timestamp).

- Enable **bias audits**, especially for fairness across jurisdictions.

- Ensure **GDPR compliance** for user data and logs.

- Set up regular review boards for AI ethics and legal alignment.

Generative AI Governance & Compliance Architecture

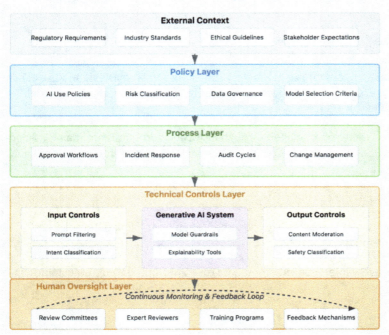

Implementing robust governance and compliance frameworks is essential when deploying generative AI applications, particularly in regulated industries or when handling sensitive data. These frameworks ensure responsible AI use, mitigate risks, and maintain alignment with legal and ethical standards.

Understanding AI Governance

AI governance encompasses the policies, processes, and structures that guide how an organization develops, deploys, and manages AI systems. For generative AI specifically, governance addresses unique challenges like potential hallucinations, bias, intellectual property concerns, and privacy implications.

Effective governance begins with clear policies that establish boundaries around AI use cases, required approval processes, and accountability structures. These policies should identify which applications require human oversight, define acceptable model behaviors, and establish procedures for handling edge cases or failures.

Key Elements of a Compliance Framework

Compliance for generative AI extends beyond traditional software compliance and encompasses several distinct dimensions:

1. Regulatory Compliance

Organizations must navigate a complex landscape of AI-specific and adjacent regulations that vary by region, including:

- GDPR (Europe) and CCPA/CPRA (California) for data privacy

- AI Act (Europe) which categorizes AI systems by risk level

- Industry-specific regulations like HIPAA for healthcare or GLBA for financial services

- Emerging transparency requirements like watermarking or disclosure rules

2. Ethical Compliance

Beyond legal requirements, organizations should establish ethical standards for their AI applications, addressing:

- Fairness and bias mitigation across demographic groups

- Transparency about AI use and limitations

- Prevention of harmful outputs or applications

- Respect for intellectual property and creative works

3. Technical Compliance

The technical architecture must enforce compliance through:

- Input filtering to prevent harmful prompts

- Output moderation to catch inappropriate content

- Content classification systems to flag sensitive materials

- Auditability mechanisms that log decisions and explanations

Governance Architecture for Generative AI

A comprehensive governance architecture includes multiple interconnected layers:

Policy Layer

- Acceptable use policies

- Risk classification frameworks

- Model selection and evaluation criteria

- Data handling policies

Process Layer

- Model evaluation and approval workflows

- Incident response procedures

- Regular audit and assessment cycles

- Feedback collection and improvement processes

Technical Controls Layer

- Prompt engineering guardrails

- Output moderation systems

- Monitoring and logging infrastructure

- Explainability tools

Human Oversight Layer

- Review committees for high-risk applications

- Expert reviewers for domain-specific content

- User feedback mechanisms

- Training programs for AI users

Implementing a Risk-Based Approach

A risk-based governance approach tailors controls to the potential impact of AI applications:

Low-Risk Applications

For applications with minimal potential harm, like internal document summarization:

- Basic input/output monitoring

- Standard model selection policies

- Regular but less frequent audits

Medium-Risk Applications

For customer-facing or business-critical applications:

140

- Enhanced monitoring and logging

- Pre-deployment testing against bias and hallucination benchmarks

- Regular review cycles for model performance

High-Risk Applications

For applications in regulated domains or with significant impact potential:

- Comprehensive human review processes

- Extensive testing for edge cases

- Detailed documentation of model decision-making

- Regular third-party audits

Practical Implementation Steps

Establishing a governance framework typically involves:

1. **Assessment**: Evaluate your organization's AI use cases and regulatory requirements

2. **Policy Development**: Create comprehensive policies addressing model selection, data handling, and use limitations

3. **Control Implementation**: Deploy technical safeguards including:

   o Input validation systems to prevent harmful prompts

   o Output filtering to catch problematic content

   o Logging mechanisms to enable auditability

   o Authentication and authorization controls

4. **Training**: Educate teams on responsible AI use and compliance requirements

5. **Monitoring**: Implement systems to track model behavior, detect drift, and identify potential issues

6. **Response Planning**: Establish procedures for handling compliance violations or unexpected outputs

Regulatory Considerations by Region

Compliance needs vary significantly by geographic region and industry:

- **European Union**: The AI Act classifies AI systems by risk categories with corresponding requirements

- **United States**: Sector-specific regulations apply (HIPAA, FCRA, etc.) with emerging state-level AI laws

- **China**: Comprehensive AI regulations with strong emphasis on content monitoring and national security

- **Canada**: PIPEDA for data protection with AI-specific guidance being developed

Industry-Specific Considerations

Different sectors face unique compliance challenges:

- **Healthcare**: Patient privacy, medical accuracy, and explainability for clinical decision support

- **Financial Services**: Fair lending practices, fraud detection, and algorithmic accountability

- **Legal**: Privilege protection, accuracy in legal analysis, and jurisdiction-specific regulations

- **Public Sector**: Transparency requirements, fairness obligations, and administrative procedure rules

Documentation and Auditability

Robust documentation is essential for compliance and includes:

- Model cards documenting capabilities, limitations, and intended uses

- Data provenance records showing training data sources and processing

- Decision logs tracking AI-generated outputs and human interventions

- Regular assessment reports evaluating ongoing compliance

Effective governance and compliance for generative AI requires a multi-layered approach that combines policy frameworks, technical controls, and human oversight. By implementing risk-based governance structures that align with both regulatory requirements and ethical principles, organizations can harness the benefits of generative AI while managing associated risks.

The frameworks should be dynamic and evolve alongside both technological capabilities and regulatory expectations. Regular reviews, stakeholder engagement, and continuous improvement processes ensure that governance structures remain effective as generative AI capabilities advance and regulatory landscapes shift.

Deployment & Monitoring

Once validated, the assistant moves to production via a secure, CI/CD-enabled deployment process. We use containerization and Kubernetes to orchestrate deployments, ensure rollback, and autoscale workloads.

For monitoring, we combine **application health metrics** with **model behavior metrics** — for example, tracking latency, uptime, and generation quality.

Deployment Architecture and Strategy

Successful generative AI deployments typically follow a layered architecture that separates concerns while maintaining flexibility. At the foundation sits the model infrastructure, which can be cloud-based API services (like OpenAI, Anthropic, or Google Vertex AI), self-hosted models on dedicated GPU clusters, or edge-deployed smaller models. This base layer connects to a middleware orchestration layer responsible for prompt management, context handling, and response processing. The application layer then integrates these capabilities into user-facing interfaces and existing business systems.

Deployment strategies generally follow one of several patterns based on risk tolerance and application criticality. Many organizations adopt a phased rollout approach, beginning with shadow deployment (where AI responses are generated but not shown to users), followed by human-in-the-loop systems (where AI suggestions require human approval), and finally graduating to fully automated systems for appropriate use cases. Each phase provides valuable feedback and builds organizational confidence.

Generative AI Deployment & Monitoring Architecture

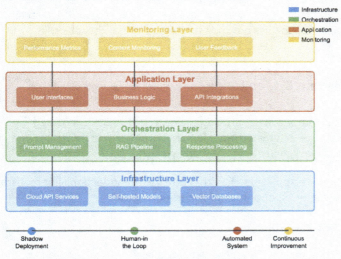

*Deployment strategies typically progress through these stages based on performance and confidence levels

Comprehensive Monitoring Framework

Monitoring generative AI systems demands a multifaceted approach that extends beyond traditional application metrics. Technical performance monitoring tracks latency, throughput, and resource utilization across the stack, with particular attention to GPU utilization for self-hosted models and token consumption for API-based services. Output quality monitoring assesses factual accuracy, hallucination rates, and adherence to safety guidelines through automated evaluation against test sets and human review processes. User interaction monitoring captures engagement metrics, satisfaction scores, and task completion rates to provide insight into real-world effectiveness.

Organizations typically implement this monitoring using a combination of specialized and general-purpose tools. LLM observability platforms like Arize AI, WhyLabs, and Arthur provide AI-specific metrics, while traditional APM tools like New Relic, Datadog, and Prometheus handle infrastructure monitoring. Custom feedback loops collect user ratings and explicit corrections. These monitoring systems feed into feedback loops that continuously improve system performance through prompt refinement, retraining on problematic examples, and knowledge base updates.

Deployment Challenges and Limitations

Deploying generative AI applications presents unique challenges not found in traditional software. Model drift occurs as real-world inputs diverge from training data, leading to degraded performance over time. System prompt leakage can expose internal instructions and guardrails to attackers through careful probing. Integration complexity arises when connecting LLMs to existing enterprise systems with different data formats and authentication requirements. Resource constraints pose particular challenges for self-hosted deployments, where GPU availability and memory limitations can impact performance and scalability.

Latency management presents a significant challenge, especially for interactive applications requiring sub-second responses. This necessitates architectural decisions like asynchronous processing for non-critical tasks, client-side caching of common responses, and potentially deploying smaller, faster models for initial responses while more capable models process complex queries in the background. Multiple environment deployments (development, staging, production) become complicated when models require significant resources or when using versioned API services.

Advanced Deployment Strategies

Sophisticated generative AI deployments often employ advanced strategies to mitigate risks and maximize benefits. Model composition approaches combine multiple specialized models rather than relying on a single general-purpose model, creating systems where different models handle different aspects of a workflow based on their strengths. Blue-green deployments maintain two identical environments with different model versions, allowing instant rollback if problems emerge with a new deployment. Canary releases direct a small percentage of traffic to new model versions before full deployment.

For critical applications, ensemble methods combine predictions from multiple models to improve reliability and reduce hallucination risk, while human-AI collaboration frameworks maintain appropriate oversight for high-stakes decisions. These strategies are increasingly implemented using ML deployment platforms like MLflow, KubeFlow, and BentoML, which provide standardized workflows for versioning, deployment, and monitoring.

Cost Management and Optimization

The economics of generative AI deployments introduce novel considerations around cost optimization. For API-based services, effective prompt engineering can significantly reduce token usage and costs. Caching common queries and responses prevents redundant API calls, while implementing tiered model selection routes simple queries to smaller, cheaper models and reserves premium models for complex tasks. For self-hosted models, appropriate hardware selection balances performance and cost, with decisions around GPU types and quantities having major implications for both throughput and operating expenses.

Ultimately, successful generative AI deployments depend on continuous feedback loops that gather signals from monitoring systems, user feedback, and business metrics to drive ongoing improvements. This creates a virtuous cycle where deployment experience informs model selection and fine-tuning approaches, which in turn enhance deployment outcomes - leading to increasingly effective AI systems that deliver tangible business value while managing the unique risks associated with generative technologies.

Deployment Tools:

- CI/CD: GitHub Actions → ArgoCD → Kubernetes (EKS)

- API Management: Kong Gateway or Apigee

- Monitoring: Prometheus + Grafana for infra; Evidently for model metrics

- Alerts: Set thresholds for drift, latency, user complaints, etc.

System Design Resource Estimation for Generative AI

Understanding Resource Estimation for Generative AI Systems

Resource estimation for generative AI systems is a critical planning process that determines the computational, storage, network, and financial resources needed to develop, deploy, and maintain AI services. Unlike traditional software systems, generative AI introduces unique estimation challenges due to its computational intensity, variable inference requirements, and evolving model architectures. Proper estimation requires understanding multiple dimensions including model selection, deployment architecture, scaling patterns, and operational considerations that collectively impact system performance and costs.

Generative AI resource planning begins with model selection decisions that set baseline requirements. Large language models (LLMs) like GPT-4, Claude, or Llama 2 have dramatically different resource profiles based on parameter count, context length capabilities, and optimization status. For example, a 70B parameter model might require 140GB of GPU memory for full-precision inference, while a quantized version might operate with 35-40GB. Input/output patterns also significantly impact resource utilization - models processing images or audio alongside text (multimodal models) require additional computational resources for processing these data types, while long-context models require proportionally more memory and computation to process lengthy inputs.

Deployment architecture represents another critical dimension of resource estimation. Organizations must determine whether to use cloud-based API services (like OpenAI, Anthropic, or cloud provider offerings), which shift resource management to the provider but introduce operational expenses and potential vendor lock-in. Alternatively, they may self-host models, requiring substantial upfront investment in specialized hardware like NVIDIA A100/H100 GPUs, but potentially reducing per-inference costs for high-volume applications. Hybrid approaches involving specialized hardware accelerators (like Amazon Trainium/Inferentia or Google TPUs) can optimize for specific workloads but require additional architecture expertise.

Generative AI Resource Estimation Framework

Model Selection	Deployment Pattern	Operational Factors	Financial Estimation
Model Size Parameter count Memory requirements	**Hosting Model** API vs Self-hosted Cloud vs on-premise	**Request Patterns** Peak QPS Average latency	**Capital Expenditure** Hardware procurement Infrastructure setup
Context Window Input/output length Memory scaling	**Hardware Selection** GPU type/count Memory configuration	**Data Flow** RAG components Vector DB sizing	**Operational Expenses** API costs Cloud resources
Optimization Level Quantization KV caching	**Scaling Strategy** Horizontal/Vertical Autoscaling rules	**Monitoring** Observability Logging volume	**Personnel Costs** Support engineers ML operations
Modality Text-only vs multimodal Input processing	**Caching Layer** Response caching Embedding storage	**Usage Growth** User adoption Expansion factors	**ROI Calculations** Cost per inference Business value metrics

Continuous Monitoring and Adjustment Based on Real Usage Patterns

Traffic patterns and usage characteristics form another estimation dimension that significantly impacts resource planning. Organizations must consider peak queries per second (QPS), average and P95/P99 latency requirements, concurrent user counts, and token generation volumes. Estimations for these factors must account for both steady-state operations and potential traffic spikes that might occur during marketing campaigns, product launches, or seasonal events. For complex generative AI applications utilizing Retrieval-Augmented Generation (RAG), additional resources must be allocated for vector databases, embedding models, retrieval engines, and the increased computational workload associated with processing retrieved context windows.

Financial estimation represents a synthesis of all technical requirements translated into budgetary terms. This includes capital expenditures (CapEx) for self-hosted solutions including GPU hardware, networking infrastructure, and facility requirements; operational expenditures (OpEx) including cloud service costs, API usage fees, personnel costs for ML engineers and operations staff; and scaling costs that account for future growth in user adoption and feature expansion. Organizations increasingly adopt hybrid approaches that blend API services for experimentation and lower-volume workloads with self-hosted solutions for high-volume, cost-sensitive applications where control over infrastructure is essential.

Resource estimation tools and methodologies have emerged to address these complex planning requirements. Specialized calculators like NVIDIA's GPU memory estimators help determine hardware needs based on model parameters, while cloud providers offer cost calculators for specific AI service offerings. Monitoring tools like Prometheus and Grafana with specialized ML metrics plugins allow for continuous observation of resource utilization patterns that inform future estimations. Frameworks like MLOps cost tracking solutions from vendors like Weights & Biases and Neptune.ai provide deeper visibility into training and inference costs across model deployment lifecycle stages.

The estimation process typically follows a structured methodology beginning with workload characterization that defines usage patterns, throughput requirements, latency constraints, and expected data volumes. This is followed by model profiling to establish baseline resource consumption per inference across different hardware configurations, often through prototype deployments and benchmarking. Resource planning templates encompass compute resources (GPU/CPU types and counts), memory requirements (VRAM, system RAM), storage needs (model weights, embeddings, caching), networking capacity, and supporting infrastructure requirements. The process culminates in capacity planning that accounts for peak load handling, redundancy requirements, geographical distribution, and growth projections.

Key challenges in resource estimation for generative AI include the rapid evolution of model architectures that may invalidate previous estimations, unpredictable scaling of resource needs with longer inputs or more complex prompts, and difficulty accurately modeling how techniques like quantization, distillation, or speculative decoding affect resource requirements in production. Organizations often struggle with the limited historical data available for novel AI applications, making it difficult to project user adoption rates and usage patterns that significantly impact long-term resource needs. Balancing performance objectives with budgetary constraints represents an ongoing challenge that requires continuous monitoring and adjustment based on real-world usage.

Best practices for accurate resource estimation include staging deployments with gradually increasing scale to gather operational metrics, implementing comprehensive monitoring across all system components, developing scenario-based planning that accounts for different growth trajectories, and maintaining flexibility in infrastructure design to accommodate rapid changes in model architecture or deployment patterns. Organizations should establish close collaboration between ML engineers, infrastructure teams, and financial planners to ensure estimates comprehensively address technical and budgetary considerations, while allowing for both conservative baseline planning and contingencies for unexpected scaling requirements.

The limitations of current estimation approaches include inherent variability in generative AI workloads where token generation times can vary significantly based on content complexity, immature benchmarking methodologies that may not accurately represent production workloads, and the difficulty predicting how model architectural improvements will affect resource requirements. Organizations must also contend with vendor-specific variations in how resources are allocated and billed, making cross-platform comparisons challenging. These limitations underscore the importance of building monitoring systems that can refine estimations based on actual production metrics rather than relying solely on theoretical projections.

In conclusion, effective resource estimation for generative AI systems requires a multidimensional approach that accounts for model characteristics, deployment architectures, operational patterns, and financial considerations. Organizations that develop systematic estimation processes gain competitive advantages through more efficient resource allocation, better cost management, and improved ability to scale AI capabilities in response to evolving business needs. As the field matures, standardized benchmarking methodologies and more sophisticated estimation tools will likely emerge to address current limitations and provide more accurate resource projections for increasingly complex generative AI applications.

Sample example.

Component	Value
Model Type (e.g., GPT-4, custom model)	GPT-4
Tokens per Month	1000000
Token Cost per 1K Tokens (USD)	0.03

Monthly Inference Cost (USD)	30
Training Hours	10
Training Cost per Hour (USD)	5
Monthly Fine-tuning Cost (USD)	50
Monthly Storage (GB)	50
Storage Cost per GB (USD)	0.02
Monthly Storage Cost (USD)	1
Other Monthly Costs (e.g., API Gateway, Security)	100
Total Monthly Cost (USD)	181

Generative AI Design Patterns

Why We Need AI Patterns

When building something new, we often rely on proven methods, established approaches, and familiar patterns—especially in software engineering. However, this isn't always the case with emerging technologies like generative AI. The field still lacks well-documented and standardized patterns to guide solution development.

In this article, I share a curated set of patterns and approaches for generative AI, drawn from my analysis of numerous real-world LLM implementations. These patterns aim to address key challenges in generative AI projects—such as high costs, latency issues, and hallucinations—and provide a more grounded foundation for building effective AI solutions.

Generative AI Design Patterns

1. **Layered Caching Strategy Leading to Fine-Tuning**
    Implement progressive caching (prompt-level, embedding-level, response-level) to reduce latency and costs—eventually feeding insights into targeted fine-tuning.

2. **Multiplexing AI Agents for a Panel of Experts**
    Route queries to specialized AI agents (each fine-tuned or prompted for a specific domain), mimicking a panel of experts to improve precision and reduce hallucinations.

3. **Fine-Tuning LLMs for Multiple Tasks**
    Customize a base model for multiple downstream tasks using task-specific fine-tuning to balance performance and reuse.

4. **Blending Rule-Based Systems with Generative AI**
    Combine deterministic rules (for known, high-risk scenarios) with LLM flexibility to ensure safety, compliance, and grounded outputs.

5. **Utilizing Knowledge Graphs with LLMs**
    Integrate structured knowledge (ontologies, graphs) with LLMs to enrich reasoning, context retention, and factual grounding.

6. **Swarm of Generative AI Agents**
    Deploy multiple generative agents that collaborate or compete (e.g., via voting or consensus) to improve reliability and creativity.

7. **Modular Monolith LLM Architecture with Composability**
    Design your system as a composable "monolith" of modular capabilities—

standardized interfaces, reusable prompt components, and API-bound tasks.

8. **Memory Cognition Layer for LLMs**
   Introduce a memory layer that tracks user history, task context, and feedback loops to enhance personalization and context continuity across sessions.

9. **Red & Blue Team Dual-Model Evaluation**
   Use adversarial evaluation setups—one model generates, the other critiques (or defends)—to test robustness, detect flaws, and improve trust.

1) Layered Caching Strategy Leading To Fine-Tuning

A layered caching strategy combined with model fine-tuning creates an intelligent system that becomes more efficient and specialized over time. Let me explain how this approach works:

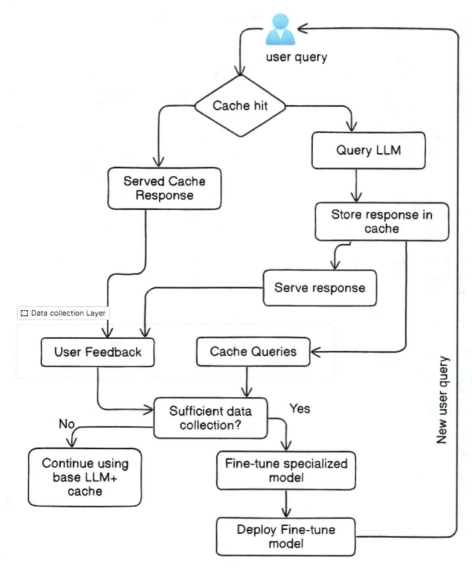

This architecture addresses key challenges of cost, redundancy, and training data quality through a progressive system:

1. **Initial Caching Layer**: Stores responses from the base language model, eliminating redundant processing for similar queries and significantly reducing both latency and operational costs.

2. **Data Collection System**: Continuously gathers both the cached query-response pairs and user feedback, building a valuable dataset for future optimization.

3. **Fine-Tuning Transition**: Once sufficient high-quality data is collected, the system uses it to fine-tune a specialized model tailored to the specific use case.

4. **Specialized Deployment**: The fine-tuned model delivers more precise responses for domain-specific tasks, creating a virtuous cycle of improved performance.

This approach is particularly valuable in specialized environments like customer support platforms or content personalization systems where both efficiency and contextual accuracy matter.

When introducing a caching strategy for large language models, we aim to balance several key factors—cost, redundancy, and the availability of training data.

By caching initial responses, the system can deliver answers much faster for repeated queries, significantly improving efficiency. The real advantage emerges when we layer in fine-tuning: once enough interaction data is collected, this feedback helps refine a more specialized model.

This specialized model not only accelerates performance but also enhances task-specific accuracy, making it ideal for high-precision use cases like customer support or personalized content generation.

To get started, you can leverage ready-made solutions like **GPTCache**, or build a custom setup using common caching tools such as **Redis, Apache Cassandra**, or **Memcached**. Just be sure to monitor performance carefully—particularly latency—as additional services are integrated.

2) Multiplexing AI Agents For A Panel Of Experts

Multiplexing AI Agents: Creating a Panel of Expert Systems
The multiplexing approach to AI systems creates a collaborative ecosystem of specialized models working together to solve complex problems through distributed expertise.

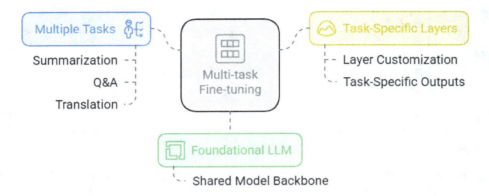

How Multiplexed AI Systems Work

This architecture creates a panel of AI experts that collaborate to address complex queries through a structured process:

1. **Query Analysis & Task Decomposition**
   - A powerful orchestrator model (like GPT-4) receives and analyzes the initial query
   - The orchestrator breaks down the problem into discrete sub-tasks requiring different expertise
   - Each sub-task is routed to the most appropriate specialized agent

2. **Parallel Processing by Specialized Agents**
   - Multiple smaller, domain-focused AI models process their assigned tasks simultaneously
   - These specialized agents can be:
     - Fine-tuned small models (Phi-2, TinyLlama) for specific domains
     - Larger models with specialized prompting (Llama variants)
     - Custom models with unique capabilities or access to specific tools

3. **Response Integration & Coherence**
   - Individual agent responses are collected and synthesized into a unified answer
   - Contradictions are resolved and overlapping information is harmonized
   - The final response maintains a consistent voice and logical structure

This approach mirrors how human expert panels function, with specialists collaborating to address multifaceted problems while maintaining efficiency through parallelization.

Key Benefits

- **Expertise Diversity**: Each agent brings specialized knowledge to specific aspects of the problem

- **Resource Efficiency**: Smaller models handle appropriate tasks while the orchestrator manages complexity
- **Scalability**: New specialized agents can be added as needed for emerging domains
- **Contextual Understanding**: The orchestrator ensures the holistic perspective isn't lost among specialized viewpoints

This architecture is particularly valuable for complex scenarios requiring diverse expertise, such as comprehensive research questions, multidisciplinary problem-solving, or situations requiring both technical and contextual understanding.

Multi-Task Fine-Tuning for Language Models: Shared Architecture with Task-Specific Outputs

Multi-task fine-tuning is a training technique where a single **foundational large language model** is fine-tuned on **multiple tasks at once** (e.g., summarization, Q&A, translation). Instead of training a separate model for each task, a **shared model backbone** is used with **task-specific layers** added on top.

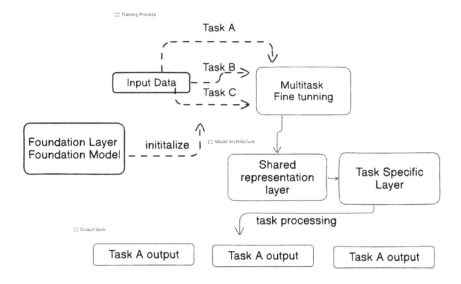

What a Multi-Task Fine-Tuning Works

This architecture leverages cross-domain knowledge transfer by simultaneously training a language model on multiple objectives:

1. Foundation Model Initialization

    o   The process begins with a pre-trained large language model (like GPT, LLaMA, or other foundation models)

    o   This model already contains broad linguistic knowledge and general reasoning capabilities

2. **Integrated Training Approach**

    o   Input data from multiple distinct tasks (A, B, C) is used concurrently during training

    o   The model learns to handle diverse objectives within a unified architecture

    o   Parameters are updated based on performance across all tasks simultaneously

3. **Architectural Design**

    o   **Shared Layer Structure**: The majority of the model's parameters are shared across all tasks

    o   **Task-Specific Components**: Specialized layers or attention mechanisms handle unique requirements of each task

    o   **Joint Optimization**: The training objective balances performance across all target tasks

4. **Output Generation**

    o   Task-specific layers interpret the shared representation for each particular application

    o   The model produces specialized outputs for each distinct task while leveraging knowledge from all domains

Implementation Advantages

*   **Knowledge Transfer**: Skills learned for one task often enhance performance on others

*   **Efficiency**: A single model can replace multiple specialized models, reducing operational complexity

- **Robustness**: Exposure to diverse data helps prevent overfitting to any single domain

- **Resource Optimization**: Training one multi-capable model requires fewer computational resources than separate models

Development Resources

Multi-task fine-tuning can be implemented using:

- HuggingFace's Transformers library with customized training loops

- DeepSpeed for memory-efficient training across multiple tasks

- Microsoft's MT-DNN (Multi-Task Deep Neural Networks) framework

- Google's T5 approach to framing diverse tasks within a text-to-text framework

This technique is particularly valuable for creating versatile AI assistants, content generation platforms, or analytical tools that need to perform well across multiple domains while maintaining a coherent underlying knowledge base.

Blending Rules Based & Generative

Blending rules-based systems with generative AI combines the precision of traditional logic with the flexibility of large language models (LLMs).

Large Language Model (rule creation)

↓

Human Verifications

user query

Pre-populated rules

Rules Based Engine

fetch applicable rule

Generated content request

Generative AI Model

Rules validation ←

Log & Feedback Loop

valid output

invalid output

Final Output

Many existing business systems and enterprise applications still rely heavily on rule-based logic. By integrating generative AI with this structured, rules-driven approach, we can create solutions that are both imaginative and compliant.

This hybrid pattern is especially effective in industries where outputs must meet strict standards or regulatory requirements. It ensures that AI stays within defined boundaries while still offering flexibility and creativity. A practical example of this is using generative AI to create user intents or conversational flows for IVR systems or traditional rule-based chatbots.

How the Hybrid Rules-Based and Generative AI System Works

This architecture bridges traditional enterprise systems with modern AI capabilities through a structured workflow:

1. **Rule Creation and Management**

   o   Large language models help draft initial rules based on business requirements and regulations

   o   Human experts verify and refine these rules before implementation

   o   The verified ruleset forms the governance framework for the system

2. **Query Processing Pipeline**

   o   User queries are first interpreted by the rules-based engine

   o   The engine identifies applicable constraints and parameters for the specific context

   o   Instead of producing rigid, templated responses, the system delegates content creation to a generative AI

3. **AI-Powered Response Generation**

   o   The generative model creates creative, human-like responses while receiving context about applicable rules

   o   This produces content that maintains compliance while leveraging the AI's linguistic capabilities

4. **Validation and Quality Control**

   o   All generated outputs undergo validation against the established ruleset

   o   Valid responses proceed to delivery

   o   Invalid outputs trigger a feedback loop for rule refinement or content adjustment

5. **Continuous Improvement**

- The system logs performance data and validation results

- This feedback informs adjustments to both rule definitions and AI parameters

- Over time, the system becomes increasingly adept at balancing creativity with compliance

Practical Applications

This hybrid approach is particularly valuable in regulated environments such as:

- **Interactive Voice Response (IVR) Systems**: Creating natural-sounding dialog flows while ensuring they follow call centre protocols and legal requirements

- **Traditional Chatbots**: Enhancing rule-based conversation trees with more natural language while maintaining predictable paths

- **Healthcare Communication**: Generating patient information that remains medically accurate while being conversational

- **Financial Services**: Creating marketing content that adheres to strict regulatory guidelines

- **Legal Document Generation**: Producing contracts with customized language while ensuring all required clauses are included

By combining the predictability of rules-based systems with the fluidity of generative AI, organizations can modernize legacy systems without sacrificing reliability or compliance.

Utilizing Knowledge Graphs with LLM's

Many enterprise systems and organizational applications continue to rely on **structured, rule-based logic** to ensure reliability, traceability, and compliance. While effective for control and precision, such systems often lack the flexibility and adaptability of modern **Generative AI** models.

By **integrating Knowledge Graphs (KGs) with Large Language Models (LLMs)**, we create a hybrid approach that combines **structured factual data** with the **reasoning**

and creative generation capabilities of LLMs. This pattern is designed to deliver outputs that are both **informative and trustworthy**, while still being able to adapt and respond naturally.

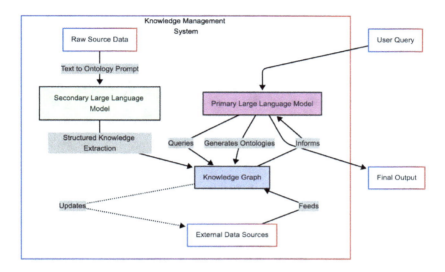

How Knowledge Graph-Enhanced LLMs Work

This architecture creates a symbiotic relationship between structured knowledge representation and neural language models:

1. Dual LLM System

    o **Primary LLM**: Handles user interactions and generates responses

    o **Secondary LLM**: Processes raw data to extract structured knowledge

2. **Knowledge Graph as Structured Repository**

    o Stores information as interconnected entities and relationships

    o Maintains semantic connections between concepts

    o Provides verifiable, structured data to enhance LLM outputs

- Can be implemented using graph databases like Neo4j, ArangoDB, or Amazon Neptune

3. **Bidirectional Information Flow**

    - **LLM → Knowledge Graph**: The primary LLM queries the knowledge graph for factual information

    - **Knowledge Graph → LLM**: Structured data enhances the LLM's responses with verified information

    - **LLM → Knowledge Graph Creation**: LLMs help generate ontologies and extract relationships from text

4. **Dynamic Knowledge Integration**

    - External data sources continuously update the knowledge graph

    - The knowledge graph provides factual grounding for the LLM's responses

    - New information discovered during user interactions can update the knowledge graph

Key Benefits

- **Factual Accuracy**: Knowledge graphs provide verified information to reduce hallucinations

- **Reasoning Transparency**: Graph structures make decision paths more traceable

- **Domain Adaptation**: Knowledge graphs can encode specialized domain knowledge

- **Up-to-date Information**: The graph can be updated without retraining the entire LLM

Practical Applications

This architecture excels in scenarios requiring both factual precision and natural language capabilities:

- **Enterprise Knowledge Management**: Connecting organizational data while providing conversational access

- **Scientific Research Assistants**: Grounding responses in verified research while maintaining accessibility

- **Healthcare Systems**: Connecting medical knowledge while communicating naturally with practitioners

- **Financial Advisory Services**: Linking complex financial data while providing understandable guidance

By combining the structured precision of knowledge graphs with the linguistic capabilities of LLMs, this approach delivers responses that are both accurate and engaging.

Swarm Of AI Agents: Collective Intelligence for Complex Tasks

Inspired by the behavior of natural swarms—like flocks of birds, schools of fish, or colonies of ants—this pattern uses a **distributed network of AI agents**, each operating semi-independently to solve parts of a problem. These agents bring different **perspectives, skills, or heuristics** to the table, and their individual outputs are then **aggregated into a single, more refined solution**.

This swarm-based approach results in a form of **collective AI intelligence** that is often more powerful, diverse, and adaptable than any single model or agent working in isolation.

Technical Backbone

To scale this approach, especially in **high-volume or real-time environments**, you can integrate:

- **Message brokers** like **Apache Kafka**, RabbitMQ, or NATS to handle:
    - Asynchronous communication between agents
    - Load balancing
    - Fault tolerance

- **Microservices** or **containerized AI agents** that can be orchestrated via Kubernetes or similar tools.

How AI Swarm Intelligence Works

This architecture implements a decentralized approach to problem-solving through coordinated autonomous agents:

1. **Distributed Processing**

    o   The initial query is routed to multiple generative AI agents

    o   Each agent analyses the problem from a distinct perspective or using different methodologies

    o   Agents operate simultaneously, creating a parallel processing environment

2. **Diverse Agent Configurations**

    o   Agents can differ in their:

        ▪   Prompting strategies (adversarial, supportive, analytical)

        ▪   Parameter settings (temperature, top-p sampling)

        ▪   Access to specialized knowledge or tools

        ▪   Assigned personas or expertise domains

3. **Consensus Formation**

    o   The ensemble layer aggregates individual outputs through methods such as:

        ▪   Majority voting on factual elements

        ▪   Confidence-weighted averaging

        ▪   Cross-validation between agent responses

        ▪   Pattern recognition across multiple solutions

4. **Output Integration**

    o   The aggregated insights are synthesized into a comprehensive solution

    o   Contradictions are resolved and complementary ideas are unified

    o   The final output represents an emergent intelligence greater than any single agent

5. **Adaptive Improvement**

- Performance feedback flows back to both individual agents and consensus rules

- The system evolves over time, strengthening successful patterns

- Failed approaches are identified and modified or discarded

Implementation Considerations

For high-volume implementations:

- **Message Handling**: Apache Kafka can manage the high-throughput communication between agents

- **Orchestration**: Kubernetes can coordinate agent deployment and scaling

- **Agent Communication**: gRPC or message queues enable efficient inter-agent interactions

Practical Applications

This architecture excels in scenarios requiring both breadth and depth:

- **Research Analysis**: Multiple "expert" perspectives evaluate academic papers from different disciplines

- **Fraud Detection**: Parallel agents apply different detection methods simultaneously

- **Customer Analytics**: Various use-case specialists examine interactions for opportunities and risks

- **Creative Ideation**: Diverse creative agents generate a wide spectrum of novel solutions

- **Risk Assessment**: Multiple risk models evaluate scenarios from different angles

By leveraging collective intelligence principles, swarm AI architectures can achieve robustness, creativity, and accuracy beyond what any single model can provide.

Modular Monolith LLM Approach with Composability

This design emphasizes **flexibility and adaptability** by structuring your AI system as a **modular monolith**—a unified system composed of interchangeable, task-specific components. Think of it like a **Swiss Army knife**, where each blade (or module) is purpose-built and can be activated when needed. This makes the architecture especially effective for businesses needing **customized solutions** across a wide range of workflows or customer interactions.

Modular Agents for Task Specialization

Each module in the system is represented by an **autonomous AI agent**, designed to handle a specific function. These agents can be developed using modern frameworks such as:

- CrewAI

- LangChain

- Microsoft AutoGen

- SuperAGI

These platforms allow for building, orchestrating, and scaling AI agents that can collaborate, share tools, and adapt to changing requirements.

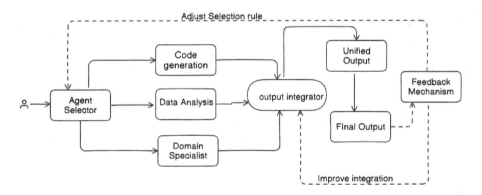

How the Modular Monolith LLM Approach Works

This system functions as a cohesive yet adaptable framework that intelligently assembles specialized components for each user interaction:

1. Intelligent Agent Selection

   o The Agent Selector analyzes incoming queries to determine which specialized agents are required

   o Selection criteria include query intent, complexity, domain, and historical performance

   o Only the most appropriate agents for the specific task are activated

2. Specialized Agent Repository

   o A collection of purpose-built AI agents with distinct capabilities:

     ▪ Domain-specific knowledge (sales, support, technical)

     ▪ Function-specific skills (data analysis, content creation, scheduling)

     ▪ Tool integration capabilities (database access, API connections)

   o Each agent maintains focused expertise rather than generalized capabilities

3. Dynamic Composition

   o Selected agents work in concert to address different aspects of the query

   o The system adapts its configuration based on task requirements

   o Interactions between agents are coordinated through standardized interfaces

4. Unified Response Generation

   o The Output Integrator synthesizes contributions from all activated agents

   o Conflicting information is reconciled and redundancies are eliminated

   o The final output maintains a consistent voice and logical structure

5. Continuous Refinement

- Feedback mechanisms adjust both agent selection rules and integration processes

- The system learns which agent combinations work best for specific query types

- Performance metrics drive ongoing optimization

Implementation Frameworks

The architecture can be implemented using several agent orchestration frameworks:

- **LangChain**: For connecting agents with external tools and data sources

- **CrewAI**: For creating collaborative agent teams with defined roles

- **Microsoft AutoGen**: For multi-agent conversation orchestration

- **SuperAGI**: For long-running autonomous agent processes

Business Applications

This approach excels in complex business environments requiring diverse capabilities:

- **Sales Operations**: Different agents handle prospecting, scheduling, content creation, and CRM updates

- **Customer Support**: Specialized agents for technical troubleshooting, policy questions, and escalation management

- **Content Production**: Dedicated agents for research, drafting, editing, and formatting

The architecture's modular nature ensures future-proofing, allowing individual components to be upgraded or replaced with specialized third-party services as AI technology evolves, without disrupting the overall system.

Approach To Memory Cognition For LLM's : Building Smarter, More Context-Aware AI

This design pattern introduces a **memory mechanism** to large language models (LLMs), enabling them to remember and **build context over time**—similar to how humans recall past conversations or experiences. Rather than treating each interaction as isolated, the AI **learns from previous exchanges**, which allows for **deeper, more coherent, and personalized responses** in long-running dialogues or continuous learning environments.

This is especially powerful for:

- **Ongoing conversations** (like in customer support or therapy bots)

- **Adaptive learning systems**

- **Personal AI assistants** that evolve with user behavior

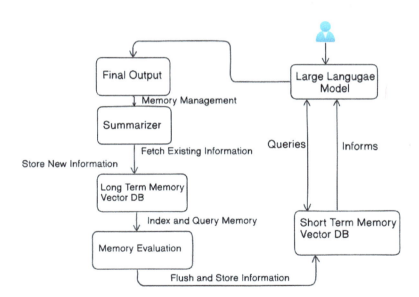

How Memory-Enhanced LLM Systems Work

This architecture creates AI systems with persistent memory capabilities through a sophisticated multi-tiered approach:

1. **Dual Memory Structure**

- Short-Term Memory: Maintains immediate context for current interactions

- Long-Term Memory: Preserves important information across extended timelines

- Both implemented using vector databases for semantic similarity search

2. Interaction Processing Pipeline

- The primary LLM handles user queries while accessing relevant memory

- During responses, the system references both short-term context and long-term knowledge

- Each interaction enriches both memory systems with new information

3. Memory Management System

- Summarization: Distills key information from interactions using efficient NLP tools

  - Light processing through spaCy for basic extraction

  - BART or T5 models for more complex summarization needs

- Memory Evaluation: Determines information importance and relevance

- Decay Mechanism: Gradually reduces prominence of less relevant information

4. Retrieval-Augmented Generation

- Before generating responses, the system performs similarity searches across memory stores

- Contextually relevant information is injected into the generation process

- This creates continuity and personalization in ongoing conversations

Implementation Components

- **Vector Databases**: Pinecone, Weaviate, Milvus, or Chroma for semantic storage

- **Summarization Tools**: spaCy for lightweight processing, BART for complex summaries

- **Memory Management**: Custom algorithms for importance scoring and memory decay

- **Integration Framework**: Similar to the open-source MemGPT project

Practical Applications

This architecture excels in scenarios requiring persistent understanding:

- **Personal Assistants**: Systems that learn user preferences and history over time

- **Educational Platforms**: Tutoring systems that track student progress and adapt accordingly

- **Customer Support**: Agents that remember previous issues and resolution attempts

- **Collaborative Work**: Systems that maintain project context across multiple sessions

By incorporating both short and long-term memory structures, these systems provide increasingly relevant and personalized interactions that build upon previous knowledge, creating a more human-like experience with each interaction.

Red & Blue Team Dual-Model Evaluation: AI vs AI for Smarter Validation

This pattern draws inspiration from cybersecurity and military defense strategies, where **"Red Teams"** attack and **"Blue Teams"** defend. In the context of AI, this becomes a **dual-model evaluation loop** where:

- The Red Team AI is responsible for **generating content or outputs**—like answering questions, summarizing articles, or writing creative content.
- The Blue Team AI plays the role of a **critical evaluator or reviewer**, checking the red team's outputs for **accuracy, logic, safety, fairness, tone, and factuality.**

This creates an **automated feedback loop**—resembling a peer-review or QA process—ensuring **high-quality, safe, and reliable AI responses.**

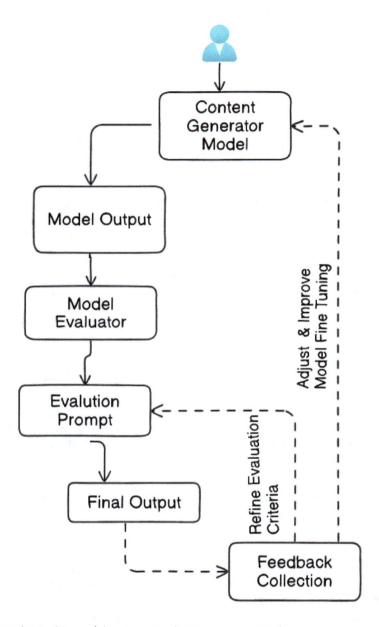

How the Red Team/Blue Team Evaluation System Works

This architecture creates a self-improving AI system through structured adversarial collaboration:

1. **Specialized Model Roles**
   - **Student Model ("Blue Team")**: Generates initial content in response to queries

- Optimized for creative production and problem-solving
- Trained to handle complex task requirements
  - **Teacher Model ("Red Team")**: Critically evaluates the generated content
    - Fine-tuned specifically for assessment and critique
    - Looks for errors, bias, factual inaccuracies, and logical inconsistencies

2. **Sequential Processing Pipeline**
   - The user query first goes to the Student Model for initial content generation
   - The complete output is then passed to the Teacher Model for thorough evaluation
   - The Teacher applies structured evaluation criteria to identify strengths and weaknesses
   - Final output includes both the original content and quality assessment

3. **Continuous Improvement Cycle**
   - Feedback from the Teacher Model informs refinements to both models
   - The Student Model's training adapts to avoid common critique points
   - The Teacher Model's evaluation criteria evolve based on emerging patterns
   - This creates a virtuous cycle of increasing quality over time

Real-World Applications

This approach is particularly valuable in scenarios requiring high-quality, verified outputs:

- **Educational Content Development**: Ensuring learning materials are accurate and comprehensive
- **Professional Document Creation**: Checking legal documents, medical literature, or technical specifications
- **News and Media Production**: Verifying factual accuracy and identifying potential bias
- **Scientific Research**: Validating methodologies and findings before publication
- **Creative Content**: Evaluating narrative coherence and stylistic consistency

Implementation Strategy

To implement this architecture effectively:

- Fine-tune the Teacher Model on human evaluation data to approximate expert review processes
- Develop structured evaluation rubrics for different content types and quality dimensions
- Create feedback integration mechanisms that maintain model improvements over time

By formalizing the evaluation process within the AI system itself, this architecture reduces dependency on human review while maintaining rigorous quality standards, effectively creating an automated peer-review system.

System Design Use Cases

Text-to- Video Generation System

The system design for a **Text-to-Video Generation System** addresses a growing demand for transforming textual input into dynamic, high-quality visual content. This technology is particularly useful in a range of industries where creating video manually is either resource-intensive or creatively limiting.

One of the primary use cases is **content creation**, where individuals or teams can generate short-form videos from simple text prompts, eliminating the need for expensive equipment, editing software, or technical expertise. It's a game-changer for **storyboarding**, allowing writers, directors, and game designers to quickly visualize scenes, plot sequences, or character interactions without waiting on production teams. In the **education sector**, it enables the automatic creation of animated explanations or simulations based on technical or academic descriptions, supporting various learning styles and improving engagement.

Marketing and advertising teams can also benefit by using the system to **generate product demos, explainer videos, or campaign visuals** directly from a brief. This streamlines content pipelines and accelerates time-to-market. Additionally, the system enhances **accessibility** by converting text into visual media, offering new modes of content consumption for users who prefer or require visual learning experiences.

The technology serves a broad set of users. These include **content creators**—such as YouTubers, independent artists, and small studios—who may not have the resources for full video production. It's also valuable to **game and film development teams** needing quick, visual prototypes to iterate on ideas, and **educational platforms** looking to scale their content offering without a proportional increase in design efforts. Even **software developers** can integrate this capability into applications where media-rich experiences enhance user engagement, such as in interactive storytelling or personalized video generation.

From a business perspective, the value is significant. Automating video generation can **reduce production costs**, as fewer human hours and tools are needed to produce high-quality results. It also **speeds up the creative process**, allowing teams to move from idea to execution in a fraction of the time. The system enables **rapid experimentation**, helping creators test and revise visual concepts on the fly. Ultimately, this democratizes access to video production, empowering individuals and smaller teams to produce compelling visual media without the traditional barriers of cost, skill, or time.

Primary Use Cases

- **Content Creation**: Enabling creators to generate video content from text descriptions

- **Storyboarding**: Visualizing scripts and narrative concepts rapidly

- **Educational Material**: Creating animated explanations from technical descriptions

- **Advertising**: Generating product demos and concept videos from marketing briefs

- **Accessibility**: Converting text-based content to visual media for different learning styles

Targeted Users

- Content creators with limited video production resources

- Game and film development teams for rapid prototyping

- Educational platforms requiring visual content generation

- Marketing teams needing quick concept visualization

- Software developers building media-rich applications

Business Value

- Reducing production costs by automating video generation

- Decreasing time-to-market for visual content

- Enabling rapid iteration on visual concepts

- Democratizing video production capabilities

2. Functional Requirements

A robust Text-to-Video Generation System must support a wide range of functionalities to translate user prompts into meaningful, coherent video outputs. At the foundation, it begins with **text input processing**—the ability to interpret natural language descriptions and extract relevant scene elements. This includes support for structured text formats like Markdown or XML, where users might embed specific directives to guide generation. Whether the input is a screenplay, technical instruction, or creative writing, the system should parse it intelligently to guide the video synthesis process.

The heart of the system lies in its **video generation capabilities**. It needs to produce coherent video sequences that maintain visual and thematic consistency from frame to frame. The generated videos should reflect the scene's intended actions, moods, and transitions—accurately interpreting motion cues and ensuring smooth animation across a range of durations, from brief five-second clips to more elaborate multi-minute videos.

A key feature of such systems is **content control**. Users should be able to specify scene elements such as characters, objects, and environments, while also tailoring the visual style—whether cinematic, cartoonish, or hyper-realistic. Beyond aesthetics, control over camera movements like panning, zooming, and tracking shots, as well as temporal pacing like slow-motion or time-lapse, enhances the creative flexibility offered by the platform.

On the output side, the system should support **diverse resolution and format requirements**, including 720p, 1080p, and even 4K, with the ability to generate MP4, WebM, or GIF outputs. It should also offer customization around frame rates (24fps, 30fps, 60fps) and embed metadata about the prompt and generation parameters for traceability and reproducibility.

User feedback integration is essential to making the system iterative and user-friendly. Users should be able to refine previously generated videos with new prompts, selectively regenerate parts of a video while preserving others, and even apply style references from existing media. This supports a creative feedback loop where users can progressively refine results rather than starting from scratch each time.

To enhance the immersive experience, **audio integration** plays a valuable role. The system should be capable of generating background music aligned with the scene's mood, adding voice narration directly from the text, and incorporating synchronized sound effects.

Finally, **editing controls** allow for precision adjustments. Developers and creators should be able to target specific scenes for regeneration, control object persistence across different shots, and even edit keyframes directly for fine-tuning the generated video sequences.

Core Requirements

1. **Text Input Processing**

   o   Parse natural language descriptions and extract scene elements

   o   Support for structured text formats (markdown, XML) with specific directives

   o   Handle creative writing, screenplays, and technical descriptions

2. **Video Generation**

   o   Generate coherent video sequences from text descriptions

   o   Maintain visual consistency across frames

   o   Support various durations (5 seconds to 3 minutes)

   o   Generate appropriate motion patterns based on text descriptions

3. **Content Control**

   o   Scene composition control (characters, objects, environment)

   o   Style control (cinematic, cartoon, realistic, etc.)

   o   Camera movement control (pan, zoom, tracking shots)

   o   Temporal pacing control (slow motion, time-lapse)

4. **Output Management**

   o   Multiple resolution support (720p, 1080p, 4K)

   o   Various output formats (MP4, WebM, GIF)

   o   Frame rate control (24fps, 30fps, 60fps)

    ○ Metadata inclusion (generation parameters, prompt information)

5. **User Feedback Integration**

    ○ Accept refinement prompts for generated videos

    ○ Support iterative generation with preserved elements

    ○ Allow segmented regeneration (keep some scenes, regenerate others)

    ○ Enable style transfer from reference materials

Extended Requirements

1. **Audio Integration**

    ○ Generate appropriate background music based on scene mood

    ○ Support for adding voice narration from text

    ○ Sound effect generation and synchronization

2. **Edit Controls**

    ○ Scene-specific regeneration without affecting the entire video

    ○ Keyframe editing for fine-tuning generated sequences

    ○ Object persistence control across scenes

3. Non-Functional Requirements

Beyond features, the system must meet a set of **non-functional requirements** to ensure it performs reliably and at scale. In terms of **performance**, it should be able to generate a base 30-second video within five minutes, even under load. The system must handle hundreds of concurrent generation requests efficiently, maximizing GPU or TPU usage while intelligently prioritizing jobs to avoid bottlenecks.

Quality is paramount. The system must ensure visual coherence, where characters and settings remain consistent across frames. Temporal stability is equally important—flickering, unexpected transitions, or inconsistencies must be minimized. Videos should support resolutions up to 4K with high detail preservation and generate realistic or stylistically fitting motion throughout the scene.

On the **reliability** front, the system needs to gracefully handle errors. This includes preserving partial outputs when generation fails, saving progress through checkpoints, and maintaining near-constant availability (targeting 99.9% uptime). Importantly, it must ensure that jobs aren't lost during updates or restarts, preserving user trust.

Security features must be in place to prevent misuse. This includes filtering out inappropriate content, validating inputs to guard against injection attacks, scanning outputs for harmful elements, and enforcing access controls through authentication mechanisms like API keys.

Lastly, **scalability** is critical for production environments. The system should scale horizontally, adding new generation nodes as needed. Load balancing mechanisms must distribute tasks evenly, and caching strategies should optimize reuse of frequently generated components. A robust queue management system ensures fair scheduling and prioritization of requests, supporting both individual users and enterprise-level demands.

Performance

- **Generation Time**: Base video (30s) generated within 5 minutes

- **Scaling**: System capable of handling concurrent generation jobs

- **Resource Utilization**: Efficient GPU/TPU usage with job prioritization

- **Throughput**: Support for at least 100 concurrent generation jobs

Quality

- **Visual Coherence**: Maintain consistent character appearance and scene composition

- **Temporal Stability**: Minimal flickering or unexpected scene transitions

- **Resolution Support**: Up to 4K output with appropriate detail preservation

- **Motion Naturalness**: Realistic or stylistically appropriate movement patterns

Reliability

- **Error Recovery**: Graceful handling of generation failures with partial results preservation

- **Checkpointing**: Regular saving of intermediate generation states

- **Availability**: 99.9% system uptime for generation services

- **Job Persistence**: No job loss during system updates or restarts

Security

- **Content Filtering**: Prevention of harmful or inappropriate content generation

- **Input Validation**: Protection against prompt injection and other attacks

- **Output Scanning**: Detection of potentially problematic generated content

- **Access Control**: API keys and user authentication for generation jobs

Scalability

- **Horizontal Scaling**: Ability to add generation nodes to increase capacity

- **Load Balancing**: Distribute generation jobs across available resources

- **Caching**: Reuse of common elements and similar generations

- **Queue Management**: Prioritization and fair scheduling of generation jobs

Architecture Overview

The architecture of a Text-to-Video Generation System is designed as a modular, service-oriented pipeline that transforms raw text into polished, high-quality video content. Each component plays a specialized role, and together they form a scalable, intelligent system capable of handling complex media generation tasks.

At the entry point, the **API Gateway** acts as the main interface for all incoming user requests. It handles user authentication, enforces rate limits to prevent abuse, and routes each request to the appropriate internal services. This gateway also maintains session information, allowing users to return to previous jobs or apply consistent preferences across multiple generations.

Once a request is received, it's handed off to the **Job Manager**, which acts as the central coordinator. This component is responsible for scheduling video generation jobs, assigning priorities, and ensuring that all tasks are fairly managed across available system resources. It also monitors the state of each job and handles failure recovery if anything goes wrong during processing.

The first major step in content generation happens within the **Text Processing Service**. This service reads the user's prompt or structured text input and breaks it down into actionable components. It uses natural language understanding to convert the text into **scene graphs**, identifying key objects, actions, emotions, and the relationships between them. It also extracts any temporal sequences (e.g., what happens before or after) to inform the flow of the video.

Based on this structured representation, the **Shot Planning Service** takes over to plan the visual storytelling. It determines how each scene should be composed: where the camera should be positioned, how it should move (pans, zooms, tracking shots), and how scenes should transition. It produces a blueprint of keyframes that will guide the video creation process.

Next, the **Frame Generation Service** takes these shot plans and uses advanced generative models—often diffusion-based—to create high-quality individual frames. This service also allows users to control visual styles, from photorealistic to stylized or animated, and ensures the presence of the right characters, environments, and visual themes based on the original prompt.

To bring these static frames to life, the **Motion Generation Service** steps in. It generates smooth transitions and natural motion between frames using techniques like optical flow or animation modeling. This ensures that the final video is temporally coherent and visually engaging, avoiding jarring or inconsistent frame changes.

After all the frames and motion elements are created, the **Video Assembly Service** compiles everything into a final video file. This includes stitching frames together, encoding the output in the desired format (MP4, WebM, etc.), and applying final polish like visual effects or transitions. The service supports multiple resolutions and frame rates, from casual 720p GIFs to professional-grade 4K videos.

All media—both intermediate and final outputs—are stored and managed by the **Media Storage Service**. This service ensures that content can be cached for efficiency, re-used for iteration, and delivered to users quickly and reliably. It integrates with content delivery networks to provide seamless playback or download.

A unique strength of the system is its responsiveness to feedback, handled by the **Feedback Service**. This component lets users refine videos by pointing out what to keep, change, or regenerate. It processes user suggestions, converts them into structured parameters, and routes them to the right part of the pipeline for reprocessing—whether it's re-generating a scene, adjusting pacing, or applying a new style.

Behind the scenes, the **Model Registry** keeps track of all AI models used in the system—frame generators, motion synthesizers, style models, etc. It handles model versioning, manages A/B testing for performance improvements, and ensures that the most effective models are deployed based on usage and quality metrics.

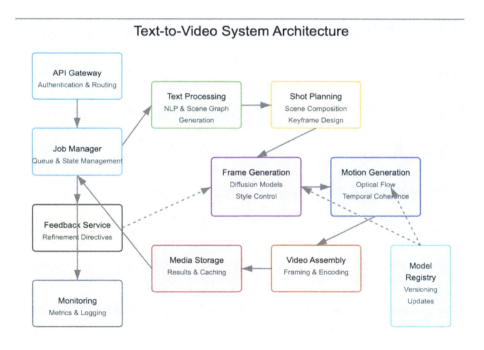

Implementation Plan & Practical Steps

Designing and building a text-to-video generation system is a complex, multi-stage process that spans natural language processing, computer vision, and video rendering. Below is a step-by-step roadmap that developers can follow to go from concept to deployment.

1. Define Scope and Requirements

Start by clearly outlining your product goals. Will the system support realistic video generation, or stylized animations? What's the maximum video length, resolution, or supported input formats? Defining this early helps constrain the technical complexity and hardware needs. Collect requirements across:

- **User input types** (plain text, structured scripts, storyboards)

- **Target output** (MP4, WebM, GIF; 720p–4K)

- **System capacity** (e.g., concurrent users, processing time)

- **Feedback and refinement capabilities**

2. Choose Foundation Models and Tools

Select your AI backbone models and supporting frameworks:

- **Text Processing**: Use NLP models like BERT, T5, or GPT for extracting semantic structures.

- **Scene Graph Generation**: Tools like SpaCy, SceneGraphParser, or custom rule-based parsers.

- **Frame Generation**: Leverage diffusion models like **Stable Video Diffusion**, **SVD-XT**, or **Pika**, depending on quality and licensing.

- **Motion Generation**: Use models like **RAFT** for optical flow, or animation models like MoCoGAN.

- **Audio Synthesis (optional)**: Integrate with TTS (e.g., Tacotron, Bark) and sound generation models.

Frameworks: PyTorch or TensorFlow for modeling; Hugging Face for transformer models; FFmpeg for encoding and video composition.

3. Build the Text Processing Pipeline

Implement a service that:

- Parses input text

- Extracts key objects, actions, emotions, and timelines

- Generates a scene graph or sequence plan

Example:

Prompt: "A boy runs through a forest as the sun sets."
→ Scene Graph: {character: boy, action: runs, setting: forest, time: sunset}
→ Timeline: Frame 1–30: running; Frame 31–60: camera pans up to sunset.

4. Implement Shot Planning Engine

Based on the parsed structure:

- Define camera positions and scene transitions

- Create keyframes that anchor major changes (e.g., boy enters frame, camera pans, background fades)

- Store shot plan in a structured format (e.g., JSON)

5. Develop Frame Generation Service

Use a generative model like **Stable Video Diffusion** to create high-quality still frames. Apply:

- **Style conditioning** (cartoon, cinematic, watercolor, etc.)

- **Scene elements** (background, character details, lighting)

You may first generate base images using a text-to-image model (like SDXL), then interpolate between them with a video model.

6. Integrate Motion Generation

Bridge frames using motion synthesis models:

- Apply **optical flow** to predict in-between frames

- Train or fine-tune models to maintain consistency in motion, lighting, and detail

Temporal coherence is critical—ensure that characters don't "flicker" or deform across frames.

7. Assemble Final Video

Use FFmpeg or similar tools to:

- Combine frames at target framerate (e.g., 30fps)

- Add motion blur or camera effects

- Insert transitions, audio, subtitles if needed

- Encode into target format and resolution

Store metadata (e.g., prompt, model version, seed) for reproducibility.

8. Set Up Storage & Delivery

Use cloud object storage (e.g., AWS S3, GCP Cloud Storage) for:

- Intermediate assets (frames, scene plans, etc.)

- Final videos Integrate a CDN for fast video delivery, and implement caching for repeated jobs or similar prompts.

9. Add Feedback Loop

Create UI or API hooks to:

- Accept user feedback (e.g., "change background," "add camera zoom")

- Route edits to the appropriate stage (text re-parsing, keyframe replan, partial regeneration)

- Allow users to lock certain scenes while regenerating others

This makes the system more interactive and iterative.

10. Test, Monitor, and Optimize

Implement end-to-end testing with various input types. Then monitor:

- Generation success rate

- Latency and GPU usage

- Frame coherence and visual quality

Use logging and alerting tools (e.g., Prometheus, Grafana) to catch issues early. Continuously profile performance to optimize runtime and GPU efficiency.

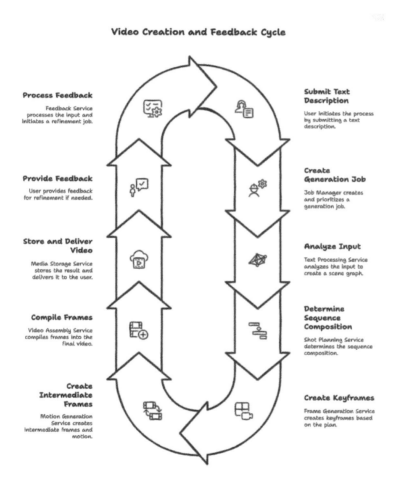

Video Creation and Feedback Cycle

Process Feedback
Feedback Service processes the input and initiates a refinement job.

Submit Text Description
User initiates the process by submitting a text description.

Provide Feedback
User provides feedback for refinement if needed.

Create Generation Job
Job Manager creates and prioritizes a generation job.

Store and Deliver Video
Media Storage Service stores the result and delivers it to the user.

Analyze Input
Text Processing Service analyzes the input to create a scene graph.

Compile Frames
Video Assembly Service compiles frames into the final video.

Determine Sequence Composition
Shot Planning Service determines the sequence composition.

Create Intermediate Frames
Motion Generation Service creates intermediate frames and motion.

Create Keyframes
Frame Generation Service creates keyframes based on the plan.

Phase 1: Text Processing Implementation

```python
# Text processing service core implementation

class TextProcessingService:

    def __init__(self, llm_client, graph_generator):

        self.llm_client = llm_client

        self.graph_generator = graph_generator


    def process_text(self, text_prompt, style_params=None):
        """

        Process text prompt into structured scene representation


        Args:

            text_prompt (str): Raw text description

            style_params (dict): Optional style parameters


        Returns:

            dict: Scene graph representation
        """

        # Step 1: Extract narrative elements using LLM

        narrative_elements = self._extract_narrative_elements(text_prompt)


        # Step 2: Identify temporal sequence and scene transitions

        temporal_sequence = self._extract_temporal_sequence(narrative_elements)
```

```python
    # Step 3: Generate formal scene graph representation
    scene_graph = self.graph_generator.create_graph(
        narrative_elements,
        temporal_sequence,
        style_params
    )

    return scene_graph


def _extract_narrative_elements(self, text_prompt):
    """Extract characters, objects, settings, and actions from text"""
    prompt_template = """
    Extract the following elements from the text:
    1. Main characters/entities and their attributes
    2. Settings/environments and their properties
    3. Actions and events in sequence
    4. Emotional tones and atmosphere
    5. Visual style indicators


    Text: {text}
    """

    response = self.llm_client.generate(
```

```python
            prompt_template.format(text=text_prompt),

            temperature=0.2,

            max_tokens=1000

        )


        return self._parse_llm_response(response)


    def _extract_temporal_sequence(self, narrative_elements):
        """Determine temporal sequence and pacing from narrative elements"""
        # Identify scene transitions and timing
        scenes = []
        current_scene = {"elements": [], "duration": 0}


        for element in narrative_elements["actions"]:
            # Check if this action indicates a scene change
            if self._is_scene_transition(element, current_scene):
                scenes.append(current_scene)
                current_scene = {"elements": [element], "duration": 0}
            else:
                current_scene["elements"].append(element)


            # Calculate approximate duration for this action
            action_duration = self._estimate_action_duration(element)
```

```python
        current_scene["duration"] += action_duration

    # Add the last scene
    if current_scene["elements"]:
        scenes.append(current_scene)

    return {
        "scenes": scenes,
        "total_duration": sum(scene["duration"] for scene in scenes),
        "transitions": self._identify_transition_types(scenes)
    }


def _is_scene_transition(self, action, current_scene):
    """Determine if an action indicates a scene transition"""
    # Implementation depends on action ontology
    # For example, actions like "cut to", "fade to", "meanwhile" indicate transitions
    transition_indicators = ["moves to", "arrives at", "later", "meanwhile"]

    for indicator in transition_indicators:
        if indicator in action["description"].lower():
            return True

    # Location change indicates scene transition
```

```python
        if current_scene["elements"] and "location" in action:

            if "location" in current_scene["elements"][0]:

                if action["location"] != current_scene["elements"][0]["location"]:

                    return True


        return False


    def _estimate_action_duration(self, action):

        """Estimate duration for an action in seconds"""

        # Simple heuristic based on action type and description length

        base_duration = 2.0  # Base duration in seconds


        # Adjust based on action type

        if "type" in action:

            if action["type"] == "dialogue":

                # Dialogue typically takes longer

                base_duration = len(action["description"].split()) * 0.3

            elif action["type"] == "movement":

                base_duration = 3.0

            elif action["type"] == "emotion":

                base_duration = 2.5


        return max(1.0, base_duration)  # Minimum 1 second per action
```

```python
def _identify_transition_types(self, scenes):
    """Identify appropriate transition types between scenes"""
    transitions = []

    for i in range(len(scenes) - 1):
        current = scenes[i]
        next_scene = scenes[i + 1]

        # Default transition
        transition = {"type": "cut", "duration": 0}

        # Check for time passage
        if self._has_time_passage(current, next_scene):
            transition = {"type": "fade", "duration": 1.0}

        # Check for location change
        if self._has_location_change(current, next_scene):
            if self._is_dramatic_change(current, next_scene):
                transition = {"type": "dissolve", "duration": 1.5}
            else:
                transition = {"type": "crossfade", "duration": 1.0}
```

```python
            transitions.append(transition)

        return transitions

    def _parse_llm_response(self, response):
        """Parse the LLM response into structured data"""
        # Implementation depends on LLM response format
        # This is a simplified version
        sections = response.split("\n\n")
        parsed = {
            "characters": [],
            "settings": [],
            "actions": [],
            "tones": [],
            "styles": []
        }

        current_section = None
        for line in response.split("\n"):
            line = line.strip()
            if not line:
                continue
```

```python
        if line.startswith("1. Main characters"):

            current_section = "characters"

        elif line.startswith("2. Settings"):

            current_section = "settings"

        elif line.startswith("3. Actions"):

            current_section = "actions"

        elif line.startswith("4. Emotional"):

            current_section = "tones"

        elif line.startswith("5. Visual"):

            current_section = "styles"

        elif current_section and line.startswith("- "):

            parsed[current_section].append(line[2:])


    # Further processing to structure the data

    parsed["actions"] = [{"description": action, "type":
self._infer_action_type(action)}

                for action in parsed["actions"]]


    return parsed


def _infer_action_type(self, action):

    """Infer the type of action from its description"""

    action_lower = action.lower()

    if "says" in action_lower or "speaks" in action_lower or "tells" in action_lower:
```

```python
            return "dialogue"

        elif "moves" in action_lower or "walks" in action_lower or "runs" in
action_lower:

            return "movement"

        elif "feels" in action_lower or "emotional" in action_lower:

            return "emotion"

        else:

            return "action"


    def _has_time_passage(self, scene1, scene2):

        """Check if there's a time passage between scenes"""

        time_indicators = ["later", "after", "before", "meanwhile", "during"]


        for element in scene2["elements"]:

            desc = element.get("description", "").lower()

            for indicator in time_indicators:

                if indicator in desc:

                    return True

        return False


    def _has_location_change(self, scene1, scene2):

        """Check if there's a location change between scenes"""

        if scene1["elements"] and scene2["elements"]:

            loc1 = scene1["elements"][0].get("location")
```

```python
        loc2 = scene2["elements"][0].get("location")

        if loc1 and loc2 and loc1 != loc2:

            return True

    return False


    def _is_dramatic_change(self, scene1, scene2):

        """Check if the change between scenes is dramatic"""

        # Dramatic changes might be day/night shifts, indoor/outdoor, etc.

        # Implementation would depend on specific scene attributes

        return False  # Simplified implementation
```

Phase 2: Shot Planning Implementation

python

```python
class ShotPlanningService:

    def __init__(self, style_engine, camera_planner):

        self.style_engine = style_engine

        self.camera_planner = camera_planner


    def create_shot_plan(self, scene_graph):
        """

        Create a detailed shot plan from scene graph


        Args:

            scene_graph (dict): Structured scene representation
```

Returns:

dict: Shot plan with keyframes and transitions

```python
"""

# Step 1: Identify key moments for keyframes
key_moments = self._identify_key_moments(scene_graph)


# Step 2: Determine appropriate camera shots for each moment
camera_plan = self.camera_planner.design_shots(key_moments, scene_graph)


# Step 3: Create composition guidelines for each shot
compositions = self._create_compositions(camera_plan, scene_graph)


# Step 4: Apply visual style to shot specifications
styled_shots = self.style_engine.apply_style(
    compositions,
    scene_graph.get("style_parameters", {})
)


# Step 5: Plan transitions between shots
transitions = self._plan_transitions(styled_shots, scene_graph)


return {
    "keyframes": styled_shots,
```

```python
        "transitions": transitions,

        "duration": scene_graph["temporal_sequence"]["total_duration"],

        "style_profile": self.style_engine.get_style_profile()

    }


def _identify_key_moments(self, scene_graph):
    """Identify key moments in the narrative for keyframe generation"""

    key_moments = []


    # Scene starts are always key moments
    for i, scene in enumerate(scene_graph["temporal_sequence"]["scenes"]):
        # Scene start
        key_moments.append({

            "scene_index": i,

            "moment_type": "scene_start",

            "elements": scene["elements"][:1],  # First element in scene

            "timestamp": self._calculate_timestamp(scene_graph, i, 0)

        })


    # Important actions within scene
    important_actions = self._filter_important_actions(scene["elements"])
    for j, action in enumerate(important_actions):
        position = scene["elements"].index(action)
```

```python
            key_moments.append({
                "scene_index": i,
                "moment_type": "key_action",
                "elements": [action],
                "timestamp": self._calculate_timestamp(scene_graph, i, position)
            })

        # Scene end
        if scene["elements"]:
            key_moments.append({
                "scene_index": i,
                "moment_type": "scene_end",
                "elements": scene["elements"][-1:],  # Last element in scene
                "timestamp": self._calculate_timestamp(
                    scene_graph, i, len(scene["elements"]) - 1
                )
            })

    return key_moments

def _filter_important_actions(self, elements):
    """Filter out the most important actions from scene elements"""
    important_actions = []
```

```python
for element in elements:

    # Check if this is an important action

    if element.get("type") == "action":

        importance = self._calculate_action_importance(element)

        if importance > 0.7:  # Threshold for importance

            important_actions.append(element)


    # Dialogue is usually important

    elif element.get("type") == "dialogue":

        important_actions.append(element)


# Limit the number of important actions to avoid too many keyframes

if len(important_actions) > 3:

    # Sort by importance and take top 3

    important_actions = sorted(

        important_actions,

        key=self._calculate_action_importance,

        reverse=True

    )[:3]


return important_actions
```

```python
def _calculate_action_importance(self, action):
    """Calculate the narrative importance of an action"""
    # Simple heuristic based on action type and description
    importance = 0.5  # Default importance

    # Action with emotional impact is important
    emotional_indicators = ["suddenly", "dramatically", "surprisingly"]
    for indicator in emotional_indicators:
        if indicator in action.get("description", "").lower():
            importance += 0.2

    # Actions involving main characters are important
    if action.get("subject_type") == "main_character":
        importance += 0.2

    return min(1.0, importance)  # Cap at 1.0

def _calculate_timestamp(self, scene_graph, scene_index, element_position):
    """Calculate timestamp for an element in the scene graph"""
    timestamp = 0.0

    # Add durations of all previous scenes
    for i in range(scene_index):
```

```python
        timestamp += scene_graph["temporal_sequence"]["scenes"][i]["duration"]


    # Add durations of elements in current scene up to position

    scene = scene_graph["temporal_sequence"]["scenes"][scene_index]

    for i in range(element_position):

        element_duration = self._estimate_element_duration(scene["elements"][i])

        timestamp += element_duration


    return timestamp


def _estimate_element_duration(self, element):

    """Estimate duration for a scene element"""

    # Use predefined duration if available

    if "duration" in element:

        return element["duration"]


    # Fallback to type-based estimation

    if element.get("type") == "dialogue":

        # Estimate based on dialogue length

        text = element.get("description", "")

        return max(1.0, len(text.split()) * 0.3)


    return 2.0  # Default duration
```

```python
def _create_compositions(self, camera_plan, scene_graph):
    """Create detailed composition guidelines for each shot"""
    compositions = []

    for shot in camera_plan:
        # Get scene elements relevant to this shot
        elements = shot["elements"]

        # Create basic composition
        composition = {
            "shot_type": shot["shot_type"], # e.g., "wide", "medium", "close-up"
            "camera_position": shot["camera_position"],
            "camera_movement": shot.get("camera_movement", "static"),
            "focus_point": self._determine_focus_point(elements),
            "framing": self._determine_framing(shot["shot_type"], elements),
            "depth": self._determine_depth(elements),
            "timestamp": shot["timestamp"],
            "duration": shot.get("duration", 3.0),
            "lighting": self._determine_lighting(shot, scene_graph),
        }

        # Add subject positioning
        if elements:
```

```python
        subjects = self._extract_subjects(elements)

        composition["subjects"] = subjects

        composition["subject_positions"] = self._position_subjects(

            subjects,

            composition["shot_type"]

        )


        # Add environment details

        composition["environment"] = self._extract_environment(elements,
scene_graph)


        compositions.append(composition)


    return compositions


def _determine_focus_point(self, elements):
    """Determine the focal point of the shot"""
    # Default to center focus
    focus = {"x": 0.5, "y": 0.5, "z": 0.0}


    if not elements:
        return focus


    # If there's a primary subject, focus on it
```

```python
        primary = self._find_primary_subject(elements)

        if primary:

            # Adjust focus based on subject type

            if primary.get("type") == "character":

                # Focus on face for characters

                focus["y"] = 0.4  # Slightly above center


        return focus


    def _find_primary_subject(self, elements):
        """Find the primary subject in the elements"""
        # First look for subjects marked as primary

        for element in elements:

            if element.get("is_primary", False):

                return element


        # Otherwise use first element with a subject

        for element in elements:

            if "subject" in element:

                return element.get("subject")

            elif element.get("type") in ["character", "object"]:

                return element
```

```python
        return None

    def _determine_framing(self, shot_type, elements):
        """Determine appropriate framing based on shot type and elements"""
        framing = {
            "rule_of_thirds": True,
            "headroom": 0.1,  # 10% headroom
            "lookroom": 0.15,  # 15% lookroom
        }

        # Adjust based on shot type
        if shot_type == "close-up":
            framing["headroom"] = 0.05 # Less headroom for close-ups
        elif shot_type == "wide":
            framing["headroom"] = 0.2 # More headroom for wide shots

        # Check for special framing needs
        for element in elements:
            if element.get("action_type") == "looking":
                # Ensure lookroom in the direction they're looking
                direction = element.get("direction", "right")
                framing["look_direction"] = direction
```

```python
        return framing

    def _determine_depth(self, elements):
        """Determine depth information for the shot"""
        depth = {
            "foreground": [],
            "midground": [],
            "background": []
        }

        # Place elements in appropriate depth planes
        for element in elements:
            position = element.get("depth_position", "midground")
            if position in depth:
                depth[position].append(element)

        return depth

    def _determine_lighting(self, shot, scene_graph):
        """Determine appropriate lighting for the shot"""
        # Default lighting
        lighting = {
            "key_light": {"intensity": 0.8, "position": {"x": 0.7, "y": 0.7, "z": 0.5}},
```

```python
        "fill_light": {"intensity": 0.4, "position": {"x": -0.7, "y": 0.5, "z": 0.3}},

        "back_light": {"intensity": 0.6, "position": {"x": 0.0, "y": 0.8, "z": -0.5}}
    }


    # Adjust based on scene time and mood
    scene_index = shot.get("scene_index", 0)
    if scene_index < len(scene_graph["temporal_sequence"]["scenes"]):
        scene = scene_graph["temporal_sequence"]["scenes"][scene_index]


        # Check for time of day
        time_of_day = self._extract_time_of_day(scene)
        if time_of_day == "night":
            lighting["key_light"]["intensity"] = 0.5

            lighting["fill_light"]["intensity"] = 0.2

        elif time_of_day == "evening":
            lighting["key_light"]["intensity"] = 0.7

            lighting["key_light"]["color"] = "#FFB46B"  # Warm sunset color


        # Check for mood
        mood = self._extract_mood(scene)
        if mood == "dramatic":
            # High contrast for dramatic scenes
            lighting["key_light"]["intensity"] = 0.9
```

```python
            lighting["fill_light"]["intensity"] = 0.2

        elif mood == "mysterious":

            # Uneven lighting for mystery

            lighting["key_light"]["position"]["x"] = 0.9  # More from the side

            lighting["fill_light"]["intensity"] = 0.1  # Less fill


        return lighting


    def _extract_time_of_day(self, scene):

        """Extract time of day from scene elements"""

        # Look for time indicators in scene description

        time_indicators = {

            "night": ["night", "evening", "dark", "moonlight"],

            "morning": ["morning", "dawn", "sunrise"],

            "evening": ["sunset", "dusk", "evening"],

            "day": ["day", "afternoon", "daylight", "sun"]

        }


        for element in scene["elements"]:

            description = element.get("description", "").lower()


            for time, indicators in time_indicators.items():

                for indicator in indicators:
```

```python
        if indicator in description:

            return time


    return "day"  # Default


def _extract_mood(self, scene):
    """Extract mood from scene elements"""
    # Look for mood indicators in scene
    mood_indicators = {

        "dramatic": ["dramatic", "intense", "shocking", "confrontation"],

        "mysterious": ["mysterious", "eerie", "suspicious", "strange"],

        "peaceful": ["peaceful", "calm", "serene", "tranquil"],

        "tense": ["tense", "nervous", "anxious", "scared"]

    }


    mood_counts = {mood: 0 for mood in mood_indicators}


    for element in scene["elements"]:
        description = element.get("description", "").lower()


        for mood, indicators in mood_indicators.items():

            for indicator in indicators:

                if indicator in description:
```

```python
            mood_counts[mood] += 1


        # Return most common mood

        if any(mood_counts.values()):

            return max(mood_counts, key=mood_counts.get)


        return "neutral"  # Default


    def _extract_subjects(self, elements):
        """Extract all subjects from elements"""
        subjects = []


        for element in elements:
            if element.get("type") in ["character", "object"]:
                subjects.append(element)
            elif "subject" in element:
                subjects.append(element["subject"])


        return subjects


    def _position_subjects(self, subjects, shot_type):
        """Determine appropriate positioning for subjects in frame"""
        positions = []
```

```python
# Position based on number of subjects and shot type

if len(subjects) == 1:

    # Single subject positioning

    subject = subjects[0]

    position = {

        "subject_id": subject.get("id", "unknown"),

        "screen_position": {"x": 0.5, "y": 0.5}  # Center by default

    }


    # Adjust based on shot type

    if shot_type == "close-up":

        position["screen_position"]["y"] = 0.4  # Slightly higher for face


    positions.append(position)


elif len(subjects) == 2:
    # Two subjects - position for dialogue/interaction
    positions.append({

        "subject_id": subjects[0].get("id", "unknown"),

        "screen_position": {"x": 0.35, "y": 0.5}

    })

    positions.append({
```

```python
                "subject_id": subjects[1].get("id", "unknown"),

                "screen_position": {"x": 0.65, "y": 0.5}

            })


        else:

            # Multiple subjects - distribute evenly

            for i, subject in enumerate(subjects):

                x_pos = 0.2 + (0.6 * i / (len(subjects) - 1)) if len(subjects) > 1 else 0.5

                positions.append({

                    "subject_id": subject.get("id", "unknown"),

                    "screen_position": {"x": x_pos, "y": 0.5}

                })


    return positions


def _extract_environment(self, elements, scene_graph):

    """Extract environment details from elements and scene graph"""

    environment = {

        "setting": "unknown",

        "props": [],

        "atmosphere": "neutral"

    }
```

```python
    # Look for setting in elements
    for element in elements:
        if element.get("type") == "setting":
            environment["setting"] = element.get("description", "unknown")
            break

    # Look for props in elements
    for element in elements:
        if element.get("type") == "object" and "subject_id" not in element:
            environment["props"].append(element)

    # Extract atmosphere from scene
    for scene in scene_graph["temporal_sequence"]["scenes"]:
        for element in scene["elements"]:
            if element.get("type") == "atmosphere":
                environment["atmosphere"] = element.get("description", "neutral")


    return environment


def _plan_transitions(self, styled_shots, scene_graph):
    """Plan transitions between shots"""
    transitions = []
```

```python
for i in range(len(styled_shots) - 1):

    current = styled_shots[i]

    next_shot = styled_shots[i + 1]


    transition = {

        "from_shot": i,

        "to_shot": i + 1,

        "type": "cut",  # Default transition

        "duration": 0.0

    }


    # Check if shots are from different scenes

    if self._are_different_scenes(current, next_shot):

        scene_transitions = scene_graph["temporal_sequence"]["transitions"]


        # Find corresponding scene transition

        scene_index = current.get("scene_index", 0)

        if scene_index < len(scene_transitions):

            scene_transition = scene_transitions[scene_index]

            transition["type"] = scene_transition["type"]

            transition["duration"] = scene_transition["duration"]

    else:

        # Within-scene transitions
```

```python
            if self._is_perspective_change(current, next_shot):

                transition["type"] = "cut"

            elif self._is_subject_change(current, next_shot):

                transition["type"] = "cut"

            elif self._is_time_jump(current, next_shot):

                transition["type"] = "dissolve"

                transition["duration"] = 1.0


            transitions.append(transition)


        return transitions


    def _are_different_scenes(self, shot1, shot2):

        """Check if two shots belong to different scenes"""

        return shot1.get("scene_index") != shot2.get("scene_index")


    def _is_perspective_change(self, shot1, shot2):

        """Check if perspective changes significantly between shots"""

        # Compare shot types (wide to close-up is a perspective change)

        shot_types = ["extreme wide", "wide", "medium", "close-up", "extreme close-up"]


        if shot1.get("shot_type") in shot_types and shot2.get("shot_type") in shot_types:
```

```python
        type1_index = shot_types.index(shot1["shot_type"])

        type2_index = shot_types.index(shot2["shot_type"])


        # If difference is more than one step, it's a perspective change

        return abs(type1_index - type2_index) > 1



    return False



def _is_subject_change(self, shot1, shot2):

    """Check if main subject changes between shots"""

    subjects1 = shot1.get("subjects", [])

    subjects2 = shot2.get("subjects", [])


    if not subjects1 or not subjects2:

        return False


    # Get primary subjects

    primary1 = subjects1[0] if subjects1 else None

    primary2 = subjects2[0] if subjects2 else None


    if primary1 and primary2:

        return primary1.get("id") != primary2.get("id")
```

```python
        return False


    def _is_time_jump(self, shot1, shot2):

        """Check if there's a time jump between shots"""

        time1 = shot1.get("timestamp", 0)

        time2 = shot2.get("timestamp", 0)


        # if time difference is significant (e.g., more than 5 seconds)

        return abs(time2 - time1) > 5.0
```

Phase 3: Frame Generation Implementation

python

```python
class FrameGenerationService:

    def __init__(self, diffusion_model, style_adapter):

        self.diffusion_model = diffusion_model

        self.style_adapter = style_adapter


    def generate_keyframes(self, shot_plan):

        """

        Generate keyframes based on shot plan


        Args:

            shot_plan (dict): Detailed shot plan with compositions


        Returns:
```

```python
        list: Generated keyframes with metadata
    """

    keyframes = []

    for shot in shot_plan["keyframes"]:
        # Step 1: Create prompt for this specific keyframe
        prompt = self._create_frame_prompt(shot)

        # Step 2: Apply style conditioning
        style_conditioning = self.style_adapter.create_conditioning(
            shot,
            shot_plan["style_profile"]
        )

        # Step 3: Generate the base frame
        frame = self.diffusion_model.generate_image(
            prompt=prompt,
            style_conditioning=style_conditioning,
            guidance_scale=7.5,
            num_inference_steps=50
        )

        # Step 4: Apply post-processing specific to this frame
```

```python
        processed_frame = self._post_process_frame(frame, shot)

        # Save frame with metadata
        keyframes.append({
            "frame": processed_frame,
            "timestamp": shot["timestamp"],
            "duration": shot.get("duration", 3.0),
            "shot_data": shot,
            "prompt": prompt
        })

    return keyframes

def _create_frame_prompt(self, shot):
    """Create detailed text prompt for frame generation"""
    prompt_parts = []

    # Environment/setting description
    if "environment" in shot and shot["environment"]:
        setting = shot["environment"].get("setting", "")
        if setting:
            prompt_parts.append(f"A {setting}")
```

```python
    # Atmosphere
    atmosphere = shot["environment"].get("atmosphere", "")
    if atmosphere:
        prompt_parts.append(f"with {atmosphere} atmosphere")


# Add subjects/characters
if "subjects" in shot and shot["subjects"]:
    subject_descriptions = []
    for subject in shot["subjects"]:
        desc = subject.get("description", "")
        if desc:
            # Add position context if available
            for position in shot.get("subject_positions", []):
                if position.get("subject_id") == subject.get("id"):
                    pos_x = position["screen_position"]["x"]
                    if pos_x < 0.4:
                        desc += " on the left side"
                    elif pos_x > 0.6:
                        desc += " on the right side"

            subject_descriptions.append(desc)


    if subject_descriptions:
```

```python
        prompt_parts.append("with " + ", ".join(subject_descriptions))


# Add action/moment context
if "elements" in shot:
    actions = [e.get("description", "") for e in shot["elements"]
               if e.get("type") == "action" and "description" in e]
    if actions:
        prompt_parts.append(actions[0])  # Use the primary action


# Add shot type
shot_type = shot.get("shot_type", "")
if shot_type:
    prompt_parts.append(f"{shot_type} shot")


# Add camera movement
camera_movement = shot.get("camera_movement", "")
if camera_movement and camera_movement != "static":
    prompt_parts.append(f"with {camera_movement} camera movement")


# Add lighting
if "lighting" in shot:
    key_intensity = shot["lighting"].get("key_light", {}).get("intensity", 0)
    if key_intensity < 0.4:
```

```python
        prompt_parts.append("with dim lighting")
    elif key_intensity > 0.8:
        prompt_parts.append("with bright lighting")


    key_color = shot["lighting"].get("key_light", {}).get("color", "")
    if key_color:
        # Convert hex color to description
        color_desc = self._color_to_description(key_color)
        if color_desc:
            prompt_parts.append(f"with {color_desc} lighting")


    # Combine all parts
    prompt = ", ".join(prompt_parts)


    # Add style qualifiers
    style_qualifiers = shot.get("style_qualifiers", [])
    if style_qualifiers:
        prompt += ", " + ", ".join(style_qualifiers)


    return prompt


def _color_to_description(self, hex_color):
    """Convert hex color to text description"""
```

```python
        # Simple mapping of common colors
        color_map = {
            "#FFB46B": "warm orange",
            "#6B90FF": "ccol blue",
            "#FF6B6B": "warm red",
            "#6BFF9E": "soft green"
        }

        return color_map.get(hex_color, "")


    def _post_process_frame(self, frame, shot):
        """Apply post-processing to the generated frame"""
        # Apply framing adjustments based on shot data
        framing = shot.get("framing", {})
        if framing.get("rule_of_thirds", False):
            frame = self._apply_rule_of_thirds(frame)


        # Apply depth of field based on shot type
        if shot.get("shot_type") in ["close-up", "extreme close-up"]:
            frame = self._apply_depth_of_field(
                frame,
                focus_point=shot.get("focus_point", {"x": 0.5, "y": 0.5})
            )
```

```python
        # Apply color grading based on mood and atmosphere
        atmosphere = shot.get("environment", {}).get("atmosphere", "neutral")
        frame = self._apply_color_grading(frame, atmosphere)

        return frame


    def _apply_rule_of_thirds(self, frame):
        """Apply rule of thirds adjustment to frame"""
        # Implementation would depend on image processing library
        # This is a placeholder for the concept
        return frame


    def _apply_depth_of_field(self, frame, focus_point):
        """Apply depth of field effect"""
        # Implementation would depend on image processing library
        # This is a placeholder for the concept
        return frame


    def _apply_color_grading(self, frame, atmosphere):
        """Apply color grading based on atmosphere"""
        # Implementation would depend on image processing library
        grading_params = {
```

```python
    "dramatic": {"contrast": 1.2, "saturation": 0.9, "temperature": -5},

    "mysterious": {"contrast": 1.1, "saturation": 0.7, "temperature": -15},

    "peaceful": {"contrast": 0.9, "saturation": 1.1, "temperature": 5},

    "tense": {"contrast": 1.3, "saturation": 0.8, "temperature": -10},

    "neutral": {"contrast": 1.0, "saturation": 1.0, "temperature": 0}

}


params = grading_params.get(atmosphere, grading_params["neutral"])


# Apply parameters (implementation would use actual image processing)

# This is a placeholder for the concept

return frame
```

Phase 4: Motion Generation Implementation

python

```python
class MotionGenerationService:

    def __init__(self, motion_model, interpolation_model):

        self.motion_model = motion_model

        self.interpolation_model = interpolation_model


    def generate_video_sequence(self, keyframes, shot_plan):

        """

        Generate complete video sequence from keyframes


        Args:
```

keyframes (list): Generated keyframes with metadata

shot_plan (dict): The original shot plan

Returns:

dict: Video frames with timing information

```python
    """

    video_sequence = []


    # Step 1: Sort keyframes by timestamp

    sorted_keyframes = sorted(keyframes, key=lambda k: k["timestamp"])


    # Step 2: Process each pair of consecutive keyframes

    for i in range(len(sorted_keyframes) - 1):

        current_keyframe = sorted_keyframes[i]

        next_keyframe = sorted_keyframes[i + 1]


        # Find transition between these shots

        transition = self._find_transition(

            current_keyframe["shot_data"],

            next_keyframe["shot_data"],

            shot_plan["transitions"]

        )
```

```python
# Generate frames for current keyframe duration
duration_frames = self._generate_duration_frames(
    current_keyframe,
    fps=24  # Standard film frame rate
)
video_sequence.extend(duration_frames)


# Generate transition frames
if transition:
    transition_frames = self._generate_transition_frames(
        current_keyframe,
        next_keyframe,
        transition,
        fps=24
    )
    video_sequence.extend(transition_frames)


# Add final keyframe duration
if sorted_keyframes:
    final_frames = self._generate_duration_frames(
        sorted_keyframes[-1],
        fps=24
    )
```

```python
        video_sequence.extend(final_frames)


    return {
        "frames": video_sequence,

        "fps": 24,

        "total_frames": len(video_sequence),

        "total_duration": video_sequence[-1]["timestamp"] if video_sequence else 0

    }



def _find_transition(self, shot1, shot2, transitions):
    """Find transition between two shots"""

    shot1_index = shot1.get("index")

    shot2_index = shot2.get("index")


    for transition in transitions:

        if transition["from_shot"] == shot1_index and transition["to_shot"] ==
shot2_index:

            return transition


    # Default transition (cut)

    return {"type": "cut", "duration": 0.0}



def _generate_duration_frames(self, keyframe, fps):

    """Generate frames for a keyframe's duration"""
```

```python
frames = []

shot_data = keyframe["shot_data"]


# Calculate number of frames for this duration

duration = shot_data.get("duration", 3.0)

frame_count = int(duration * fps)


# Generate each frame with appropriate motion

base_frame = keyframe["frame"]


for i in range(frame_count):
    # Calculate progress through this shot (0.0 to 1.0)

    progress = i / frame_count if frame_count > 0 else 0

    timestamp = keyframe["timestamp"] + progress * duration


    # Apply any camera movement for this shot

    camera_movement = shot_data.get("camera_movement", "static")


    if camera_movement == "static":
        # No movement, use base frame

        frame = base_frame
    else:
        # Apply camera movement effect
```

```python
        frame = self._apply_camera_movement(
            base_frame,
            camera_movement,
            progress
        )


        # Apply any subject movement for this shot
        frame = self._apply_subject_movement(
            frame,
            shot_data.get("subjects", []),
            progress
        )


        frames.append({
            "frame": frame,
            "timestamp": timestamp,
            "index": i,
            "shot_index": shot_data.get("index")
        })


    return frames


def _apply_camera_movement(self, frame, movement_type, progress):
```

```python
        """Apply camera movement effect to frame"""
        if movement_type == "pan":
            # Pan from left to right (or right to left)
            offset_x = progress * 0.1  # 10% pan
            return self._shift_frame(frame, offset_x, 0)
        elif movement_type == "tilt":
            # Tilt up or down
            offset_y = progress * 0.1  # 10% tilt
            return self._shift_frame(frame, 0, offset_y)
        elif movement_type == "zoom_in":
            # Zoom in effect
            zoom_factor = 1.0 + (progress * 0.2)  # Up to 20% zoom
            return self._zoom_frame(frame, zoom_factor)
        elif movement_type == "zoom_out":
            # Zoom out effect
            zoom_factor = 1.0 - (progress * 0.15)  # Up to 15% zoom out
            return self._zoom_frame(frame, zoom_factor)

        return frame

    def _shift_frame(self, frame, offset_x, offset_y):
        """Shift frame by offset (simulating camera movement)"""
        # Implementation would depend on image processing library
```

```python
        # This is a placeholder for the concept

        return frame


    def _zoom_frame(self, frame, zoom_factor):
        """Apply zoom effect to frame"""
        # Implementation would depend on image processing library
        # This is a placeholder for the concept
        return frame


    def _apply_subject_movement(self, frame, subjects, progress):
        """Apply movement to subjects in frame"""
        # For each subject with movement data
        for subject in subjects:
            movement = subject.get("movement")
            if not movement:
                continue


            # Apply movement based on type
            if movement["type"] == "walk":
                direction = movement.get("direction", "right")
                speed = movement.get("speed", 1.0)


                # Calculate position change
```

```python
        offset_x = speed * progress * (1.0 if direction == "right" else -1.0)

        # Apply movement (implementation would use actual image processing)

        # This is a placeholder for the concept

        pass

    return frame


    def _generate_transition_frames(self, from_keyframe, to_keyframe, transition,
fps):

        """Generate transition frames between keyframes"""

        frames = []

        # Skip if this is a cut (no transition frames needed)

        if transition["type"] == "cut" or transition["duration"] <= 0:

            return frames

        # Calculate number of frames for this transition

        frame_count = int(transition["duration"] * fps)

        # Get source frames

        source_frame = from_keyframe["frame"]

        target_frame = to_keyframe["frame"]
```

```python
        # Generate transition frames
    for i in range(frame_count):
        # Calculate progress through transition (0.0 to 1.0)
        progress = i / frame_count if frame_count > 0 else 0


        # Calculate timestamp
        from_time = from_keyframe["timestamp"] +
from_keyframe["shot_data"].get("duration", 0)
        timestamp = from_time + progress * transition["duration"]


        # Generate frame based on transition type
        if transition["type"] == "dissolve" or transition["type"] == "crossfade":
            frame = self._blend_frames(source_frame, target_frame, progress)
        elif transition["type"] == "fade":
            if progress < 0.5:
                # Fade out
                fade_progress = progress * 2  # 0.0 -> 1.0 over first half
                frame = self._fade_frame(source_frame, 1.0 - fade_progress)
            else:
                # Fade in
                fade_progress = (progress - 0.5) * 2  # 0.0 -> 1.0 over second half
                frame = self._fade_frame(target_frame, fade_progress)
        else:
            # Default to crossfade
```

```python
        frame = self._blend_frames(source_frame, target_frame, progress)

    frames.append({
        "frame": frame,
        "timestamp": timestamp,
        "transition_type": transition["type"],
        "transition_progress": progress
    })

    return frames


def _blend_frames(self, frame1, frame2, blend_factor):
    """Blend two frames with the given factor"""
    # Implementation would depend on image processing library
    # This is a placeholder for the concept
    return frame1  # Simplified return


def _fade_frame(self, frame, opacity):
    """Fade frame to/from black"""
    # Implementation would depend on image processing library
    # This is a placeholder for the concept
    return frame  # Simplified return
```

Phase 5: Video Assembly Implementation

python

```python
class VideoAssemblyService:

    def __init__(self, encoder_config):

        self.encoder_config = encoder_config


    def assemble_video(self, video_sequence, output_config):
        """

        Assemble final video from sequence of frames


        Args:

            video_sequence (dict): Generated video sequence with frames

            output_config (dict): Configuration for final video


        Returns:

            dict: Output video information
        """
        # Step 1: Apply final color grading and post-processing

        processed_frames = self._process_frames(

            video_sequence["frames"],

            output_config.get("post_processing", {})

        )


        # Step 2: Generate any required audio elements
```

```python
audio_track = self._generate_audio(

    video_sequence,

    output_config.get("audio", {})

)


# Step 3: Encode video with specified parameters

video_path = self._encode_video(

    processed_frames,

    video_sequence["fps"],

    output_config.get("encoding", {})

)


# Step 4: Combine video and audio if needed

if audio_track:

    final_path = self._combine_audio_video(

        video_path,

        audio_track,

        output_config.get("encoding", {})

    )

else:

    final_path = video_path


return {
```

```
    "video_path": final_path,

    "duration": video_sequence["total_duration"],

    "frame_count": video_sequence["total_frames"],

    "fps": video_sequence["fps"],

    "resolution": output_config.get("encoding", {}).get("resolution", "1080p"),

    "format": output_config.get("encoding",
```

Text-to-Speech System Design: End-to-End Solution

Get a deep, hands-on understanding of how cutting-edge speech synthesis models are designed, trained, and evaluated.

Text-to-speech (TTS) models are neural networks that turn written text into natural-sounding speech. This technology powers more human-like and engaging interactions by enabling machines to "speak" in a way that feels lifelike and personal. From digital assistants to accessibility tools, TTS is transforming how we interact with technology.

Thanks to rapid progress in natural language processing and audio synthesis, today's TTS systems can produce incredibly expressive and realistic voices. Models like NVIDIA's Tacotron2 and xTTS are leading the charge—capable of controlling tone, emotion, and even accents to create highly personalized speech. This level of customization is a game-changer for use cases like content narration, real-time translation, and assistive communication. You'll find these systems at the core of everything from Siri to modern AI chatbots like ChatGPT.

In this guide, we'll walk through how to build a flexible, high-quality TTS system that takes in text and outputs clear, intelligible speech.

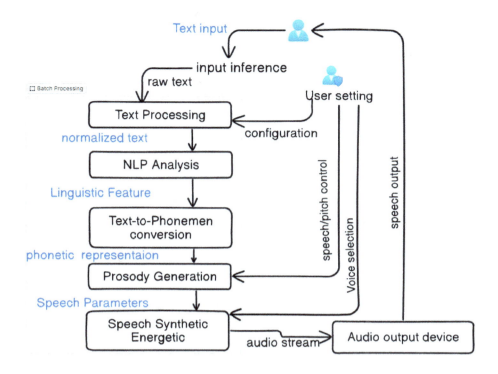

This diagram illustrates the typical flow in a text-to-speech (TTS) system:

1. **User Interaction**: The user enters text through an interface and can adjust settings.

2. **Text Processing Pipeline**:

   o Text preprocessing normalizes the input (handling abbreviations, numbers, etc.)

   o NLP analysis identifies linguistic features (sentence boundaries, part-of-speech)

   o Text-to-phoneme conversion translates text into pronunciation symbols

   o Prosody generation adds natural rhythm, stress, and intonation

3. **Speech Generation**:

   o The synthesis engine converts all this information into audio

   o Output is delivered through speakers or headphones

4. **User Controls**: Settings allow customization of voice, speed, pitch, and other parameters

1. Use Case

Text-to-Speech (TTS) technology converts written text into natural-sounding speech. Modern TTS systems are used across various applications:

- **Accessibility tools** for people with visual impairments or reading difficulties

- **Voice assistants** like Siri, Alexa, and Google Assistant

- **Navigation systems** providing spoken directions

- **Audiobook production** automating narration

- **Content consumption** allowing users to listen to articles or documents while multitasking

- **Video content** automated voiceovers for educational or entertainment content

For this research, we'll focus on designing a TTS system for a developer platform that allows integration of high-quality speech synthesis into applications via API.

2. Functional Requirements

The core functionalities that our TTS system should support include:

1. **Text Processing**

   o Accept plain text and SSML (Speech Synthesis Markup Language) inputs

   o Support for multiple languages and dialects

   o Handle abbreviations, numbers, dates, and special characters

   o Process formatting cues (commas, periods, question marks) for natural pauses

2. **Voice Synthesis**

   o Generate natural-sounding speech with appropriate prosody

   o Support multiple voices (gender varieties, age differences)

- o Control speech parameters (speed, pitch, volume)

- o Express emotions in voice (happiness, sadness, etc.)

3. **API Integration**

   - o RESTful API for synchronous requests

   - o Streaming API for real-time synthesis

   - o Batch processing for large volumes of text

   - o Client libraries for major programming languages

4. **Audio Output**

   - o Support for common audio formats (MP3, WAV, OGG)

   - o Adjustable audio quality settings

   - o Custom audio profiles for different devices

---

3. Non-Functional Requirements

The nonfunctional requirements ensure that the TTS system performs reliably, scales effectively, and maintains security:

1. **Performance**

   - o Low latency (<300ms) for short text conversion

   - o Efficient processing for long-form content

   - o Scalable to handle concurrent requests

2. **Quality**

   - o Natural-sounding speech with minimal robotic artifacts

   - o Proper pronunciation of domain-specific terminology

   - o Consistent voice characteristics across sessions

3. **Reliability**

   - o 99.9% uptime for the TTS service

   - o Graceful degradation under heavy load

　　　　　○　　　Appropriate error handling and fallback mechanisms

4.　Security

　　　　　○　　　Data encryption in transit and at rest

　　　　　○　　　Authentication and authorization for API access

　　　　　○　　　Protection against injection attacks in input text

5.　Compliance

　　　　　○　　　Adherence to accessibility standards

　　　　　○　　　Data handling in compliance with privacy regulations

---

4. System Architecture

A comprehensive TTS system consists of these major components:

High-Level Architecture

Text Input → Text Normalization → Linguistic Analysis → Acoustic Model → Vocoder → Audio Output

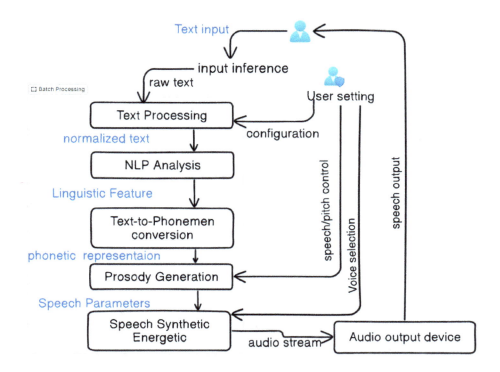

Detailed Component Breakdown

1. **Frontend Services**

   o   API Gateway for request handling

   o   Authentication and rate limiting

   o   Request validation and preprocessing

2. **Text Processing Pipeline**

   o   Text normalization (converting numbers, dates, etc.)

   o   Linguistic analysis (part-of-speech tagging)

   o   Grapheme-to-phoneme conversion

3. **Speech Synthesis Engine**

   o   Acoustic model (neural network for speech parameters)

   o   Prosody and intonation modeling

o   Voice selection and parameter application

4.   **Audio Backend**

o   Vocoder for waveform generation

o   Audio encoding and format conversion

o   Audio quality optimization

5.   **Infrastructure Components**

o   Load balancers for distributing requests

o   Caching for frequently requested phrases

o   Monitoring and logging systems

5. Model Selection

Modern TTS systems generally use one of these approaches:

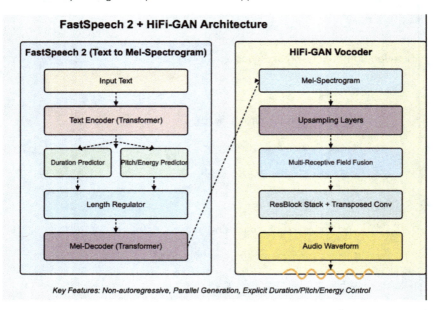

This diagram illustrates your selected TTS system architecture using FastSpeech 2 with a HiFi-GAN vocoder, following a structure similar to the Fish-Speech model diagram you provided.

The left side shows the FastSpeech 2 component, which handles the text-to-mel-spectrogram conversion through:

- Text encoding via transformer layers

- Parallel predictors for duration, pitch, and energy

- A length regulator that expands features based on predicted durations

- A mel-decoder that generates the spectrogram representation

The right side shows the HiFi-GAN vocoder, which converts mel-spectrograms to high-quality audio waveforms through:

- Upsampling layers to increase temporal resolution

- Multi-receptive field fusion for capturing patterns at different scales

- A stack of residual blocks and transposed convolutions

This combination offers several advantages for your use case:

- Fast, non-autoregressive generation (unlike autoregressive models like Tacotron 2)

- Explicit control over speech attributes (duration, pitch, energy)

- High-quality audio synthesis with the efficient HiFi-GAN architecture

- Good balance between quality, speed, and model size compared to concatenative synthesis

Concatenative Synthesis

- Uses recorded speech fragments stitched together

- Good quality but limited flexibility

- Large storage requirements for voice database

Parametric Synthesis

- Statistical models (HMMs) or neural networks generate speech parameters

- More flexible but can sound less natural

- Smaller footprint than concatenative methods

Neural TTS Models

- **Tacotron 2**: Sequence-to-sequence model with attention for spectrogram prediction

- **WaveNet/WaveRNN**: Neural vocoders for high-quality waveform generation

- **FastSpeech 2**: Non-autoregressive model for faster inference

- **VITS**: End-to-end model combining text-to-spectrogram and vocoder

For our use case, we'll select **FastSpeech 2** with **HiFi-GAN** vocoder:

- FastSpeech 2 provides fast, non-autoregressive generation

- Explicit duration modeling for controlling speech rate

- HiFi-GAN offers efficient, high-quality waveform generation

- Good balance between quality, speed, and flexibility

6. Implementation Example

Let's build a simple Python-based TTS system using the FastSpeech 2 model with HiFi-GAN vocoder through Hugging Face's Transformers library:

```python
import torch
from transformers import SpeechT5Processor, SpeechT5ForTextToSpeech, SpeechT5HifiGan
from datasets import load_dataset
import soundfile as sf
from flask import Flask, request, jsonify, send_file
import os
import uuid
import logging
from pathlib import Path
import time

# Configure logging
```

```python
logging.basicConfig(level=logging.INFO, format='%(asctime)s - %(name)s - %(levelname)s - 
%(message)s')
logger = logging.getLogger(__name__)

app = Flask(__name__)

# Create output directory
output_dir = Path("./audio_output")
output_dir.mkdir(exist_ok=True)

# Load models
class TTSEngine:
    def __init__(self):
        logger.info("Loading TTS models...")
        start_time = time.time()

        # Load processor, model and vocoder
        self.processor = SpeechT5Processor.from_pretrained("microsoft/speecht5_tts")
        self.model = SpeechT5ForTextToSpeech.from_pretrained("microsoft/speecht5_tts")
        self.vocoder = SpeechT5HifiGan.from_pretrained("microsoft/speecht5_hifigan")

        # Load speaker embeddings
        self.embeddings_dataset = load_dataset("Matthijs/cmu-arctic-xvectors", 
split="validation")

        # Speaker mapping
        self.speakers = {
            "male": 0,    # bdl speaker
            "female": 1,  # clb speaker
        }

        logger.info(f"Models loaded in {time.time() - start_time:.2f} seconds")

    def preprocess_text(self, text):
        """Normalize text and prepare for synthesis"""
        # Basic normalization - in production, this would be more complex
        text = text.replace('\n', ' ').strip()
        return text

    def synthesize(self, text, speaker="female", speed=1.0):
        """Generate speech from text"""
```

```python
        try:
            # Preprocess text
            text = self.preprocess_text(text)
            logger.info(f"Processing text: {text[:50]}{'...' if len(text) > 50 else ''}")

            # Get speaker embedding
            speaker_idx = self.speakers.get(speaker.lower(), 0)
            speaker_embeddings =
torch.tensor(self.embeddings_dataset[speaker_idx]["xvector"]).unsqueeze(0)

            # Prepare inputs
            inputs = self.processor(text=text, return_tensors="pt")

            # Generate speech with adjusted speed
            speech = self.model.generate_speech(
                inputs["input_ids"],
                speaker_embeddings,
                vocoder=self.vocoder
            )

            # Adjust speed (resample if needed)
            if speed != 1.0:
                # Simple speed adjustment by changing the sample rate during saving
                # More sophisticated approaches would use proper resampling
                pass

            return speech

        except Exception as e:
            logger.error(f"Speech synthesis error: {str(e)}")
            raise

# Initialize TTS engine
tts_engine = TTSEngine()

@app.route("/synthesize", methods=["POST"])
def synthesize_speech():
    """API endpoint for speech synthesis"""
    try:
        data = request.json
```

```python
    # Extract parameters
    text = data.get("text", "")
    speaker = data.get("speaker", "female")
    speed = float(data.get("speed", 1.0))
    audio_format = data.get("format", "wav")

    if not text:
        return jsonify({"error": "No text provided"}), 400

    # Generate speech
    speech = tts_engine.synthesize(text, speaker, speed)

    # Save to file with unique ID
    file_id = str(uuid.uuid4())
    file_path = output_dir / f"{file_id}.{audio_format}"

    # Save audio file
    sf.write(str(file_path), speech.numpy(), samplerate=16000)

    # Return file or download link
    return send_file(
        str(file_path),
        mimetype=f"audio/{audio_format}",
        as_attachment=True,
        download_name=f"speech_{file_id}.{audio_format}"
    )

    except Exception as e:
        logger.error(f"API error: {str(e)}")
        return jsonify({"error": str(e)}), 500

@app.route("/health", methods=["GET"])
def health_check():
    """Health check endpoint"""
    return jsonify({"status": "healthy"})

# Streaming API endpoint (simplified version)
@app.route("/stream", methods=["POST"])
def stream_speech():
    """Simplified streaming API - in production this would use proper streaming"""
    return jsonify({"error": "Streaming not implemented in this example"}), 501
```

```
if __name__ == "__main__":
    # For production, use a proper WSGI server like gunicorn
    app.run(host="0.0.0.0", port=5000, debug=False)
```

7. Deployment Architecture

A production-ready TTS system would use a more sophisticated deployment:

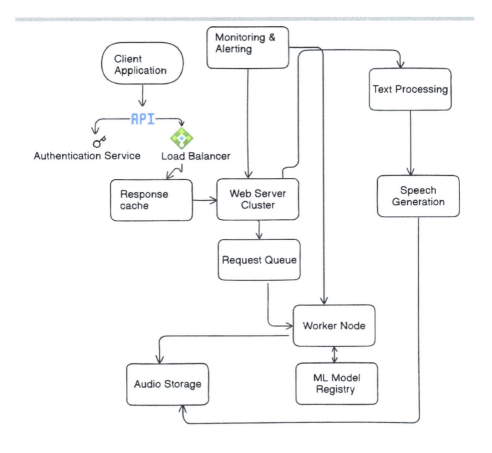

8. Time Estimation for Implementation

Phase	Task	Time Estimate
Research & Planning	Requirements analysis	2 weeks
	Architecture design	2 weeks
	Model selection and evaluation	3 weeks
Data Preparation	Data collection for training	4-8 weeks
	Data cleaning and preprocessing	3-4 weeks
	Data annotation	4-6 weeks
Development	Text processing pipeline	4-6 weeks
	Model training and fine-tuning	6-10 weeks

Phase	Task	Time Estimate
	Vocoder integration	3-4 weeks
	API development	4-6 weeks
Testing	Unit and integration testing	3-4 weeks
	Performance benchmarking	2-3 weeks
	Quality evaluation	3-4 weeks
Deployment	Infrastructure setup	2-3 weeks
	Monitoring implementation	1-2 weeks
	Production deployment	2-3 weeks
Total		45-68 weeks

Note: These timelines assume a small dedicated team. Larger teams can parallelize work to reduce calendar time but may increase coordination overhead.

9. Model Training Process

Training a modern FastSpeech 2 + HiFi-GAN text-to-speech system involves several sophisticated stages that work together to produce natural-sounding speech from text input.

Data Preparation

The foundation of effective TTS training lies in high-quality labeled data. A diverse corpus of professionally recorded speech with corresponding text transcriptions is meticulously processed through forced alignment. This crucial step maps each phoneme to its precise temporal position in the audio, establishing ground truth alignments. From these recordings, mel-spectrograms are extracted to serve as intermediate representations, capturing the frequency content of speech while reducing dimensionality. Additional acoustic features including pitch contours, energy profiles, and phoneme durations are also extracted to facilitate the training of explicit variance predictors.

FastSpeech 2 Training

FastSpeech 2 training employs a knowledge distillation approach where a pre-trained autoregressive teacher model (typically Tacotron 2) provides alignments between text and acoustic features. This eliminates the need for attention mechanisms that can cause instability. The model is trained with a multi-task learning objective comprising several loss components: a mel-reconstruction loss that ensures spectral accuracy, and separate losses for duration, pitch, and energy predictors. This explicit modeling of speech attributes enables fine-grained control over the generated speech characteristics. Unlike autoregressive models that generate frames sequentially, FastSpeech 2's feed-forward architecture enables parallel generation, dramatically improving inference speed.

HiFi-GAN Training

The HiFi-GAN vocoder is trained using adversarial learning techniques. The generator converts mel-spectrograms into raw waveforms through a series of transposed convolutions and residual blocks with multi-receptive field fusion. This architecture efficiently captures both local and global acoustic patterns. Training employs multiple discriminators operating at different scales to distinguish between real and synthetic audio. The loss function combines adversarial loss with feature matching loss and mel-spectrogram reconstruction loss. This hybrid approach ensures that the generated audio maintains both perceptual quality and spectral accuracy. The multi-period discriminator structure is particularly effective at capturing the periodic patterns essential for natural speech reproduction.

Integration and Fine-tuning

After individual training, the FastSpeech 2 and HiFi-GAN models are integrated into a complete pipeline. The mel-spectrograms generated by FastSpeech 2 serve as input to HiFi-GAN, which converts them into waveforms. Optional end-to-end fine-tuning can further improve coherence between the two components. The integrated system undergoes rigorous evaluation using both objective metrics (such as PESQ and STOI) and subjective assessment through Mean Opinion Score (MOS) tests. These evaluations focus on speech naturalness, intelligibility, and speaker similarity. Special attention is given to challenging phonetic contexts and prosodic elements to ensure the model generalizes well across diverse linguistic patterns.

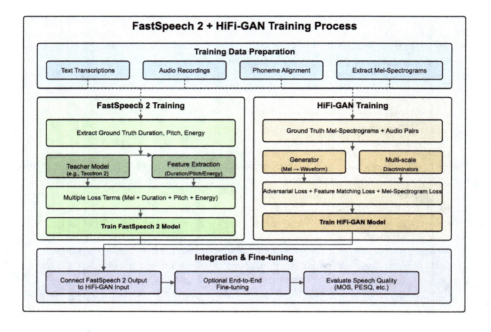

1. Training Data Preparation

- **Text Transcriptions**: The textual input that corresponds to recorded speech

- **Audio Recordings**: High-quality voice recordings for training

- **Phoneme Alignment**: Converting text to phonemes and aligning them with audio timestamps

- **Extract Mel-Spectrograms**: Converting audio to mel-spectrogram format for model training

2. FastSpeech 2 Training (Left Side)

- **Ground Truth Extraction**: Obtaining duration, pitch, and energy values from audio

- **Teacher Model**: Using a pre-trained autoregressive model (e.g., Tacotron 2) to help extract alignment information

- **Feature Extraction**: Computing duration, pitch, and energy features from aligned data

- **Multiple Loss Terms**: Training with separate losses for mel-spectrograms, duration, pitch, and energy predictions

- **Model Training**: Optimizing the FastSpeech 2 model parameters

3. HiFi-GAN Training (Right Side)

- **Training Data**: Pairs of ground truth mel-spectrograms and corresponding audio waveforms

- **Generator**: The network that converts mel-spectrograms to audio waveforms

- **Multi-scale Discriminators**: Networks that distinguish between real and synthesized audio

- **Loss Functions**: Combination of adversarial loss, feature matching loss, and mel-spectrogram loss

- **Model Training**: Optimizing the HiFi-GAN parameters using GAN training techniques

4. Integration & Fine-tuning

- **Connect Models**: Linking FastSpeech 2 output to HiFi-GAN input

- **End-to-End Fine-tuning**: Optional joint training to improve overall system performance

- **Evaluation**: Assessing speech quality using metrics like Mean Opinion Score (MOS) and PESQ

This two-stage training approach is common for modern TTS systems. FastSpeech 2 is trained first to convert text to mel-spectrograms with appropriate duration, pitch, and energy. Then, HiFi-GAN is trained separately to convert those mel-spectrograms into high-quality audio waveforms. The two models can be integrated and optionally fine-tuned together for the best performance.

Data Requirements

- **Speech corpus**: 10-50 hours of high-quality recorded speech per voice

- **Text-audio alignments**: Time-aligned transcriptions

- **Text corpus**: Large text corpus for language modeling

Training Steps

1. **Text preprocessing model training** (1-2 weeks)

   o   Train text normalization components

   o   Build grapheme-to-phoneme models

2. **Acoustic model training** (4-6 weeks)

   o   Train FastSpeech 2 model

   o   GPU compute requirements: 4-8 high-end GPUs

   o   Expected training time: 1-2 weeks per voice

3. **Vocoder training** (2-3 weeks)

   o   Train HiFi-GAN vocoder

   o   GPU compute requirements: 2-4 high-end GPUs

4. **Fine-tuning and optimization** (2-3 weeks)

   o   Hyperparameter optimization

   o   Model compression for deployment

10. Comprehensive Evaluation Framework for TTS Systems

Objective Metrics

Objective evaluation of TTS systems employs computational methods that quantify speech quality without human judgment. Mel Cepstral Distortion (MCD) serves as a foundational metric that calculates the spectral distance between synthesized and reference speech in the mel-frequency domain, with lower values indicating better spectral reconstruction. For linguistic accuracy assessment, Word Error Rate (WER) and Character Error Rate (CER) leverage automatic speech recognition (ASR) systems to transcribe synthesized speech and measure deviation from the original text input, effectively evaluating intelligibility from a machine perspective. The Perceptual Evaluation of Speech Quality (PESQ), an ITU-standardized metric, models human perception to provide a quality score that correlates well with subjective assessments. Additionally, F0 Frame Error (FFE) specifically targets prosodic accuracy by measuring pitch prediction errors, crucial for natural intonation patterns in synthesized speech.

Subjective Metrics

Subjective evaluation captures human perception aspects that objective metrics often miss. The Mean Opinion Score (MOS) remains the gold standard, where human evaluators rate speech samples on a 1-5 scale across dimensions like naturalness and clarity. For comparative analysis, MUSHRA (Multiple Stimuli with Hidden Reference and Anchor) testing enables simultaneous evaluation of multiple systems against hidden references and quality anchors, providing fine-grained preference data. ABX testing offers a simplified approach where listeners indicate preference between pairs of samples, yielding statistically significant preference trends. Dedicated naturalness ratings specifically measure how human-like the synthesized speech sounds, while intelligibility testing—often conducted in challenging acoustic conditions—ensures the speech remains understandable across various contexts. These human-centered evaluations remain essential despite their resource-intensive nature, as they capture nuanced perceptual qualities that computational metrics cannot fully address.

System Performance Metrics

Beyond speech quality, practical deployment considerations are quantified through system performance metrics. Real-time Factor (RTF) calculates the ratio of audio duration to generation time, with values below 1.0 indicating faster-than-real-time processing—essential for interactive applications. Latency measurements capture the critical time delay between request submission and the start of audio output, directly impacting user experience in conversational systems. For high-volume applications, throughput assessment determines system capacity by measuring requests processed per unit time. Resource utilization analysis tracks CPU/GPU consumption during inference, helping optimize deployment configurations and identify performance bottlenecks. These technical metrics are particularly valuable when balancing quality requirements against hardware constraints, enabling informed decisions about model size, quantization strategies, and computing infrastructure needed for successful TTS deployment across different use cases ranging from embedded devices to cloud services.

Objective Metrics

1. **Mel Cepstral Distortion (MCD)**: Measures spectral distance between synthesized and reference speech

2. **Word Error Rate (WER)**: When using ASR to transcribe synthesized speech

3. **Character Error Rate (CER)**: Similar to WER but at character level

4. **PESQ (Perceptual Evaluation of Speech Quality)**: ITU standard for speech quality assessment

5. **F0 Frame Error (FFE)**: Measures accuracy of fundamental frequency prediction

Subjective Metrics

1. **Mean Opinion Score (MOS)**: Human ratings of speech quality (1-5 scale)

2. **MUSHRA (Multiple Stimuli with Hidden Reference and Anchor)**: Comparative quality evaluation

3. **ABX Testing**: Preference tests between pairs of samples

4. **Naturalness**: How human-like the speech sounds

5. **Intelligibility**: How well the speech can be understood

System Performance Metrics

1. **Real-time Factor (RTF)**: Ratio of audio duration to generation time

2. **Latency**: Time from request to first audio output

3. **Throughput**: Number of requests processed per unit time

4. **CPU/GPU utilization**: Resource usage during inference

11. Challenges and Mitigations

Challenge	Impact	Mitigation
Pronunciation errors	Poor user experience	Custom pronunciation dictionaries
Resource constraints	High inference costs	Model quantization, distillation
Multilingual support	Complexity, cost	Language-specific models, transfer learning
Voice consistency	Quality issues	Speaker embedding consistency checks
Long text processing	Latency	Chunking strategies, progressive output
Scalability	Service failures	Containerization, auto-scaling

12. Future Enhancements

1. **Voice cloning**: Ability to clone voices with minimal data

2. **Emotion control**: More granular control over emotional expression

3. **Style transfer**: Apply speaking styles across different voices

4. **Zero-shot voice synthesis**: Generate new voices without specific training

5. **Multi-speaker conversations**: Synthesize dialogues with different speakers

6. **Real-time adaptation**: Adjust speaking style based on context

System Design of a Text-to-image generation system

To help you select an optimal text-to-image model, I'll analyze the leading options, provide a comparative assessment, and create architecture diagrams for both general text-to-image generation and training workflows.

Use Case Definition

Content Creation & Illustration

Text-to-Image systems can instantly generate artwork, illustrations, and visual stories based on user prompts. Content creators, authors, and designers can use them to prototype ideas, create comic books, or visually enrich blog posts without needing a graphic artist.

E-Commerce & Marketing

Marketers can generate promotional banners, product mockups, or seasonal themes from brief descriptions. This is especially useful for A/B testing creative variations or personalizing visuals for different regions and audiences.

Education & Visualization

T2I can help visualize complex topics like physics, biology, or math concepts. Teachers or instructional designers can convert learning material into engaging imagery for books or slide decks.

Developer Tools & Game Design

Game developers can prototype environments, characters, or items by generating visual references from descriptive lore or mechanics. This accelerates ideation and asset design before final 3D modeling.

Functional Requirements

Prompt Handling

The system should support both short and long descriptive prompts. Users may input styles ("in watercolor"), objects, scenes, or narrative elements. The model must parse this context effectively to control the generated image composition.

Semantic Control

Support semantic consistency — e.g., if a prompt says "a red apple on a table," the output should capture both the object, color, and scene. Advanced support includes grounding, multiple object arrangement, and perspective understanding.

Style & Resolution Control

Allow users to specify:

- Artistic style: photorealistic, anime, sketch, oil painting
- Image resolution: Low (256x256) to high (1024x1024 or more)
- Aspect ratio or framing: portrait, landscape, square

Iterative Refinement

Enable users to modify or extend prompts and regenerate while preserving scene context. For example, a follow-up like "make the sky darker" should re-render with minimal deviation from the original except the requested change.

1. **Text Input Processing**:
   - Accept and parse natural language descriptions
   - Support for style modifiers and compositional prompts
   - Handle multi-language support
2. **Image Generation**:
   - Generate high-resolution images (minimum 512×512, scalable to 1024×1024)
   - Support various artistic styles and visual aesthetics
   - Generate photorealistic and abstract content

3. **User Controls**:
    - Adjustable parameters for image refinement (style weight, color palette, composition)
    - Seed management for reproducibility
    - Image variations from a base prompt
4. **Output Management**:
    - Multiple format support (PNG, JPEG, WebP)
    - Metadata retention for traceability
    - Image download and sharing capabilities

Non-Functional Requirements

Latency & Throughput
Real-time preview generation (<5s) is ideal for interactive apps. Batch processing should scale to thousands of images with distributed GPU queues. Efficient batching and prompt deduplication can reduce load.

GPU Utilization
Use GPU-efficient models (e.g., quantized diffusers, LoRA-enabled transformers). Support mixed precision (FP16) for memory savings. Prioritize job queueing with cost-based routing for optimized multi-tenant workloads.

Reliability & Resilience
The system should:
- Retry or recover from generation failures
- Save intermediate latent vectors for partial re-renders
- Offer versioned image generations for traceability

Safety & Abuse Prevention
Text prompts must be scanned for toxic, biased, or NSFW intent. Generated images should be post-processed or filtered using classifiers (e.g., nude detection, facial realism validators) to block inappropriate content.

Performance:
- Response time under 5 seconds for standard generation
- Support for batch processing
- Scaling capabilities for high request volumes

Reliability:
- System uptime of 99.9%
- Graceful degradation under high load
- Proper error handling with informative messages

Security:
- Content filtering for inappropriate imagery
- Rate limiting to prevent abuse
- Secure API authentication

Scalability:
- Horizontal scaling for handling peak loads
- Resource allocation optimization for GPU utilization
- Queue management for request prioritization

Compliance:

- Content moderation and filtering
- GDPR and privacy compliance
- Copyright considerations for generated content

Comprehensive Model Comparison

Model	Architecture	Strengths	Limitations	Image Quality	Training Resources	Open Source	Customization Options
Stable Diffusion v2	Latent Diffusion	- Strong open community - Extensive fine-tuning options - Reasonable compute requirements - Active ecosystem	- Some NSFW limitations - Less coherent text rendering - Can struggle with complex prompts	High (512-768px)	Moderate >(24GB+ VRAM recommended)	Yes (Model weights & code)	LoRA, Textual Inversion, DreamBooth, Hypernetworks
DALL·E 3	Diffusion + Transformer	- Superior text understanding - Exceptional prompt following - Advanced composition - Excellent text rendering	- Closed source - API-only access - Limited customization - Usage costs	Very High (1024px+)	N/A (Not trainable by users)	No	Limited to API parameters

Model	Architecture	Strengths	Limitations	Image Quality	Training Resources	Open Source	Customization Options
Midjourney	Proprietary	- Outstanding aesthetic quality - Consistent style coherence - Intuitive prompting - Strong community	- Closed source - Discord-based interface - Limited control over outputs - Subscription required	Very High (1024 px+)	N/A (Not trainable by users)	No	Style parameters only
Kandinsky 2.2	Prior-Decoder Architecture	- Strong semantic understanding - Multi-language support - Good creative interpretation	- Less community support - Higher resource requirements - Smaller ecosystem	High (768px)	High (32GB+ VRAM for full model)	Yes	LoRA, DreamBooth
DeepFloyd IF	Multi-stage Diffusion	- Exceptional detail at high resolutions - Superior text rendering - Strong consistency	- Extremely resource intensive - Multi-step generation pipeline - Slower inference	Very High (1024 px+)	Very High (40GB+ VRAM)	Yes (with license)	Limited documentation for fine-tuning
PixArt-α	Transformer Diffusion	- Fast generation - Good composition - Efficient architecture	- Newer with less community support - Limited fine-tuning resources	High (512-1024px)	Moderate-High (24GB+ VRAM)	Yes	LoRA

Recommended Model: Stable Diffusion v2/XL

For most practical applications balancing quality, customizability, and resource requirements, **Stable Diffusion v2/XL** stands out as the optimal choice. Key advantages include:

1. **Open Ecosystem**: Fully open-source with extensive community resources, tutorials, and pre-built tools
2. **Customization Options**: Supports all major fine-tuning approaches (DreamBooth, LoRA, Textual Inversion)
3. **Reasonable Resource Requirements**: Can be fine-tuned on consumer GPUs with 24GB VRAM (16GB with optimization techniques)
4. **Deployment Flexibility**: Can be deployed on-premises or via various hosted
5. **Active Development**: Continuous improvements and model variants from both Stability AI and the community

While DALL·E 3 produces superior results in terms of prompt adherence and composition, its closed nature prevents customization beyond API parameters. DeepFloyd IF offers higher quality in some aspects but demands significantly more computational resources that may be impractical for many use cases.

For specialized use cases where aesthetic quality is paramount and customization isn't needed, Midjourney remains compelling despite its closed nature. However, for projects requiring any level of model adaptation or controlled deployment, Stable Diffusion provides the most versatile foundation.

System Architecture Design for text-to-image

The system architecture shown in the diagram represents a **Text-to-Image Generation Platform** built with modular components across **Client, API, Application, ML Infrastructure, Storage, and Monitoring layers**.

At the top, the **Client Layer** includes various interfaces like a **User Interface, Mobile Application**, and **API Client**, all of which interact through the **API Gateway**. Requests are routed through an **Authentication** service followed by a **Rate Limiter**, ensuring secure and controlled access.

Next, the **Application Layer** handles incoming prompts using a **Text Processor**, which passes data to a **Prompt Enhancer**. Enhanced prompts are queued in a **Job Queue** for further processing. Meanwhile, prompt metadata is stored in the **Prompt Database**.

The **ML Infrastructure Layer** contains the intelligence behind the system. An **Orchestrator** coordinates the flow, selecting appropriate models via the **Model Selector** and passing jobs to the **Text-to-Image Service**, which generates the image outputs. A **Post Processor** then refines these outputs.

The resulting images are stored in **Image Storage** and also sent to the **Result Cache** for faster future access. Additionally, all system activities are tracked using a **Monitoring Layer** that includes a **Logging Service, Analytics,** and an **Alert System** for operational insights and health checks.

Finally, **Storage Layer** components like the **User Database** and **Prompt Database** maintain user and prompt data, completing the full circle of the system's operation. The architecture is scalable, modular, and designed for performance and observability at every step.

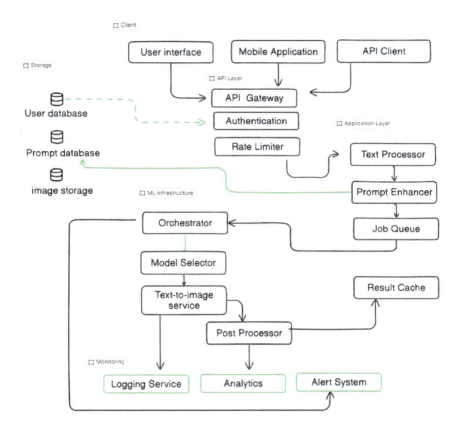

Model Selection

Pretrained Models

- **Stable Diffusion v2**: Open-source, popular, latent diffusion model with high quality and flexible fine-tuning.

- **DALL·E 2 / 3**: Commercial-grade generation with advanced prompt conditioning and creativity.

- **Kandinsky / Parti**: Transformer-based image generators with complex reasoning ability.

- **DeepFloyd IF**: High fidelity, multi-stage diffusion model with rich semantic understanding.

Fine-Tuning Options

- **DreamBooth**: Fine-tune models on user-provided objects or people for personalization.

- **LoRA (Low-Rank Adaptation)**: Efficient fine-tuning on specific styles or domains

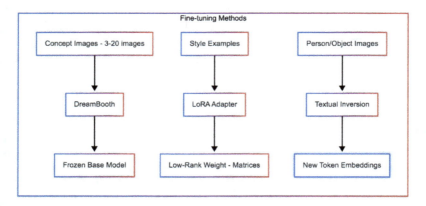

Let's evaluate the primary model options for text-to-image systems:

Model	Architecture	Strengths	Weaknesses	Use Case Fit
Stable Diffusion	Latent Diffusion	Open source, highly customizable, active community	Resource intensive, complex tuning	General-purpose deployment with fine-tuning capabilities
DALL-E 3	Transformer-based	High quality results, good for realism	Closed source, API costs	Production systems with budget for API costs
Midjourney	Proprietary	Excellent aesthetic quality	Limited API access, less control	Artistic and creative applications
ControlNet	Diffusion + Control	Precise control over composition	Additional complexity	Applications requiring spatial control

For our implementation, **Stable Diffusion XL** offers the best balance of quality, control, and open-source accessibility.

Key Implementation Considerations

1. **Computing Requirements**:

   o Full model training: Multiple high-end GPUs (A100s or equivalent) with 80GB+ total VRAM

   o Fine-tuning: Consumer GPUs with 24GB+ VRAM (or 16GB with optimization techniques)

   o Inference: Minimum 8GB VRAM for basic usage, 12GB+ recommended

2. **Training Optimizations**:

   o Gradient checkpointing to reduce memory requirements

   o Mixed precision training (FP16/BF16) for faster computation

   o Efficient fine-tuning techniques (LoRA/QLoRA) for resource-constrained environments

3. **Evaluation Metrics**:

   o FID (Fréchet Inception Distance) for overall image quality

Time Estimation

Phase	Activities	Estimated Time
Research & Planning	Requirements gathering, architecture design	2-3 weeks
Infrastructure Setup	Cloud resources, CI/CD pipelines, monitoring	1-2 weeks
Model Integration	Base model setup, pipeline configuration	2-3 weeks
Backend Development	API development, queue management, database	3-4 weeks
Frontend Development	User interface, controls, preview features	3-4 weeks
Data Processing Pipeline	Text preprocessing, image postprocessing	2-3 weeks
Testing & Optimization	Performance testing, bottleneck identification	2-3 weeks
Security & Compliance	Content filtering, rate limiting	1-2 weeks
Deployment	Staging, production rollout	1-2 weeks
Total		17-26 weeks

Practical Implementation

```
import os
import time
import torch
import logging
from fastapi import FastAPI, HTTPException, Depends, BackgroundTasks
from fastapi.security import OAuth2PasswordBearer
from pydantic import BaseModel
```

```python
from typing import Optional, List
from diffusers import StableDiffusionXLPipeline
from transformers import CLIPTokenizer
import boto3
from PIL import Image
import uuid
import redis
from prometheus_client import Counter, Histogram

# Initialize logging
logging.basicConfig(level=logging.INFO)
logger = logging.getLogger(__name__)

# Initialize FastAPI app
app = FastAPI(title="Text-to-Image API")

# Security
oauth2_scheme = OAuth2PasswordBearer(tokenUrl="token")

# Redis for caching and rate limiting
redis_client = redis.Redis(host="localhost", port=6379, db=0)

# S3 for image storage
s3_client = boto3.client(
    's3',
    aws_access_key_id=os.environ.get("AWS_ACCESS_KEY_ID"),
    aws_secret_access_key=os.environ.get("AWS_SECRET_ACCESS_KEY"),
    region_name=os.environ.get("AWS_REGION", "us-east-1")
)
S3_BUCKET = os.environ.get("S3_BUCKET", "text-to-image-results")

# Prometheus metrics
GENERATION_COUNTER = Counter('image_generation_total', 'Total number of images
generated')
GENERATION_TIME = Histogram('image_generation_seconds', 'Time spent generating
images')

# Model cache - use singleton pattern to avoid loading multiple times
class ModelCache:
    _instance = None
```

```python
    @classmethod
    def get_instance(cls):
        if cls._instance is None:
            cls._instance = cls._load_model()
        return cls._instance

    @classmethod
    def _load_model(cls):
        logger.info("Loading Stable Diffusion XL model...")
        pipe = StableDiffusionXLPipeline.from_pretrained(
            "stabilityai/stable-diffusion-xl-base-1.0",
            torch_dtype=torch.float16,
            use_safetensors=True,
            variant="fp16"
        )
        # Move to GPU if available
        if torch.cuda.is_available():
            pipe = pipe.to("cuda")
        logger.info("Model loaded successfully")
        return pipe

# Request/Response models
class GenerationRequest(BaseModel):
    prompt: str
    negative_prompt: Optional[str] = ""
    width: Optional[int] = 1024
    height: Optional[int] = 1024
    num_inference_steps: Optional[int] = 50
    guidance_scale: Optional[float] = 7.5
    seed: Optional[int] = None

class GenerationResponse(BaseModel):
    job_id: str
    status: str
    image_url: Optional[str] = None
    created_at: float

class JobStatus(BaseModel):
    job_id: str
    status: str
    image_url: Optional[str] = None
```

274

```python
    created_at: float
    completed_at: Optional[float] = None

# Background job processing
def process_generation_job(job_id: str, request: GenerationRequest):
    start_time = time.time()

    try:
        # Get model
        pipe = ModelCache.get_instance()

        # Set seed for reproducibility
        generator = None
        if request.seed is not None:
            generator = torch.Generator("cuda").manual_seed(request.seed)

        # Generate the image
        with GENERATION_TIME.time():
            image = pipe(
                prompt=request.prompt,
                negative_prompt=request.negative_prompt,
                width=request.width,
                height=request.height,
                num_inference_steps=request.num_inference_steps,
                guidance_scale=request.guidance_scale,
                generator=generator
            ).images[0]

        # Save image
        image_filename = f"{job_id}.png"
        image_path = f"/tmp/{image_filename}"
        image.save(image_path)

        # Upload to S3
        s3_client.upload_file(
            image_path,
            S3_BUCKET,
            image_filename,
            ExtraArgs={'ContentType': 'image/png', 'ACL': 'public-read'}
        )
```

```python
        # Generate URL
        image_url = f"https://{S3_BUCKET}.s3.amazonaws.com/{image_filename}"

        # Update job status
        redis_client.hset(
            f"job:{job_id}",
            mapping={
                "status": "completed",
                "image_url": image_url,
                "completed_at": str(time.time())
            }
        )

        # Increment counter
        GENERATION_COUNTER.inc()

        # Cleanup
        os.remove(image_path)

        logger.info(f"Job {job_id} completed successfully in {time.time() - start_time:.2f}s")

    except Exception as e:
        logger.error(f"Error processing job {job_id}: {str(e)}")
        redis_client.hset(
            f"job:{job_id}",
            mapping={
                "status": "failed",
                "error": str(e),
                "completed_at": str(time.time())
            }
        )

# Dependency for authentication
async def get_current_user(token: str = Depends(oauth2_scheme)):
    # In a real implementation, verify the token
    # For simplicity, we'll just return a user ID
    return "user-123"

# Rate limiting middleware
def check_rate_limit(user_id: str):
    # Basic rate limiting: 10 requests per minute
```

```python
    rate_key = f"rate:{user_id}"
    current = redis_client.get(rate_key)

    if current and int(current) >= 10:
        raise HTTPException(status_code=429, detail="Rate limit exceeded")

    pipe = redis_client.pipeline()
    pipe.incr(rate_key)
    pipe.expire(rate_key, 60)  # 1 minute expiry
    pipe.execute()

# API endpoints
@app.post("/generate", response_model=GenerationResponse)
async def generate_image(
    request: GenerationRequest,
    background_tasks: BackgroundTasks,
    user_id: str = Depends(get_current_user)
):
    # Check rate limit
    check_rate_limit(user_id)

    # Create job
    job_id = str(uuid.uuid4())
    created_at = time.time()

    # Store job info
    redis_client.hset(
        f"job:{job_id}",
        mapping={
            "user_id": user_id,
            "prompt": request.prompt,
            "status": "pending",
            "created_at": str(created_at)
        }
    )

    # Add to processing queue
    background_tasks.add_task(process_generation_job, job_id, request)

    return GenerationResponse(
        job_id=job_id,
```

```python
        status="pending",
        created_at=created_at
    )

@app.get("/jobs/{job_id}", response_model=JobStatus)
async def get_job_status(job_id: str, user_id: str = Depends(get_current_user)):
    # Get job info
    job_info = redis_client.hgetall(f"job:{job_id}")

    if not job_info:
        raise HTTPException(status_code=404, detail="Job not found")

    # Convert bytes to string
    job_info = {k.decode('utf-8'): v.decode('utf-8') for k, v in job_info.items()}

    # Check permission
    if job_info.get("user_id") != user_id:
        raise HTTPException(status_code=403, detail="Not authorized to access this job")

    return JobStatus(
        job_id=job_id,
        status=job_info.get("status", "unknown"),
        image_url=job_info.get("image_url"),
        created_at=float(job_info.get("created_at", 0)),
        completed_at=float(job_info.get("completed_at", 0)) if "completed_at" in job_info else
None
    )

@app.get("/health")
async def health_check():
    return {"status": "healthy"}

if __name__ == "__main__":
    import uvicorn
    uvicorn.run(app, host="0.0.0.0", port=8000)
```

Evaluation Metrics

For text-to-image systems, evaluation focuses on both technical performance and output quality:

Latency

This measures the total time taken from the moment a user submits a prompt to when the final image is returned. In an ideal, interactive experience—like an art generator or creative tool—this should be under **5 seconds for 512x512 images**, ensuring users don't feel a lag. High latency might frustrate users or cause backlogs in a production setting.

latency = end_time - start_time # in seconds

```python
import time

start_time = time.time()
# call your image generation function here
generate_image(prompt="a cat in a spacesuit")
end_time = time.time()

print(f"Latency: {end_time - start_time:.2f} seconds")
```

Throughput

Throughput refers to how many images your system can generate per minute or per hour—often expressed in terms of GPU performance. For instance, a strong benchmark is **10 images per minute per A100 GPU**. This is crucial for batch generation scenarios, like marketing creatives or dataset expansion.

```python
throughput = total_images / total_time  # images per second or per minute
```

```python
import time

start = time.time()
for _ in range(20):
    generate_image(prompt="a futuristic city")
end = time.time()

throughput = 20 / (end - start)
print(f"Throughput: {throughput:.2f} images/sec")
```

GPU Utilization

You want to keep GPUs busy, but not overloaded. This metric shows how effectively the compute resources are being used. Ideally, utilization should hover around **80– 95%**, which suggests your pipeline is well-optimized. Underutilization may hint at I/O bottlenecks, inefficient code, or unnecessary model overhead.

watch -n 1 nvidia-smi

```
from pynvml import *

nvmlInit()
handle = nvmlDeviceGetHandleByIndex(0)
util = nvmlDeviceGetUtilizationRates(handle)
print(f"GPU Utilization: {util.gpu}%")
nvmlShutdown()
```

Memory Usage

Here, we measure both **RAM** (CPU-side) and **VRAM** (GPU-side) usage during generation. Text-to-Image models—especially diffusion-based ones—can be memory-hungry. Efficient memory management (e.g., using mixed precision or checkpointing) can significantly lower your **VRAM footprint**, enabling larger batch sizes or multiple concurrent jobs per GPU.

```
import torch

print(f"VRAM used: {torch.cuda.memory_allocated() / 1024**2:.2f} MB")
print(f"Max VRAM used: {torch.cuda.max_memory_allocated() / 1024**2:.2f} MB")
```

Error Rate

This tracks how often the generation pipeline fails—either due to malformed prompts, OOM (Out Of Memory) crashes, or internal model exceptions. A **low error rate (<1%)** is essential for production reliability, especially when scaling to thousands of requests.

```
error_rate = failed_requests / total_requests
failed = 0
total = 100
```

```
for _ in range(total):
    try:
        generate_image(prompt="some prompt")
    except:
        failed += 1

print(f"Error rate: {failed/total:.2%}")
```

Technical Metrics

1. **Latency**: Time from request to image generation (target: <5s for standard resolutions)

2. **Throughput**: Number of images generated per time unit (e.g., 10/minute/GPU)

3. **GPU Utilization**: Percentage of GPU resources effectively used

4. **Memory Usage**: RAM and VRAM consumption during generation

5. **Error Rate**: Percentage of failed generations

Quality Metrics

FID (Fréchet Inception Distance)
This is a widely accepted metric for measuring how close the generated images are to real-world photos. It uses features extracted from a pre-trained Inception network to compare statistical distributions. Lower FID scores (e.g., **<15**) indicate more realistic outputs. FID is particularly useful for benchmarking model performance across training runs.

```
Installation:

pip install pytorch-fid
Code:
# Assuming you have two folders: "real" and "generated"
pytorch-fid real/ generate/
#Custom code (simplified):

from pytorch_fid import fid_score
```

```
score = fid_score.calculate_fid_given_paths(['real_images/', 'generated_images/'],
batch_size=50, device='cuda', dims=2048)
print(f"FID: {score}")
```

CLIP Score

CLIP Score measures how well the generated image semantically matches the input text. It does this by comparing the embeddings of the prompt and image using OpenAI's CLIP model. Higher scores mean the visual content reflects the described scene more accurately—crucial for prompt-to-image alignment.

```
Installation:


pip install openai-clip
pip install torchvision
#Code:

import clip
import torch
from PIL import Image


device = "cuda" if torch.cuda.is_available() else "cpu"
model, preprocess = clip.load("ViT-B/32", device=device)

text = clip.tokenize(["a futuristic city"]).to(device)
image = preprocess(Image.open("generated.png")).unsqueeze(0).to(device)

with torch.no_grad():
    image_features = model.encode_image(image)
    text_features = model.encode_text(text)

    similarity = torch.nn.functional.cosine_similarity(image_features, text_features)
    print(f"CLIP Score: {similarity.item():.4f}")
```

User Satisfaction Rating

This is qualitative feedback collected from real users through surveys, thumbs-up/down ratings, or reaction emojis. It provides insight into perceived image quality, prompt relevance, and overall enjoyment. This is especially useful when A/B testing models or prompt engineering techniques.

```
##Backend logging example (Flask):
```

```
@app.route("/rate", methods=["POST"])
def rate_image():
    data = request.json
    log_feedback(user_id=data["user"], rating=data["stars"], prompt=data["prompt"])
    return {"status": "success"}
##You can store this in a DB and compute:

average_rating = sum(all_ratings) / len(all_ratings)
```

NSFW Detection Rate

A must-have metric for public-facing systems. This tracks how effectively the model or filtering layer can block inappropriate or harmful content. It typically involves a secondary classifier (like NSFW detectors or moderation APIs). A **high detection rate with a low false positive rate** is ideal—blocking bad content while keeping creative freedom intact.

```
pip install nsfw-detector

from nsfw_detector import predict

model = predict.load_model("nsfw.299x299.h5")
predictions = predict.classify(model, ["img1.png", "img2.png"])
print(predictions)

#Then calculate:

nsfw_detected = sum(1 for pred in predictions.values() if pred["nsfw"] > 0.5)
detection_rate = nsfw_detected / len(predictions)
```

Aesthetic Quality

This can be subjective, but is often scored using human raters or AI aesthetic scoring models like BLIP, NIMA, or even CLIP-based scoring. You might measure:

- Color harmony
- Composition balance
- Artistic flair These are important for applications like branding, media, or digital art tools where visual appeal matters more than realism.

  pip install git+https://github.com/salesforce/BLIP.git

1. **FID (Fréchet Inception Distance)**: Measures similarity between generated and real images

2. **CLIP Score**: Alignment between text prompt and generated image

3. **User Satisfaction Rating**: Feedback from users on image quality and prompt alignment

4. **NSFW Detection Rate**: Effectiveness of content filtering

5. **Aesthetic Quality**: Can be measured through human evaluation or specialized models

```
6.   # 📦 Step 1: Install Dependencies
7.   !pip install torch torchvision clip-by-openai pytorch-fid nsfw-detector tqdm
8.
9.   # 🕐 Step 2: Imports & Setup
10.  import torch
11.  import clip
12.  import time
13.  import os
14.  from PIL import Image
15.  from torchvision import transforms
16.  from nsfw_detector import predict
17.  from pytorch_fid import fid_score
18.  from tqdm import tqdm
19.
20.  device = "cuda" if torch.cuda.is_available() else "cpu"
21.
22.  # Load CLIP model
23.  clip_model, preprocess = clip.load("ViT-B/32", device=device)
24.
25.  # Load NSFW detector
26.  nsfw_model = predict.load_model("nsfw.299x299.h5")
27.
28.  # 🗂 Step 3: Generate and Evaluate Images
29.  # You need to provide your `generate_image(prompt)` function
30.
31.  prompts = [
32.      "a futuristic city at sunset",
33.      "a dog playing piano on stage",
34.      "a magical forest with glowing plants"
35.  ]
36.
37.  generated_dir = "generated_images/"
38.  real_images_dir = "real_images/" # Optional: for FID
```

```python
39.
40.    os.makedirs(generated_dir, exist_ok=True)
41.
42.    clip_scores = []
43.    nsfw_hits = 0
44.    latencies = []
45.
46.    # Dummy function for demonstration. Replace with your actual generation function.
47.    def generate_image(prompt):
48.        return Image.new("RGB", (256, 256), color=(73, 109, 137))
49.
50.    for idx, prompt in enumerate(tqdm(prompts)):
51.        start = time.time()
52.        image = generate_image(prompt)
53.        end = time.time()
54.        latency = end - start
55.        latencies.append(latency)
56.
57.        file_path = os.path.join(generated_dir, f"{idx}.png")
58.        image.save(file_path)
59.
60.        tokenized_text = clip.tokenize([prompt]).to(device)
61.        image_input = preprocess(image).unsqueeze(0).to(device)
62.
63.        with torch.no_grad():
64.            image_feat = clip_model.encode_image(image_input)
65.            text_feat = clip_model.encode_text(tokenized_text)
66.            similarity = torch.nn.functional.cosine_similarity(image_feat, text_feat).item()
67.            clip_scores.append(similarity)
68.
69.        pred = predict.classify(nsfw_model, file_path)
70.        if pred[file_path]['nsfw'] > 0.5:
71.            nsfw_hits += 1
72.
73.    # 📊 Step 4: Report Metrics
74.    import numpy as np
75.
76.    print("🔍 Evaluation Summary:")
77.    print(f"Avg Latency: {np.mean(latencies):.2f} sec")
78.    print(f"Throughput: {len(prompts) / sum(latencies):.2f} images/sec")
79.    print(f"Avg CLIP Score: {np.mean(clip_scores):.4f}")
```

```
80.    print(f"NSFW Detection Rate: {nsfw_hits / len(prompts):.2%}")
81.
82.    # 📊 Step 5: (Optional) FID Score
83.    if os.path.exists(real_images_dir):
84.        fid = fid_score.calculate_fid_given_paths(
85.            [real_images_dir, generated_dir],
86.            batch_size=8, device=device, dims=2048
87.        )
88.        print(f"FID Score: {fid:.2f}")
89.    else:
90.        print("📁 FID skipped: No real_images directory found.")
```

Detailed Implementation Guide for Text-to-Image Generation System

Let me provide you with a much more comprehensive, step-by-step implementation guide for building a production-ready text-to-image generation system.

1. Development Environment Setup

1.1 Local Development Environment

```
# Create a dedicated project directory
mkdir text-to-image-system
cd text-to-image-system

# Initialize git repository
git init

# Create virtual environment
python -m venv venv
source venv/bin/activate  # On Windows: venv\Scripts\activate

# Create requirements.txt file
cat > requirements.txt << EOL
torch==2.0.1
```

```
torchvision==0.15.2
ciffusers==0.21.4
transformers==4.33.1
accelerate==0.23.0
fastapi==0.103.1
uvicorn[standard]==0.23.2
pydantic==2.3.0
python-multipart==0.0.6
redis==4.6.0
boto3==1.28.38
pillow==10.0.0
prometheus-client==0.17.1
python-jose==3.3.0
passlib==1.7.4
python-dotenv==1.0.0
numpy==1.25.2
EOL
```

Install dependencies
```
pip install -r requirements.txt
```

Set up project structure
```
mkdir -p app/api app/core app/models app/services app/utils app/tests config
```

1.2 Docker Environment Setup

Create Dockerfile
```
cat > Dockerfile << EOL
FROM nvidia/cuda:11.8.0-cudnn8-runtime-ubuntu22.04
```

System dependencies
```
RUN apt-get update && apt-get install -y --no-install-recommends \
    python3.10 \
    python3-pip \
    python3-dev \
    git \
    && rm -rf /var/lib/apt/lists/*
```

Set working directory
```
WORKDIR /app
```

```
# Copy requirements
COPY requirements.txt .

# Install Python dependencies
RUN pip3 install --no-cache-dir -r requirements.txt

# Copy application code
COPY app/ ./app/
COPY config/ ./config/

# Expose port
EXPOSE 8000

# Run application
CMD ["uvicorn", "app.main:app", "--host", "0.0.0.0", "--port", "8000"]
EOL

# Create docker-compose.yml for local development
cat > docker-compose.yml << EOL
version: '3.8'

services:
  web:
    build: .
    ports:
     - "8000:8000"
    volumes:
     - ./app:/app/app
     - ./config:/app/config
    environment:
     - ENV_FILE=.env.dev
    depends_on:
     - redis
    deploy:
      resources:
        reservations:
          devices:
           - driver: nvidia
             count: 1
             capabilities: [gpu]
```

```
redis:
  image: redis:7.0.5-alpine
  ports:
    - "6379:6379"
  volumes:
    - redis-data:/data

volumes:
  redis-data:
EOL
```

1.3 Environment Configuration

```
# Create environment files
cat > .env.example << EOL
# App Settings
APP_NAME=text-to-image-api
DEBUG=false
LOG_LEVEL=INFO

# Security
SECRET_KEY=your-secret-key-here
ALGORITHM=HS256
ACCESS_TOKEN_EXPIRE_MINUTES=30

# Database
REDIS_HOST=redis
REDIS_PORT=6379
REDIS_DB=0

# AWS
AWS_ACCESS_KEY_ID=your-access-key
AWS_SECRET_ACCESS_KEY=your-secret-key
AWS_REGION=us-east-1
S3_BUCKET=text-to-image-results

# Model Settings
MODEL_ID=stabilityai/stable-diffusion-xl-base-1.0
USE_FP16=true
MAX_BATCH_SIZE=4
```

```
DEVICE=cuda
EOL

# Create development environment file (copy and modify for production)
cp .env.example .env.dev
```

---

2. Core Components Implementation

2.1 Configuration Management

Create a configuration management system:

```python
# app/core/config.py
import os
from pydantic import BaseSettings
from dotenv import load_dotenv

# Load environment variables from file specified by ENV_FILE
env_file = os.getenv("ENV_FILE", ".env")
load_dotenv(env_file)

class Settings(BaseSettings):
    # App Settings
    APP_NAME: str = "text-to-image-api"
    DEBUG: bool = False
    LOG_LEVEL: str = "INFO"

    # Security
    SECRET_KEY: str
    ALGORITHM: str = "HS256"
    ACCESS_TOKEN_EXPIRE_MINUTES: int = 30

    # Database
    REDIS_HOST: str = "localhost"
    REDIS_PORT: int = 6379
    REDIS_DB: int = 0
```

```python
    # AWS
    AWS_ACCESS_KEY_ID: str
    AWS_SECRET_ACCESS_KEY: str
    AWS_REGION: str = "us-east-1"
    S3_BUCKET: str = "text-to-image-results"

    # Model Settings
    MODEL_ID: str = "stabilityai/stable-diffusion-xl-base-1.0"
    USE_FP16: bool = True
    MAX_BATCH_SIZE: int = 4
    DEVICE: str = "cuda"

    # Content filtering
    SAFETY_CHECKER_ENABLED: bool = True
    NSFW_THRESHOLD: float = 0.5

    # Rate limiting
    RATE_LIMIT_ENABLED: bool = True
    RATE_LIMIT_REQUESTS: int = 10
    RATE_LIMIT_WINDOW: int = 60  # seconds

    class Config:
        env_file = env_file
        case_sensitive = True

settings = Settings()
```

2.2 Database Setup

Set up Redis connection utility:

```python
# app/core/redis.py
import redis
from app.core.config import settings

redis_client = redis.Redis(
    host=settings.REDIS_HOST,
    port=settings.REDIS_PORT,
    db=settings.REDIS_DB,
    decode_responses=True  # Automatically decode responses to strings
```

```python
)

def get_redis_client():
    return redis_client
```

2.3 S3 Storage Setup

```python
# app/core/storage.py
import boto3
from app.core.config import settings

def get_s3_client():
    return boto3.client(
        's3',
        aws_access_key_id=settings.AWS_ACCESS_KEY_ID,
        aws_secret_access_key=settings.AWS_SECRET_ACCESS_KEY,
        region_name=settings.AWS_REGION
    )

def upload_image(image_data, object_name, content_type="image/png"):
    """Upload image data to S3 bucket"""
    s3_client = get_s3_client()
    try:
        s3_client.put_object(
            Body=image_data,
            Bucket=settings.S3_BUCKET,
            Key=object_name,
            ContentType=content_type,
            ACL="public-read"
        )
        return f"https://{settings.S3_BUCKET}.s3.amazonaws.com/{object_name}"
    except Exception as e:
        raise Exception(f"S3 upload error: {str(e)}")
```

2.4 Model Management

```python
# app/models/text_to_image.py
import torch
import logging
from diffusers import StableDiffusionXLPipeline
from app.core.config import settings
```

```python
from typing import Optional, Dict, Any, List, Union
import io

logger = logging.getLogger(__name__)

class ModelManager:
    _instance = None

    def __new__(cls):
        if cls._instance is None:
            cls._instance = super(ModelManager, cls).__new__(cls)
            cls._instance._initialized = False
        return cls._instance

    def __init__(self):
        if self._initialized:
            return

        logger.info(f"Initializing ModelManager with model {settings.MODEL_ID}")
        self._model = None
        self._device = settings.DEVICE
        self._initialized = True

    def load_model(self):
        """Load model on demand to save memory when not in use"""
        if self._model is not None:
            return self._model

        logger.info(f"Loading model {settings.MODEL_ID} to {self._device}")

        # Model loading options
        model_kwargs = {}
        if settings.USE_FP16 and torch.cuda.is_available():
            model_kwargs["torch_dtype"] = torch.float16
            model_kwargs["variant"] = "fp16"

        # Load the model
        try:
            pipe = StableDiffusionXLPipeline.from_pretrained(
                settings.MODEL_ID,
                use_safetensors=True,
```

```python
            **model_kwargs
        )

        # Move to appropriate device
        if self._device == "cuda" and torch.cuda.is_available():
            pipe = pipe.to("cuda")
        else:
            logger.warning("CUDA not available, using CPU")
            self._device = "cpu"

        # Enable memory efficient attention if available
        if hasattr(pipe, "enable_xformers_memory_efficient_attention"):
            pipe.enable_xformers_memory_efficient_attention()

        # Enable attention slicing to reduce memory usage
        pipe.enable_attention_slicing()

        self._model = pipe
        logger.info("Model loaded successfully")
        return self._model
    except Exception as e:
        logger.error(f"Error loading model: {str(e)}")
        raise

def generate_image(
    self,
    prompt: str,
    negative_prompt: Optional[str] = "",
    width: int = 1024,
    height: int = 1024,
    num_inference_steps: int = 50,
    guidance_scale: float = 7.5,
    seed: Optional[int] = None,
    output_format: str = "PNG"
) -> io.BytesIO:
    """Generate image based on prompt and parameters"""
    try:
        # Load model if not loaded
        pipe = self.load_model()

        # Set seed for reproducibility if provided
```

```python
        generator = None
        if seed is not None:
            generator = torch.Generator(device=self._device).manual_seed(seed)

        # Generate the image
        image = pipe(
            prompt=prompt,
            negative_prompt=negative_prompt,
            width=width,
            height=height,
            num_inference_steps=num_inference_steps,
            guidance_scale=guidance_scale,
            generator=generator
        ).images[0]

        # Convert to in-memory binary stream
        image_byte_stream = io.BytesIO()
        image.save(image_byte_stream, format=output_format)
        image_byte_stream.seek(0)

        return image_byte_stream
    except Exception as e:
        logger.error(f"Error generating image: {str(e)}")
        raise
```

2.5 Authentication System

```python
# app/core/security.py
from datetime import datetime, timedelta
from typing import Optional
from jose import JWTError, jwt
from passlib.context import CryptContext
from fastapi import Depends, HTTPException, status
from fastapi.security import OAuth2PasswordBearer
from pydantic import BaseModel
from app.core.config import settings

# Password hashing context
pwd_context = CryptContext(schemes=["bcrypt"], deprecated="auto")
```

```python
# OAuth2 authentication scheme
oauth2_scheme = OAuth2PasswordBearer(tokenUrl="token")

# Token data model
class TokenData(BaseModel):
    username: Optional[str] = None


class User(BaseModel):
    username: str
    email: Optional[str] = None
    full_name: Optional[str] = None
    disabled: Optional[bool] = None

# Mock user database (replace with actual database in production)
fake_users_db = {
    "testuser": {
        "username": "testuser",
        "email": "testuser@example.com",
        "full_name": "Test User",
        "hashed_password": pwd_context.hash("testpassword"),
        "disabled": False,
    }
}

def verify_password(plain_password, hashed_password):
    return pwd_context.verify(plain_password, hashed_password)

def get_password_hash(password):
    return pwd_context.hash(password)

def get_user(db, username: str):
    if username in db:
        user_dict = db[username]
        return User(**user_dict)

def authenticate_user(fake_db, username: str, password: str):
    user = get_user(fake_db, username)
    if not user:
        return False
    if not verify_password(password, fake_db[username]["hashed_password"]):
        return False
```

```python
        return user

def create_access_token(data: dict, expires_delta: Optional[timedelta] = None):
    to_encode = data.copy()

    if expires_delta:
        expire = datetime.utcnow() + expires_delta
    else:
        expire = datetime.utcnow() +
timedelta(minutes=settings.ACCESS_TOKEN_EXPIRE_MINUTES)

    to_encode.update({"exp": expire})
    encoded_jwt = jwt.encode(to_encode, settings.SECRET_KEY,
algorithm=settings.ALGORITHM)
    return encoded_jwt

async def get_current_user(token: str = Depends(oauth2_scheme)):
    credentials_exception = HTTPException(
        status_code=status.HTTP_401_UNAUTHORIZED,
        detail="Could not validate credentials",
        headers={"WWW-Authenticate": "Bearer"},
    )

    try:
        payload = jwt.decode(token, settings.SECRET_KEY, algorithms=[settings.ALGORITHM])
        username: str = payload.get("sub")
        if username is None:
            raise credentials_exception

        token_data = TokenData(username=username)
    except JWTError:
        raise credentials_exception

    user = get_user(fake_users_db, username=token_data.username)
    if user is None:
        raise credentials_exception

    return user

async def get_current_active_user(current_user: User = Depends(get_current_user)):
    if current_user.disabled:
```

```
        raise HTTPException(status_code=400, detail="Inactive user")
    return current_user
```

2.6 Background Task Processing

```python
# app/services/job_service.py
import time
import uuid
import json
import asyncio
import logging
from typing import Dict, Any, Optional
from app.core.redis import get_redis_client
from app.models.text_to_image import ModelManager
from app.core.storage import upload_image
from app.core.config import settings

logger = logging.getLogger(__name__)
model_manager = ModelManager()
redis_client = get_redis_client()

class JobService:
    @staticmethod
    async def create_job(user_id: str, params: Dict[str, Any]) -> str:
        """Create a new job and return the job ID"""
        job_id = str(uuid.uuid4())
        created_at = time.time()

        # Store job information
        job_data = {
            "user_id": user_id,
            "params": json.dumps(params),
            "status": "pending",
            "created_at": str(created_at)
        }

        redis_client.hset(f"job:{job_id}", mapping=job_data)

        # Add to processing queue
        redis_client.lpush("job_queue", job_id)
```

```python
        logger.info(f"Created job {job_id} for user {user_id}")
        return job_id

    @staticmethod
    async def get_job(job_id: str) -> Dict[str, Any]:
        """Get job status and details"""
        job_data = redis_client.hgetall(f"job:{job_id}")

        if not job_data:
            return None

        # Parse stored JSON
        if "params" in job_data:
            job_data["params"] = json.loads(job_data["params"])

        # Convert created_at to float
        if "created_at" in job_data:
            job_data["created_at"] = float(job_data["created_at"])

        # Convert completed_at to float if it exists
        if "completed_at" in job_data:
            job_data["completed_at"] = float(job_data["completed_at"])

        return job_data

    @staticmethod
    async def process_jobs():
        """Background worker to process jobs from queue"""
        logger.info("Starting job processing worker")

        while True:
            try:
                # Pop job from queue with blocking wait
                result = redis_client.brpop("job_queue", timeout=1)

                if result is None:
                    await asyncio.sleep(0.1)
                    continue

                _, job_id = result
                job_id = job_id.decode() if isinstance(job_id, bytes) else job_id
```

```python
    logger.info(f"Processing job {job_id}")

    # Get job data
    job_data = await JobService.get_job(job_id)
    if not job_data:
        logger.error(f"Job {job_id} not found")
        continue

    # Update status to processing
    redis_client.hset(f"job:{job_id}", "status", "processing")

    # Extract parameters
    params = job_data["params"]

    try:
        # Generate image
        image_data = model_manager.generate_image(
            prompt=params["prompt"],
            negative_prompt=params.get("negative_prompt", ""),
            width=params.get("width", 1024),
            height=params.get("height", 1024),
            num_inference_steps=params.get("num_inference_steps", 50),
            guidance_scale=params.get("guidance_scale", 7.5),
            seed=params.get("seed")
        )

        # Upload to S3
        image_filename = f"{job_id}.png"
        image_url = upload_image(image_data, image_filename)

        # Update job with success
        redis_client.hset(
            f"job:{job_id}",
            mapping={
                "status": "completed",
                "image_url": image_url,
                "completed_at": str(time.time())
            }
        )
```

```python
            logger.info(f"Job {job_id} completed successfully")

        except Exception as e:
            logger.error(f"Error processing job {job_id}: {str(e)}")

            # Update job with error
            redis_client.hset(
                f"job:{job_id}",
                mapping={
                    "status": "failed",
                    "error": str(e),
                    "completed_at": str(time.time())
                }
            )

    except Exception as e:
        logger.error(f"Error in job processing loop: {str(e)}")
        await asyncio.sleep(1)  # Prevent tight loop on persistent errors
```

2.7 Rate Limiting Service

```python
# app/services/rate_limit.py
from fastapi import HTTPException, status
from app.core.redis import get_redis_client
from app.core.config import settings
import time

redis_client = get_redis_client()

class RateLimitService:
    @staticmethod
    async def check_rate_limit(user_id: str):
        """
        Check if user has exceeded rate limits
        Raises HTTPException if limit is exceeded
        """
        if not settings.RATE_LIMIT_ENABLED:
            return
```

```python
        rate_key = f"rate:{user_id}"

        # Get current request count
        current = redis_client.get(rate_key)
        current_count = int(current) if current else 0

        if current_count >= settings.RATE_LIMIT_REQUESTS:
            # Get TTL to tell user how long to wait
            ttl = redis_client.ttl(rate_key)
            raise HTTPException(
                status_code=status.HTTP_429_TOO_MANY_REQUESTS,
                detail=f"Rate limit exceeded. Try again in {ttl} seconds."
            )

        # Increment counter and set expiry if it's the first request
        pipe = redis_client.pipeline()
        pipe.incr(rate_key)
        if current_count == 0:
            pipe.expire(rate_key, settings.RATE_LIMIT_WINDOW)
        pipe.execute()
```

2.8 Content Safety Service

```python
# app/services/safety.py
import re
from typing import List, Tuple, Set

class SafetyChecker:
    def __init__(self):
        # Simple blocklist of terms (extend with more sophisticated filtering in production)
        self.blocklist = {
            # Add blocklist terms here
            "explicit content",
            "pornography",
            # Add more terms
        }

    def check_prompt(self, prompt: str) -> Tuple[bool, str]:
        """
        Check if prompt contains unsafe content
        Returns (is_safe, reason)
```

```python
    """

    # Convert to lowercase for case-insensitive matching
    prompt_lower = prompt.lower()

    # Check against blocklist
    for term in self.blocklist:
        if term in prompt_lower:
            return False, f"Prompt contains blocked term: {term}"

    # Advanced pattern checks could be added here

    return True, ""
```

3. API Implementation

3.1 Data Models

```python
# app/api/models.py
from pydantic import BaseModel, Field, validator
from typing import Optional, List
from datetime import datetime

class Token(BaseModel):
    access_token: str
    token_type: str

class TokenData(BaseModel):
    username: Optional[str] = None

class GenerationRequest(BaseModel):
    prompt: str = Field(..., min_length=3, max_length=1000)
    negative_prompt: Optional[str] = Field("", max_length=1000)
    width: Optional[int] = Field(1024, ge=256, le=2048)
    height: Optional[int] = Field(1024, ge=256, le=2048)
    num_inference_steps: Optional[int] = Field(50, ge=10, le=150)
    guidance_scale: Optional[float] = Field(7.5, ge=1.0, le=20.0)
```

```python
    seed: Optional[int] = None

    @validator('width', 'height')
    def validate_dimensions(cls, v):
        # Ensure dimensions are multiples of 8 for stable diffusion
        if v % 8 != 0:
            rounded = ((v + 7) // 8) * 8
            return rounded
        return v


class GenerationResponse(BaseModel):
    job_id: str
    status: str
    created_at: float


class JobStatusResponse(BaseModel):
    job_id: str
    status: str
    created_at: float
    completed_at: Optional[float] = None
    image_url: Optional[str] = None
    error: Optional[str] = None
```

3.2 Auth Endpoints

```python
# app/api/auth.py
from datetime import timedelta
from fastapi import APIRouter, Depends, HTTPException, status
from fastapi.security import OAuth2PasswordRequestForm
from app.api.models import Token
from app.core.security import (
    authenticate_user,
    create_access_token,
    fake_users_db,
    get_current_active_user,
    User
)
from app.core.config import settings

router = APIRouter(tags=["authentication"])
```

304

```python
@router.post("/token", response_model=Token)
async def login_for_access_token(form_data: OAuth2PasswordRequestForm = Depends()):
    user = authenticate_user(fake_users_db, form_data.username, form_data.password)
    if not user:
        raise HTTPException(
            status_code=status.HTTP_401_UNAUTHORIZED,
            detail="Incorrect username or password",
            headers={"WWW-Authenticate": "Bearer"},
        )

    access_token_expires = timedelta(minutes=settings.ACCESS_TOKEN_EXPIRE_MINUTES)
    access_token = create_access_token(
        data={"sub": user.username}, expires_delta=access_token_expires
    )

    return {"access_token": access_token, "token_type": "bearer"}

@router.get("/users/me", response_model=User)
async def read_users_me(current_user: User = Depends(get_current_active_user)):
    return current_user
```

3.3 Text-to-Image Endpoints

```python
# app/api/text_to_image.py
from fastapi import APIRouter, Depends, HTTPException, BackgroundTasks, Path, Query
from typing import Optional
from app.api.models import GenerationRequest, GenerationResponse, JobStatusResponse
from app.core.security import get_current_active_user, User
from app.services.job_service import JobService
from app.services.rate_limit import RateLimitService
from app.services.safety import SafetyChecker
import logging

router = APIRouter(prefix="/api/v1", tags=["text-to-image"])
logger = logging.getLogger(__name__)
safety_checker = SafetyChecker()

@router.post("/generate", response_model=GenerationResponse)
async def generate_image(
    request: GenerationRequest,
    background_tasks: BackgroundTasks,
```

```python
    current_user: User = Depends(get_current_active_user)
):
    # Check rate limit
    await RateLimitService.check_rate_limit(current_user.username)

    # Check content safety
    is_safe, reason = safety_checker.check_prompt(request.prompt)
    if not is_safe:
        raise HTTPException(status_code=400, detail=reason)

    # Create job
    job_id = await JobService.create_job(
        user_id=current_user.username,
        params=request.dict()
    )

    return GenerationResponse(
        job_id=job_id,
        status="pending",
        created_at=float(await JobService.get_job(job_id))["created_at"]
    )

@router.get("/jobs/{job_id}", response_model=JobStatusResponse)
async def get_job_status(
    job_id: str = Path(..., description="Job ID"),
    current_user: User = Depends(get_current_active_user)
):
    job_data = await JobService.get_job(job_id)

    if not job_data:
        raise HTTPException(status_code=404, detail="Job not found")

    # Check permission
    if job_data["user_id"] != current_user.username:
        raise HTTPException(status_code=403, detail="Not authorized to access this job")

    return JobStatusResponse(**job_data)

@router.get("/jobs", response_model=list[JobStatusResponse])
async def list_user_jobs(
    status: Optional[str] = Query(None, description="Filter by job status"),
```

```python
    limit: int = Query(10, ge=1, le=100, description="Number of jobs to return"),
    offset: int = Query(0, ge=0, description="Number of jobs to skip"),
    current_user: User = Depends(get_current_active_user)
):
    # Implementation would query Redis for jobs belonging to current user
    # This is a placeholder that would need actual implementation
    # You could implement this with Redis sorted sets or scan operations
    pass
```

3.4 Health Endpoints

```python
# app/api/health.py
from fastapi import APIRouter, Depends
from app.core.redis import get_redis_client
from app.models.text_to_image import ModelManager
import torch

router = APIRouter(prefix="/health", tags=["health"])

@router.get("")
async def health_check():
    # Basic health check
    return {
        "status": "healthy",
        "service": "text-to-image-api"
    }

@router.get("/ready")
async def readiness_check():
    # More detailed readiness probe
    status = {
        "redis": "unknown",
        "gpu": "unknown",
        "model": "unknown"
    }

    # Check Redis connection
    try:
        redis_client = get_redis_client()
        redis_ping = redis_client.ping()
        status["redis"] = "ok" if redis_ping else "error"
```

```python
    except Exception:
        status["redis"] = "error"

    # Check GPU availability
    try:
        status["gpu"] = "ok" if torch.cuda.is_available() else "not_available"
        if torch.cuda.is_available():
            status["gpu_info"] = {
                "device_name": torch.cuda.get_device_name(0),
                "device_count": torch.cuda.device_count(),
                "memory_allocated": f"{torch.cuda.memory_allocated(0)/1024**3:.2f} GB",
                "memory_reserved": f"{torch.cuda.memory_reserved(0)/1024**3:.2f} GB"
            }
    except Exception:
        status["gpu"] = "error"

    # Check model loading
    try:
        model_manager = ModelManager()
        # Just check if we can initialize the manager, don't actually load
        # the model here as it would be expensive for a health check
        status["model"] = "ok"
    except Exception:
        status["model"] = "error"

    # Overall status
    is_ready = all(s == "ok" for s in [status["redis"], status["model"]]) and \
            (status["gpu"] == "ok" or status["gpu"] == "not_available")

    return {
        "ready": is_ready,
        "components": status
    }
```

3.5 Main Application

```python
# app/main.py
import logging
import asyncio
from fastapi import FastAPI, Request
from fastapi.middleware.cors import CORSMiddleware
```

```python
from fastapi.responses import JSONResponse
from app.api import auth, text_to_image, health
from app.core.config import settings
from app.services.job_service import JobService
import time
import uvicorn

# Configure logging
logging.basicConfig(
    level=getattr(logging, settings.LOG_LEVEL),
    format="%(asctime)s - %(name)s - %(levelname)s - %(message)s"
)
logger = logging.getLogger(__name__)

# Create FastAPI app
app = FastAPI(
    title=settings.APP_NAME,
    description="API for text-to-image generation",
    version="1.0.0",
    debug=settings.DEBUG
)

# Add CORS middleware
app.add_middleware(
    CORSMiddleware,
    allow_origins=["*"],  # In production, limit to your frontend domains
    allow_credentials=True,
    allow_methods=["*"],
    allow_headers=["*"],
)

# Add request timing middleware
@app.middleware("http")
async def add_process_time_header(request: Request, call_next):
    start_time = time.time()
    response = await call_next(request)
    process_time = time.time() - start_time
    response.headers["X-Process-Time"] = str(process_time)
    return response

# Exception handler
```

```python
@app.exception_handler(Exception)
async def global_exception_handler(request: Request, exc: Exception):
    logger.error(f"Unhandled exception: {str(exc)}", exc_info=True)
    return JSONResponse(
        status_code=500,
        content={"detail": "Internal
    return JSONResponse(
        status_code=500,
        content={"detail": "Internal server error. Please try again later."}
    )


# Include routers
app.include_router(auth.router)
app.include_router(text_to_image.router)
app.include_router(health.router)


# Background task for job processing
@app.on_event("startup")
async def startup_event():
    logger.info("Starting application")

    # Start job processing in background
    asyncio.create_task(JobService.process_jobs())


@app.on_event("shutdown")
async def shutdown_event():
    logger.info("Shutting down application")
    # Perform cleanup if needed


if __name__ == "__main__":
    uvicorn.run("app.main:app", host="0.0.0.0", port=8000, reload=settings.DEBUG)
```

4. Testing and Quality Assurance

4.1 Unit Tests

```python
# app/tests/test_model.py
import pytest
from unittest.mock import patch, MagicMock
from app.models.text_to_image import ModelManager
```

```python
import io

@pytest.fixture
def model_manager():
    # Create a fresh instance for each test
    manager = ModelManager()
    # Reset singleton to avoid test interference
    manager._initialized = False
    manager._model = None
    return manager

def test_model_singleton():
    manager1 = ModelManager()
    manager2 = ModelManager()
    assert manager1 is manager2

@patch('app.models.text_to_image.StableDiffusionXLPipeline')
def test_load_model(mock_pipeline, model_manager):
    # Mock the pipeline
    mock_pipe = MagicMock()
    mock_pipeline.from_pretrained.return_value = mock_pipe

    # Test loading the model
    result = model_manager.load_model()

    # Verify the model was loaded with correct parameters
    mock_pipeline.from_pretrained.assert_called_once()
    assert result is mock_pipe

@patch('app.models.text_to_image.ModelManager.load_model')
def test_generate_image(mock_load_model, model_manager):
    # Mock the model
    mock_pipe = MagicMock()
    mock_load_model.return_value = mock_pipe

    # Mock image result
    mock_image = MagicMock()
    mock_pipe.return_value.images = [mock_image]

    # Mock PIL image save method
    mock_image.save = MagicMock()
```

```python
    # Test generating an image
    result = model_manager.generate_image("test prompt")

    # Verify the model was called with correct parameters
    mock_pipe.assert_called_once()
    assert isinstance(result, io.BytesIO)

# app/tests/test_api.py
from fastapi.testclient import TestClient
from app.main import app
import pytest
from unittest.mock import patch, AsyncMock

client = TestClient(app)

@pytest.fixture
def auth_headers():
    # Get auth token
    response = client.post(
        "/token",
        data={"username": "testuser", "password": "testpassword"}
    )
    token = response.json()["access_token"]
    return {"Authorization": f"Bearer {token}"}

def test_health_check():
    response = client.get("/health")
    assert response.status_code == 200
    assert response.json()["status"] == "healthy"

@patch('app.api.text_to_image.RateLimitService.check_rate_limit', new_callable=AsyncMock)
@patch('app.api.text_to_image.JobService.create_job', new_callable=AsyncMock)
@patch('app.api.text_to_image.JobService.get_job', new_callable=AsyncMock)
def test_generate_image(mock_get_job, mock_create_job, mock_rate_limit, auth_headers):
    # Mock job creation
    mock_create_job.return_value = "test-job-id"
    mock_get_job.return_value = {"created_at": 123456789.0}

    # Test request
    request_data = {
```

```python
    "prompt": "A beautiful sunset over mountains",
    "width": 1024,
    "height": 1024
  }

  response = client.post(
    "/api/v1/generate",
    json=request_data,
    headers=auth_headers
  )

  assert response.status_code == 200
  assert response.json()["job_id"] == "test-job-id"
  assert response.json()["status"] == "pending"
```

4.2 Integration Tests

```python
# app/tests/test_integration.py
import pytest
import asyncio
from fastapi.testclient import TestClient
from app.main import app
from app.core.redis import get_redis_client
import time

client = TestClient(app)
redis_client = get_redis_client()

@pytest.fixture
def auth_headers():
  # Get auth token
  response = client.post(
    "/token",
    data={"username": "testuser", "password": "testpassword"}
  )
  token = response.json()["access_token"]
  return {"Authorization": f"Bearer {token}"}

@pytest.fixture(autouse=True)
def setup_teardown():
```

```python
    # Setup - clear redis before test
    keys = redis_client.keys("job:*")
    if keys:
        redis_client.delete(*keys)
    redis_client.delete("job_queue")

    yield

    # Teardown - clean up after test
    keys = redis_client.keys("job:*")
    if keys:
        redis_client.delete(*keys)
    redis_client.delete("job_queue")


@pytest.mark.asyncio
async def test_end_to_end_flow(auth_headers):
    # Skip if no GPU available (CI environments)
    import torch
    if not torch.cuda.is_available():
        pytest.skip("No GPU available for integration test")

    # 1. Submit generation request
    request_data = {
        "prompt": "Test prompt for integration",
        "width": 512,  # Smaller for faster test
        "height": 512,
        "num_inference_steps": 20  # Fewer steps for faster test
    }

    response = client.post(
        "/api/v1/generate",
        json=request_data,
        headers=auth_headers
    )

    assert response.status_code == 200
    job_id = response.json()["job_id"]

    # 2. Wait for processing (maximum 60 seconds)
    max_wait = 60
    start_time = time.time()
```

```python
    completed = False

    while time.time() - start_time < max_wait:
        # Check job status
        status_response = client.get(
            f"/api/v1/jobs/{job_id}",
            headers=auth_headers
        )

        assert status_response.status_code == 200
        job_status = status_response.json()["status"]

        if job_status == "completed":
            completed = True
            break
        elif job_status == "failed":
            assert False, "Job failed during processing"

        # Wait before checking again
        await asyncio.sleep(2)

    assert completed, f"Job did not complete within {max_wait} seconds"

    # 3. Verify final job result
    final_response = client.get(
        f"/api/v1/jobs/{job_id}",
        headers=auth_headers
    )

    assert final_response.status_code == 200
    job_data = final_response.json()

    assert job_data["status"] == "completed"
    assert "image_url" in job_data
    assert job_data["image_url"].startswith("https://")
```

5. Infrastructure and Deployment

5.1 Kubernetes Deployment

Create deployment manifests for Kubernetes:

```yaml
# k8s/namespace.yaml
apiVersion: v1
kind: Namespace
metadata:
  name: text-to-image
```

```yaml
# k8s/configmap.yaml
apiVersion: v1
kind: ConfigMap
metadata:
  name: app-config
  namespace: text-to-image
data:
  LOG_LEVEL: "INFO"
  REDIS_HOST: "redis-service"
  REDIS_PORT: "6379"
  REDIS_DB: "0"
  MODEL_ID: "stabilityai/stable-diffusion-xl-base-1.0"
  USE_FP16: "true"
  MAX_BATCH_SIZE: "4"
  DEVICE: "cuda"
  SAFETY_CHECKER_ENABLED: "true"
```

```yaml
# k8s/secret.yaml
apiVersion: v1
kind: Secret
metadata:
  name: app-secrets
  namespace: text-to-image
type: Opaque
data:
  # Base64 encoded secrets
  SECRET_KEY: <base64-encoded-secret>
  AWS_ACCESS_KEY_ID: <base64-encoded-key>
  AWS_SECRET_ACCESS_KEY: <base64-encoded-secret>
  AWS_REGION: <base64-encoded-region>
  S3_BUCKET: <base64-encoded-bucket>
```

```yaml
# k8s/redis-deployment.yaml
```

```yaml
apiVersion: apps/v1
kind: Deployment
metadata:
 name: redis
 namespace: text-to-image
spec:
 replicas: 1
 selector:
  matchLabels:
   app: redis
 template:
  metadata:
   labels:
    app: redis
  spec:
   containers:
   - name: redis
     image: redis:7.0.5-alpine
     ports:
     - containerPort: 6379
     resources:
      requests:
       memory: "256Mi"
       cpu: "100m"
      limits:
       memory: "512Mi"
       cpu: "200m"
     volumeMounts:
     - name: redis-data
       mountPath: /data
   volumes:
   - name: redis-data
     persistentVolumeClaim:
       claimName: redis-pvc
---
apiVersion: v1
kind: Service
metadata:
 name: redis-service
 namespace: text-to-image
spec:
```

```yaml
  selector:
    app: redis
  ports:
  - port: 6379
    targetPort: 6379
---
apiVersion: v1
kind: PersistentVolumeClaim
metadata:
  name: redis-pvc
  namespace: text-to-image
spec:
  accessModes:
    - ReadWriteOnce
  resources:
    requests:
      storage: 5Gi
```

```yaml
# k8s/api-deployment.yaml
apiVersion: apps/v1
kind: Deployment
metadata:
  name: text-to-image-api
  namespace: text-to-image
spec:
  replicas: 1
  selector:
    matchLabels:
      app: text-to-image-api
  template:
    metadata:
      labels:
        app: text-to-image-api
    spec:
      containers:
      - name: api
        image: ${YOUR_REGISTRY}/text-to-image-api:latest
        ports:
        - containerPort: 8000
        resources:
```

```yaml
      requests:
        memory: "8Gi"
        cpu: "2"
      limits:
        memory: "16Gi"
        cpu: "4"
    env:
    - name: ENV_FILE
      value: .env.prod
    envFrom:
    - configMapRef:
        name: app-config
    - secretRef:
        name: app-secrets
    volumeMounts:
    - name: model-cache
      mountPath: /root/.cache/huggingface
  volumes:
  - name: model-cache
    persistentVolumeClaim:
      claimName: model-cache-pvc
  nodeSelector:
    cloud.google.com/gke-accelerator: nvidia-tesla-t4  # Adjust based on your cloud provider
---
apiVersion: v1
kind: Service
metadata:
  name: text-to-image-api-service
  namespace: text-to-image
spec:
  selector:
    app: text-to-image-api
  ports:
  - port: 80
    targetPort: 8000
---
apiVersion: v1
kind: PersistentVolumeClaim
metadata:
  name: model-cache-pvc
  namespace: text-to-image
```

```yaml
spec:
  accessModes:
    - ReadWriteOnce
  resources:
    requests:
      storage: 30Gi  # Models can be large
```

```yaml
# k8s/ingress.yaml
apiVersion: networking.k8s.io/v1
kind: Ingress
metadata:
  name: text-to-image-ingress
  namespace: text-to-image
  annotations:
    kubernetes.io/ingress.class: nginx
    cert-manager.io/cluster-issuer: letsencrypt-prod
spec:
  rules:
  - host: api.yourdomain.com
    http:
      paths:
      - path: /
        pathType: Prefix
        backend:
          service:
            name: text-to-image-api-service
            port:
              number: 80
  tls:
  - hosts:
    - api.yourdomain.com
    secretName: text-to-image-tls
```

5.2 Monitoring Setup

```yaml
# k8s/prometheus.yaml
apiVersion: v1
```

```yaml
kind: ConfigMap
metadata:
  name: prometheus-config
  namespace: text-to-image
data:
  prometheus.yml: |
    global:
      scrape_interval: 15s

    scrape_configs:
      - job_name: 'text-to-image-api'
        metrics_path: /metrics
        static_configs:
          - targets: ['text-to-image-api-service:80']
---
apiVersion: apps/v1
kind: Deployment
metadata:
  name: prometheus
  namespace: text-to-image
spec:
  replicas: 1
  selector:
    matchLabels:
      app: prometheus
  template:
    metadata:
      labels:
        app: prometheus
    spec:
      containers:
      - name: prometheus
        image: prom/prometheus:v2.40.0
        ports:
        - containerPort: 9090
        volumeMounts:
        - name: config
          mountPath: /etc/prometheus
      volumes:
      - name: config
        configMap:
```

```yaml
      name: prometheus-config
---
apiVersion: v1
kind: Service
metadata:
  name: prometheus-service
  namespace: text-to-image
spec:
  selector:
    app: prometheus
  ports:
  - port: 9090
    targetPort: 9090




# k8s/grafana.yaml
apiVersion: apps/v1
kind: Deployment
metadata:
  name: grafana
  namespace: text-to-image
spec:
  replicas: 1
  selector:
    matchLabels:
      app: grafana
  template:
    metadata:
      labels:
        app: grafana
    spec:
      containers:
      - name: grafana
        image: grafana/grafana:9.3.2
        ports:
        - containerPort: 3000
        env:
        - name: GF_SECURITY_ADMIN_PASSWORD
          valueFrom:
            secretKeyRef:
```

```yaml
        name: grafana-secrets
        key: admin-password
    volumeMounts:
    - name: grafana-storage
      mountPath: /var/lib/grafana
    volumes:
    - name: grafana-storage
      persistentVolumeClaim:
        claimName: grafana-pvc
---
apiVersion: v1
kind: Service
metadata:
  name: grafana-service
  namespace: text-to-image
spec:
  selector:
    app: grafana
  ports:
  - port: 3000
    targetPort: 3000
---
apiVersion: v1
kind: PersistentVolumeClaim
metadata:
  name: grafana-pvc
  namespace: text-to-image
spec:
  accessModes:
    - ReadWriteOnce
  resources:
    requests:
      storage: 5Gi
```

6. CI/CD Pipeline

Create GitHub Actions workflow for CI/CD:

```yaml
# .github/workflows/ci-cd.yml
name: CI/CD Pipeline

on:
  push:
    branches: [ main ]
  pull_request:
    branches: [ main ]

jobs:
  test:
    runs-on: ubuntu-latest
    steps:
    - uses: actions/checkout@v3

    - name: Set up Python
      uses: actions/setup-python@v4
      with:
        python-version: '3.10'

    - name: Install dependencies
      run: |
        python -m pip install --upgrade pip
        pip install -r requirements.txt
        pip install pytest pytest-asyncio pytest-cov

    - name: Run tests
      run: |
        pytest app/tests/ --cov=app --cov-report=xml

    - name: Upload coverage report
      uses: codecov/codecov-action@v3
      with:
        file: ./coverage.xml

  build-and-push:
    needs: test
    if: github.event_name == 'push' && github.ref == 'refs/heads/main'
    runs-on: ubuntu-latest
    steps:
    - uses: actions/checkout@v3
```

```yaml
    - name: Set up Docker Buildx
      uses: docker/setup-buildx-action@v2

    - name: Login to DockerHub
      uses: docker/login-action@v2
      with:
        username: ${{ secrets.DOCKERHUB_USERNAME }}
        password: ${{ secrets.DOCKERHUB_TOKEN }}

    - name: Build and push
      uses: docker/build-push-action@v4
      with:
        context: .
        push: true
        tags: ${{ secrets.DOCKERHUB_USERNAME }}/text-to-image:latest,${{ secrets.DOCKERHUB_USERNAME }}/text-to-image:${{ github.sha }}
        cache-from: type=registry,ref=${{ secrets.DOCKERHUB_USERNAME }}/text-to-image:buildcache
        cache-to: type=registry,ref=${{ secrets.DOCKERHUB_USERNAME }}/text-to-image:buildcache,mode=max

  deploy:
    needs: build-and-push
    runs-on: ubuntu-latest
    steps:
    - uses: actions/checkout@v3

    - name: Install kubectl
      uses: azure/setup-kubectl@v3
      with:
        version: 'v1.25.0'

    - name: Configure kubectl
      run: |
        echo "${{ secrets.KUBE_CONFIG }}" > kubeconfig.yaml
        echo "KUBECONFIG=$(pwd)/kubeconfig.yaml" >> $GITHUB_ENV

    - name: Update deployment
      run: |
        # Update the image tag in the deployment
```

```
kubectl set image deployment/text-to-image-api api=${{ secrets.DOCKERHUB_USERNAME
}}/text-to-image:${{ github.sha }} -n text-to-image

# Verify deployment
kubectl rollout status deployment/text-to-image-api -n text-to-image
```

7. Fine-tuning and Customization

Let's explore the steps for fine-tuning the Stable Diffusion model for specific use cases:

7.1 Dataset Preparation

```python
# scripts/prepare_dataset.py
import os
import json
import shutil
from PIL import Image
from tqdm import tqdm
import argparse
import random


def preprocess_dataset(source_dir, output_dir, validation_split=0.1, min_size=512):
    """
    Prepare a dataset for fine-tuning by organizing images and captions.

    Args:
        source_dir: Directory containing source images and captions
        output_dir: Output directory for the processed dataset
        validation_split: Fraction of data to use for validation
        min_size: Minimum image dimension
    """
    # Create output directories
    train_img_dir = os.path.join(output_dir, "train", "images")
```

```python
val_img_dir = os.path.join(output_dir, "validation", "images")

os.makedirs(train_img_dir, exist_ok=True)
os.makedirs(val_img_dir, exist_ok=True)

# Process image and caption pairs
train_metadata = []
val_metadata = []

# Get all image files
image_files = [f for f in os.listdir(source_dir) if f.lower().endswith(('.png', '.jpg', '.jpeg'))]

for img_file in tqdm(image_files, desc="Processing images"):
    img_path = os.path.join(source_dir, img_file)
    caption_file = os.path.splitext(img_file)[0] + ".txt"
    caption_path = os.path.join(source_dir, caption_file)

    # Skip if no caption file exists
    if not os.path.exists(caption_path):
        continue

    # Read caption
    with open(caption_path, 'r', encoding='utf-8') as f:
        caption = f.read().strip()

    # Process image
    try:
        img = Image.open(img_path)

        # Filter small images
        if img.width < min_size or img.height < min_size:
            continue

        # Decide if this goes to training or validation
        is_validation = random.random() < validation_split

        # Destination paths
        dest_dir = val_img_dir if is_validation else train_img_dir
        dest_img_path = os.path.join(dest_dir, img_file)

        # Copy image
```

```python
        shutil.copy2(img_path, dest_img_path)

        # Store metadata
        metadata_entry = {
            "file_name": img_file,
            "text": caption
        }

        if is_validation:
            val_metadata.append(metadata_entry)
        else:
            train_metadata.append(metadata_entry)

    except Exception as e:
        print(f"Error processing {img_file}: {str(e)}")

# Write metadata files
with open(os.path.join(output_dir, "train", "metadata.jsonl"), 'w', encoding='utf-8') as f:
    for entry in train_metadata:
        f.write(json.dumps(entry) + '\n')

with open(os.path.join(output_dir, "validation", "metadata.jsonl"), 'w', encoding='utf-8') as f:
    for entry in val_metadata:
        f.write(json.dumps(entry) + '\n')

print(f"Dataset prepared with {len(train_metadata)} training and {len(val_metadata)} validation samples")

if __name__ == "__main__":
    parser = argparse.ArgumentParser(description="Prepare dataset for fine-tuning")
    parser.add_argument("--source", required=True, help="Source directory with images and captions")
    parser.add_argument("--output", required=True, help="Output directory")
    parser.add_argument("--val_split", type=float, default=0.1, help="Validation split ratio")
    parser.add_argument("--min_size", type=int, default=512, help="Minimum image dimension")

    args = parser.parse_args()
    preprocess_dataset(args.source, args.output, args.val_split, args.min_size)
```

7.2 Fine-tuning Script

```python
# scripts/finetune.py
import os
import torch
import argparse
from diffusers import StableDiffusionXLPipeline, DPMSolverMultistepScheduler,
UNet2DConditionModel
from diffusers.optimization import get_scheduler
from diffusers.training_utils import EMAModel
from torch.utils.data import Dataset, DataLoader
from torchvision import transforms
from PIL import Image
from tqdm.auto import tqdm
import json
import logging
import transformers

# Configure logging
logging.basicConfig(level=logging.INFO, format='%(asctime)s - %(levelname)s - %(message)s')
logger = logging.getLogger(__name__)

class TextImageDataset(Dataset):
    def __init__(self, metadata_file, img_dir, tokenizer, max_length=77):
        self.img_dir = img_dir
        self.tokenizer = tokenizer
        self.max_length = max_length

        # Load metadata
        self.entries = []
        with open(metadata_file, 'r', encoding='utf-8') as f:
            for line in f:
                self.entries.append(json.loads(line))

        # Image transforms
        self.transforms = transforms.Compose([
            transforms.Resize((512, 512)),
            transforms.ToTensor(),
            transforms.Normalize([0.5], [0.5])
        ])
```

```python
    def __len__(self):
        return len(self.entries)

    def __getitem__(self, idx):
        entry = self.entries[idx]

        # Load and transform image
        img_path = os.path.join(self.img_dir, entry["file_name"])
        image = Image.open(img_path).convert("RGB")
        image = self.transforms(image)

        # Tokenize text
        text = entry["text"]
        encoded_text = self.tokenizer(
            text,
            padding="max_length",
            max_length=self.max_length,
            truncation=True,
            return_tensors="pt"
        )

        return {
            "pixel_values": image,
            "input_ids": encoded_text.input_ids[0],
            "attention_mask": encoded_text.attention_mask[0]
        }

def train(args):
    # Load base model
    logger.info(f"Loading base model from {args.model_path}")
    pipeline = StableDiffusionXLPipeline.from_pretrained(
        args.model_path,
        torch_dtype=torch.float16 if args.fp16 else torch.float32
    )

    # Extract components
    unet = pipeline.unet
    text_encoder = pipeline.text_encoder
    vae = pipeline.vae
    tokenizer = pipeline.tokenizer
```

```python
# Freeze VAE and text encoder
vae.requires_grad_(False)
text_encoder.requires_grad_(False)

# Move to device
device = torch.device("cuda" if torch.cuda.is_available() else "cpu")
unet.to(device)
vae.to(device)
text_encoder.to(device)

# Create datasets
train_dataset = TextImageDataset(
    os.path.join(args.data_dir, "train", "metadata.jsonl"),
    os.path.join(args.data_dir, "train", "images"),
    tokenizer
)

val_dataset = TextImageDataset(
    os.path.join(args.data_dir, "validation", "metadata.jsonl"),
    os.path.join(args.data_dir, "validation", "images"),
    tokenizer
)

# Create dataloaders
train_dataloader = DataLoader(
    train_dataset,
    batch_size=args.batch_size,
    shuffle=True,
    num_workers=args.num_workers
)

val_dataloader = DataLoader(
    val_dataset,
    batch_size=args.batch_size,
    shuffle=False,
    num_workers=args.num_workers
)

# Setup optimizer
optimizer = torch.optim.AdamW(
    unet.parameters(),
```

```python
        lr=args.learning_rate,
        weight_decay=args.weight_decay
    )

    # Setup scheduler
    num_update_steps_per_epoch = len(train_dataloader)
    num_training_steps = args.num_epochs * num_update_steps_per_epoch

    lr_scheduler = get_scheduler(
        name=args.lr_scheduler,
        optimizer=optimizer,
        num_warmup_steps=args.warmup_steps,
        num_training_steps=num_training_steps
    )

    # Setup EMA
    if args.use_ema:
        ema_unet = UNet2DConditionModel.from_pretrained(
            args.model_path,
            subfolder="unet",
            torch_dtype=torch.float16 if args.fp16 else torch.float32
        ).to(device)
        ema_model = EMAModel(
            parameters=ema_unet.parameters(),
            power=args.ema_power,
            decay=args.ema_decay
        )

    # Training loop
    global_step = 0

    for epoch in range(args.num_epochs):
        unet.train()
        train_loss = 0.0

        for step, batch in enumerate(tqdm(train_dataloader, desc=f"Epoch
{epoch+1}/{args.num_epochs}")):
            # Move batch to device
            pixel_values = batch["pixel_values"].to(device)
            input_ids = batch["input_ids"].to(device)
            attention_mask = batch["attention_mask"].to(device)
```

```python
# Encode text
with torch.no_grad():
    text_embeddings = text_encoder(
        input_ids=input_ids,
        attention_mask=attention_mask
    )[0]

# Forward pass through VAE to get latents
with torch.no_grad():
    latents = vae.encode(pixel_values).latent_dist.sample() * 0.18215

# Add noise to latents
noise = torch.randn_like(latents)
timesteps = torch.randint(0, pipeline.scheduler.num_train_timesteps,
(latents.shape[0],), device=device)
noisy_latents = pipeline.scheduler.add_noise(latents, noise, timesteps)

# Predict noise
noise_pred = unet(noisy_latents, timesteps, text_embeddings).sample

# Compute loss
loss = torch.nn.functional.mse_loss(noise_pred, noise)

# Update weights
loss.backward()
optimizer.step()
lr_scheduler.step()
optimizer.zero_grad()

# Update EMA
if args.use_ema:
    ema_model.step(unet.parameters())

# Update progress
train_loss += loss.item()
global_step += 1

# Log training progress
if global_step % args.log_steps == 0:
```

```
        logger.info(f"Epoch: {epoch+1}/{args.num_epochs}, Step: {global_step}, Loss:
{loss.item():.4f}")

        # Calculate average training loss
        avg_train_loss = train_loss / len(train_dataloader)
        logger.info(f"Epoch {epoch+1} completed. Average training loss: {avg_train_loss:.4f}")

        # Validation
        unet.eval()
        val_loss = 0.0

        with torch.no_grad():
            for batch in tqdm(val_dataloader, desc="Validation"):
                # Move batch to device
                pixel_values = batch["pixel_values"].to(device)
                input_ids = batch["input_ids"].to(device)
                attention_mask = batch["attention_mask"].to(device)
```

Transforming Text to Image Delivery

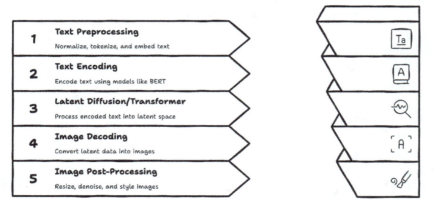

1	**Text Preprocessing** Normalize, tokenize, and embed text	
2	**Text Encoding** Encode text using models like BERT	
3	**Latent Diffusion/Transformer** Process encoded text into latent space	
4	**Image Decoding** Convert latent data into images	
5	**Image Post-Processing** Resize, denoise, and style images	

Summary

The document provides a comprehensive overview of designing large-scale systems tailored for Generative AI applications. It walks through key architectural decisions, from data collection and preprocessing to model training, fine-tuning, deployment, and inference serving. A significant focus is placed on ensuring scalability, low latency, and cost-effectiveness while supporting the unique requirements of generative workloads—like high-throughput GPUs, long context windows, and multi-modal processing.

The paper emphasizes modular design, favoring microservices and orchestration tools (like Kubernetes) to manage complex pipelines across training, retraining, and serving layers. It also underlines the importance of robust MLOps, including model monitoring, continuous evaluation, feedback loops, and secure APIs.

In terms of infrastructure, the document explores the trade-offs between using cloud-native services versus custom hardware stacks (e.g., NVIDIA DGX, TPUs). It discusses challenges like distributed training at scale, caching embeddings, handling large model checkpoints, and optimizing for different types of inference (streaming, batch, real-time).

A major section is devoted to generative modalities—text, image, audio, video, and multi-modal fusion. Each has unique system-level requirements, with examples of architectural patterns and best practices for production deployment.

Conclusion and Future Trends

Designing systems for Generative AI is no longer about just plugging in a model—it requires a deep understanding of the data pipeline, infrastructure orchestration, and inference workflows. As models grow in size and capability, system complexity increases exponentially, demanding smarter resource management, model compression strategies, and efficient fine-tuning techniques like LoRA or PEFT.

Looking ahead, **future trends** are poised to reshape generative system design:

- **Model Specialization:** Smaller, expert models working together (Mixture of Experts) to reduce latency and costs.
- **Real-time & On-device AI:** From streaming audio generation to AR/VR visual synthesis, generative systems will need to run efficiently on edge devices, bringing challenges like memory constraints and privacy-preserving computation.
- **Federated & Continual Learning:** Instead of one-off training, systems will evolve to support on-the-fly learning from user feedback, requiring robust privacy layers and adaptive pipelines.
- **Ethical AI & Governance:** As these systems generate more human-like content, monitoring misuse, hallucination, and bias becomes a core system design requirement.
- **Multi-modal Coherence:** Future systems will move from isolated text-to-image or text-to-video to deeply coherent multi-modal reasoning, demanding more integrated, synchronous processing pipelines.

The complexity of system design for Generative AI will continue to grow—not just in engineering but in aligning systems with human expectations, real-world use cases, and responsible deployment.